𝔄 Gospel for Liberals

Considering the Historical Jesus in Light of Today's Most Controversial Social Issues

By

Todd F. Eklof

ISBN 978-1449960827

Library of Congress Cataloging in Publication Data

Eklof, Todd F.

    A Gospel for Liberals

    Includes Works Cited and Index.

www.agospelforliberals.com

ACKNOWLEDGEMENTS

In his book, *Living Buddha, Living Christ*, Thich Nhat Hanh writes, "When we look into the heart of a flower, we see clouds, sunshine, minerals, time, the earth, and everything else in the cosmos in it. Without clouds, there could be no rain, and there would be no flower. Without time, the flower could not bloom. In fact, the flower is made entirely of non-flower elements; it has no independent, individual existence."[1] I sometimes feel the same way about myself when I look in the mirror. Therein I see at least 13.7 billion years of creation staring back at me. I stand on the shoulders of giants, but also in the tracks of small creatures, the first hydrogen clouds, the first cells, the countless microorganisms that share my body, and the earth beneath my feet. Likewise, I understand that, in some way, my life has been influenced by every event that has ever happened, from the heat and light of every star that's ever been, to the imperceptible breeze created by the soft flap of a butterfly's delicate wing. Any attempt, then, to acknowledge those who have helped me in writing this book, in only a few words at that, must, necessarily, remain woefully inadequate! Still, in my inadequacy, there are a few who readily stand out in my mind that I should like to mention.

Firstly, I'd like to offer my love and gratitude to my spouse and best friend ever in life, Peggy, who married me for no other reason than love, and has stayed with me throughout the years for this same reason. As a dreamer and philosopher I have not focused my energies on the sort of meaningless economic rewards and securities men of my generation are expected to emphasize. Yet you've always given me the space to be myself, and enjoyed me as I am, without complaint. Thanks for all the unconditional love!

---

[1] Hanh, Thich Nhat, *Living Buddha, Living Christ*, Riverhead Books, Berkley Publishing Group, New York, NY, 1995, p. 11.

Thanks also to our children, Julian and Cassidy, for coming to us. It would be a stroke of impossible fortune for any parent to get the best kid on the planet, but to get them both is a miracle! Thanks for all the love and goodness in each of you. Julian, you are just, witty, intelligent, and as bold as you are kind. I am honored to know you! Cassidy, even though I too often call you "little Miss," I know you're destined to do big things. There's a great soul wrapped up inside you, almost as great as your heart. You're truly a Mahatma!

I thank my parents, especially my father, who stoked the anger that fuels my passion for justice, and my compassion for all who suffer.

Thanks to my brother Chad for being a true brother.

Thanks to my friends and mentors, Phil and Sharon Smith, who helped teach this fish to look for water.

I thank those professors who, over the years, have opened my mind and heart, and helped expand my understanding. Thanks especially to Dr. Wallace Roark and Dr. Clyde Majors at Howard Payne University for teaching me how little I know, and opening my mind to infinite possibilities. Thanks to Dr. Randall Bush for being more kind than you are intelligent, which says a lot considering you're one of the most intelligent persons I've ever known! Thanks to Dr. Joe Martos, of Spalding University, for your radical and refreshing approach to education. Thanks to Dr. Adeline Fehribach, also of Spalding University, for being such a radical Christian, a profound scholar, and an inspiring teacher. Thanks also to Rev. Dr. Matthew Fox who has inspired me to live out my faith, regardless of the costs, and to help make the world a better place.

Thanks also to the many scholars who have devoted their lives to providing so much of the important research that has informed me and influenced this book, many of whom are mentioned throughout the following pages, and many in the background who are not. I include in this a special note of gratitude to William R. Herzog who seems as unpretentious as he is profound. You, more than any other, have given me a Jesus to look up to. Thanks!

Thanks to the members of Clifton Unitarian Church for trusting me and supporting me, and for having the fortitude to deal with the wounds Christianity has left so many of us with. I've enjoyed growing and healing with you over the years.

Thanks to my publicist, Bridget O'Brien for believing in this project and for believing in me. I believe in you too!

I also offer an incredible level of gratitude to my friend, Ava Sakowski, for supporting this dream. You are a light! May God provide you just a little dessert to go with your daily bread.

Finally, perhaps it is fitting that I should thank this incredible soul we call *Jesus* for continuing to reach beyond the millennium to offer us insight and inspiration. I pray our species might one day come to practice what you preached. Amen.

PREFACE

Many years ago, while I was preparing for the Southern Baptist ministry, a woman came to me in grave despair because the façade she had woven around her tragic life was unraveling. She'd been married more than 25 years to a man who's undiagnosed and untreated paranoid schizophrenia made him extremely sadistic. Throughout their lives together he regularly beat her and their sons, and did the unthinkable to their daughters. During those many miserable years she felt powerless to do anything to protect herself or her children, in part, because she was too afraid, and, in part, because of her own masochistic need to be loved. So, instead of defending herself and the children she loved, she tried the best she could to keep her "family secrets" secret. When she came to me her children were all nearly grown, with the exception of her youngest teenage daughter who had been acting out a lot and getting in trouble with the law. After the courts ordered the child to undergo professional counseling, the truth about her troubled home life came out, her father was arrested, and her mother had to finally face the reality of what had happened all those miserable years.

Prior to the day she came to me, she'd never expressed any interest in religion, and, in fact, seemed hostile toward it, probably because she was overwhelmed by guilt and did not believe God could forgive her when she could not even forgive herself. But she had become desperate, and, feeling completely helpless and hopeless, she came to me to ask, with an already defeated softness, "Todd, what do I have to do to become a Christian?" Needless to say, this is the sort of question conservative Christians only hope to hear! In fact, I was a bit taken aback by its directness. My response seemed slow and uncertain, as if, somewhere deep inside, I knew it wasn't really going to make a meaningful difference for this broken soul; as if I were ashamed to offer it. Nevertheless, it stumbled off my lips, as dispassionate as it was inadequate, "You have to believe that Jesus died for your sins, accept him into your heart as your personal Lord and savior, and ask for his forgiveness." Leaning against the doorway, as if siphoning its stability to help her sunken body stand, she gave a faint response, "Oh," then turned and slipped away. And I knew, by the forlorn look on her departing face, that I'd said nothing to offer her solace. Soon thereafter she was diagnosed with cancer and died within six short months.

This tragic experience caused me to genuinely begin asking myself, *what's so "good" about the Good News?* I realized there was nothing life changing or healing in my telling this unfortunate woman to say the "sinner's prayer." That's when I first began truly contemplating the life and teachings of Jesus. In the process I decided to forget for a while about all that Paul the Apostle had written about him, about the extraordinary miracle stories told of him in Gospels, and even about the teachings attributed to him. Instead, I began focusing my attention solely upon his interactions with the people he encountered; trying to understand what he might have done had this woman stood in his doorway. It didn't take long before I began to see what should have been obvious to me all along—Jesus never judged or rejected anybody! On the contrary, he went out of his way to make everyone, especially those his society demonized, feel worthy and loved. When he healed lepers, for instance, he did so by touch, compassionately making contact with those his culture considered unclean and unholy, risking the disease himself! When Zaccheous, so desperate to make a living that he betrayed his own people by collecting taxes for the Romans, climbed a tree just to catch a glimpse of this holy man, Jesus, not caring what the crowd might think, approached him and said, "Zaccheous, come down here, let's do lunch!"

Eating with outcasts was a particular offense to many in Jesus' culture, especially to those puritanical Pharisees who were competing against the authority of the Temple priests (Sadducees) by practicing priestly rituals outside the Temple, especially at mealtime. "The Pharisees," according to William R. Herzog, "were a table companionship sect that attempted to transform every meal into a ritual of purity equal to that of the priests consuming a meal in the temple."[1] This is the reason Jesus' willingness to eat with "toll collectors and sinners" was particularly upsetting for those who were essentially a table cult. But Jesus did not seem to care about what was being said about him, that he was being called, "a glutton and a drunkard, a friend of toll collectors and sinners," because he obviously cared more about people than social conventions.

One of the stories I found most moving about his human interactions is *John*'s fictitious account of Jesus' encounter with a Samaritan woman while she was drawing water from a well. "Give me a drink," he asks. The woman is astonished and responds, **"How is it that you, a Jew, asks a drink of me, a woman of Samaria?"**[2] She knew all too well that Jews didn't speak to Samaritans, that men didn't speak publicly to women, and that holy men, especially, didn't address "adulteresses," as is turns out this woman was considered by her community. Yet Jesus, breaking all these social conventions, asks to drink from a vessel that had surely touched her "unclean" lips a thousand times. This fictional account utilizes a betrothal type-scene common in Hebrew literature in which a male foreigner meets his future wife at a well (i.e., Isaac meets Rebekah at a well, Jacob meets Rachel at a well). In so doing, the author of *John* challenges his readers to embrace those who are ostracized and marginalized by society in the most intimate way, by uniting with them in complete solidarity and partnership. Although scholars know this story to be a historical fiction, it does, no doubt, reflect the genuine spirit of Jesus that is present whenever we manifest compassion, forgiveness, inclusion, and love among ourselves. "For where

---

[1] Herzog, William R., *Jesus, Justice and the Reign of God*, Westminster Knox Press, Louisville, KY, 2000, p. 153.
[2] John 4:9.

two or three are gathered in my name, I am there among them."[3]

Another of *John's* purely fictional, though spiritually accurate, stories about Jesus concerns a woman caught in adultery. She is accused, as you will recall, of being a prostitute and is brought to Jesus to see whether or not he will support the "Bible's" command that she be stoned to death. He brilliantly dismisses the crowd by saying, "Let anyone among you who is without sin be the first to throw a stone at her."[4] I often ask those familiar with this story if they remember the first words Jesus spoke to this unfortunate woman after the mob finally disperses and he is left alone with her. Inevitably they respond, "Go now and sin no more," proving they miss its point entirely. On the contrary, the first thing he asks is, "Where are your accusers?" implying there's no one left to judge her, including himself! I imagine this frightened woman, probably a child, forced into her occupation by abusive men who left her as "spoiled goods," with no other way to survive, had not experienced such compassion before. Unlike the woman of my encounter, this woman walked away transformed by a profound experience of unconditional love, "Neither do I condemn you. Now go your way and do what's right."

Now that's good news! "Don't be frightened, don't be ashamed; it's okay, you are loved. You deserve joy and happiness just like everyone else. God loves you, and so do I!" If only I had understood this simple, yet profoundly transforming message when my mother came to me searching for salvation so long ago. I will always wonder if she could have learned to live with herself had I understood enough about Jesus' true message to tell her that things would be okay, that she is loved, that all of us make mistakes but it doesn't mean we have to keep making them. How might things have turned out if only I had known enough to say, "There's nothing you can do to be saved Mom because you were

---

[3] Matthew 18:20.
[4] John 8:7.

never lost. 'There are no gates in heaven, everyone gets in.'" There's really nothing that can separate any of us from God's love.

CONTENTS

INTRODUCTION

"I'm not really a Christian, but I do try to follow Jesus the best I can." These were the words with which I began my question to Father Daniel Berrigan during the Q & A portion of a presentation he gave in Louisville in 2003. This famous antiwar activist, who, along with his brother Philip, had once been on the FBI's Ten Most Wanted List, appeared puzzled, as if he could not comprehend what I meant by this strange juxtaposition. Although he did not interrupt my question, his confused physical response, which brought some chuckles from the audience, spoke volumes, "But isn't 'following Jesus the best you can' precisely what it means to be a Christian?"

Perhaps this is so for Christians like Berrigan, who spent three years in prison for using "homemade" napalm to burn 378 draft files after illegally entering the Catonsville, Maryland draft board in 1969. Berrigan is among thousands of Christians throughout history who have understood the connection between faith and action; that, **"Faith without works is dead."** Unfortunately, the majority of Christians, as Christianity's violent and oppressive history proves beyond question, have managed to conveniently disconnect their beliefs from their behavior.

"I recently attended a speech given by President George Bush," I continued, "He held his arm out, as if hugging some invisible person, and said, botching an attempt to quote Jesus, 'You've got to put your arm around your neighbor and tell 'em you love 'em.' The hand selected audience thundered with applause, and, to my bewilderment," I went on, "just seconds later he was talking about 'hunting' people down, 'one by one,' and killing them, to which the same audience again roared with accolades." The room was quiet when I finally asked my question, "Do you think Christians are a little schizophrenic?" Those around me laughed. Berrigan smiled.

I can't remember his response, or if he even gave one. What could he say? I do recall, however, after his presentation was finished, a woman from the audience approached me and said, "You probably are a Christian, even if you don't realize it."

"I really don't think I am," I argued politely.

"But if you try to follow Jesus, you must be," she insisted.

"But Jesus isn't central to my theology," I explained, "I'm also inspired by the Buddha, and by Muhammad, and Lao Tzu, and Chief Seattle, and Gandhi, and Einstein, and countless others."

"Oh, I see," she agreed, before departing.

Her response confirms my suspicion that for most Christians, even the best intentioned, *behaving* like Jesus is, at best, secondary to *believing* in Christ.

A Gospel for Liberals is my effort, my longing, my prayer that Christians everywhere might begin to reconsider this position, as I have had to do in my own process. I became a "born-again" Christian when I was 14-years-old, and remained so until I was 24. During that decade of my life, I first became extremely active in an Evangelical Free church before finally settling in among the Southern Baptists. I carried a Bible with me everywhere I went, wore a "Jesus is Lord" brass belt buckle (talk about "girding your loins with truth"), and "witnessed" to nearly everyone I met. I spent the summer of my 18th year working as a missionary in Greenwich Village, NY, handing out Bible tracts, and as a camp counselor for youth raised in the housing projects on the lower eastside of Manhattan. Later that year I began studying for the Southern Baptist ministry at Howard Payne University, a Baptist college in Texas, the heart of the Bible Belt. The small country church I interned at during my senior year was kind enough to ordain me after I graduated, just before my move to Louisville, Kentucky to continue my education at Southern Baptist Theological Seminary—from which I dropped out after only a semester-and-a-half.

Christians sometimes ask me, "How did you become so *disillusioned*?" This question always seems odd to me because it implies that I was *illusioned* to begin with, a word that negatively connotes "deception" and "mockery." Is this really how Christians consider those of us who "leave the fold," as if we're no longer under a deceptive spell? And, if so, is it really their intention to suggest the best thing for us is to become deceived again? As Kant suggested, there is no return once we awaken from our "dogmatic slumber."

But I don't believe my departure from Christianity was ever the result of a single event or an abrupt shift in consciousness. Rather, it was the natural evolution of my own faith experience, which remains rooted, to this day, in the simple notion that brought me to Christianity in the first place, "God loves you." This fundamental message, that none of us are ever excluded from Divine love, was especially important to a young man like myself, having so often experienced the opposite of love at home. But as my experience in Christianity progressed I found myself becoming increasingly judgmental of others, and more ashamed of myself, especially as a young man whose hormones were naturally raging out of control. Yet as I developed intellectually and became less prone to thinking in the black and white terms typical of childhood and adolescence, and began to encounter many wonderful people with a variety of beliefs, backgrounds, and lifestyles, I had to let go of such pointless guilt and judgment. For faith rooted in love may well pass through the mire of such fear, but as we drink from that divine source, the origin of all that is, the fruit of love must eventually spring out of the mire to bloom most splendidly.

Returning to that original message, drinking in the unconditional love of God, I could not woller long among swine, among the illusion of fear, judgment, and shame. I came to my senses and found my way home to the welcome embrace of love, and, so graced, could not help but become more openhearted myself. Such openness to others, however, to non-Christians, to atheists, to gays and lesbians, and, ultimately, to all creatures, meant the Church would close its doors to me, leaving me with little choice but to leave the ministry.

The necessity of this became especially apparent one Sunday when, while still enrolled in seminary, a small country

Baptist church, much like the one that had ordained me, called me to be its minister. I knew the call was coming, and felt some trepidation given all the doubts I was having. Still, ministry was and remains my life's calling. I've known I wanted to be a minister since I was five-years-old, which seems extraordinary for a kid who wasn't brought up in church. But my need to be honest is equally as important. So, on the Sunday I expected the call to come, I delivered a sermon confessing my many doubts, fully expecting this would put an end to the proceedings. To my surprise, however, the head deacon shot towards me immediately after I gave the traditional alter call at the end of the service and said, "Todd, we want you to be our pastor." I must have looked like the proverbial dear in headlights! This wasn't the response I was expecting at all.

"You did hear my sermon didn't you? The part about me having doubts?"

"Having doubts is good," he said, to his credit, "All of us have doubts. They'll make you a better minister."

"But I have lots of doubts," I reiterated.

After a few moments of repeating the argument, he invited me home for a delicious (traditional Southern Baptist) fried chicken lunch. Later, while his spouse was doing the dishes and cleaning up the kitchen (also a SB tradition), he and I continued our conversation. I kept reaffirming my many doubts, and he kept insisting this wasn't a problem. I really wanted to believe him. I really wanted to accept this call to ministry, but I couldn't manage to shake the lingering feeling that there was still something wrong, that I hadn't yet come quite clean. Then, in a sudden moment of clarity, the solution came and I knew precisely what had to happen. "But I doubt the virgin birth" I confessed, "I doubt the resurrection. I doubt the Bible is the authoritative word of God. And I doubt the divinity of Jesus."

There, I said it! I named my doubts aloud for the first time in my life! Without missing a beat, my gracious host, who only moments ago had insisted they were of no real consequence, hollered back toward the kitchen, "Ma, Todd can't be our pastor!"

We shook hands and I left, feeling like a ton of bricks had been lifted off my shoulders! Having finally spelled it all out, I realized that if I were going to stay in my integrity and speak my truth, my days as a Christian were over, not to mention my pursuit of the Christian ministry. But that's okay, because for me, at least, living within my truth is far more important than being accepted by others—which, it turns out, has made me more accepting of myself and others.

Admittedly, however, I was a little angry after I left Christianity because I had been rejected for something as trivial as my ideas, and for something as important as expressing my truth to those who are supposed to love me unconditionally. But my resentment toward those who profess to follow him most, never resulted in the slightest animosity toward Jesus himself. In fact, it seemed, I'd come to appreciate him more than I ever did as a Christian. As a Christian I had to overlook and ignore so many of his most obvious teachings in order to maintain a position of judgment, superiority, and hostility toward the non-Christian world. Free from the burden of Christianity, however, I became free to wrestle with Jesus on his own terms.

I have since grown into a brazen liberal, not because I left Christianity, but because I've fully embraced the teachings of Jesus, which have left me much more open to others, including other ideas. *Liberal* comes from the Latin word meaning, "freedom," and, as a liberal, in the truest sense of the word, I'm free to seek inspiration from many sources, including mystics, prophets, philosophers, and teachers from all traditions and disciplines. Yet, in my particular journey, it was the truth of Jesus that first set me free to explore these unlimited possibilities. *A Gospel for Liberals* is an exploration of these liberating truths. It's also a tool for those who agree with the likes of Nietzsche, that, "There was only one Christian, and he died on the cross," and Mark Twain, who suggested, "If Christ were here now there is one thing that he would not be—a Christian!" It's for those of us who have had to restrain our innate admiration of Jesus because disentangling his profound teachings from Church dogma has seemed far too daunting. Yet *A Gospel for Liberals* accomplishes this and boldly liberates Jesus from Christianity. Although being a Christian does not exclude one from following Jesus, and there are many wonderful Christians who do, the point of this book is to make it clear that it's not necessary to be a Christian to follow Jesus, and that there are many Christians who aren't following his teachings at all. It is, therefore, a challenge to all of us, Christians and non-Christians alike, to take a second look at Jesus' life and teachings, and discover, therein, what we have known all along; that his simple philosophy of compassion, forgiveness, acceptance, justice, and sharing truly could create Heaven on Earth, the kingdom of God among us, so long as we put them into practice, regardless of whatever else we might believe about him.

CHAPTER I

Jesus Was a Man

"He who sows the good seed is the Son of Man."

Legitimate biblical scholars acknowledge there is very little reported about Jesus that actually happened. The most recent "quest" for the historical Jesus, conducted by the *Jesus Seminar*, involving hundreds of scholars over many years, suggests that around fifteen percent of everything he is reported to have said and done *may* have happened, and even this much is questionable. But early Christians, like modern scholars, also disagreed about who he really was. This is why they wrote four different Gospels, in addition to many other ancient texts describing his life and teachings that were not eventually canonized. These different texts once functioned very much like different denominations do today. Just as there are Catholic Christians, Baptist Christians, Presbyterian Christians, Methodist Christians, etc., etc., the Johannine Christians were those who favored the Jesus told of in the *Gospel of John*, and the Matthian Christians were those who liked the Jesus in *Matthew*'s Gospel. The same holds true for those Markan and Lukan Christians who preferred the Jesus presented in *Mark* and *Luke*.

Although many would like to dismiss their differences as irrelevant, the Gospel writers each tailored their own picture of Jesus to a specific audience with a specific agenda in mind, leaving us with many contradictions between them. It is most obvious, for instance, that the earlier the writing, the more human Jesus appears, and the latter, the more divine. *Mark*, the earliest of the four Gospels, written around 65 CE, for example, begins at Jesus' baptism, after he is fully grown, and suggests an *adoptionistic Christology*, meaning he became God's son at that moment; **"And just as he was coming up out of the water, he saw the heavens torn apart and the Spirit descending like a** dove on him. And a voice came from heaven, 'You are my Son, the Beloved; with you I am well pleased.'"[1]

Unlike *Mark*, which was written for a more general audience, the *Gospel of Matthew*, written between 80 and 90 CE, attempts to convince a Jewish audience that Jesus was their promised Messiah by beginning with a lengthy genealogy tracing his bloodline all the way back to Abraham, the father of Israel, through David, to whom, according to Jewish tradition, he had to be related to be considered the true Messiah. "**An account of the genealogy of Jesus the Messiah, the son of David, the son of Abraham.**"[2] In this obviously fictional account, his grandfather is named Jacob and his father Joseph, which, to a Jew, symbolizes the lineage from Abraham, to Isaac, to Jacob, to Joseph, to Jesus. Thus, in the Matthian account, Jesus is God's son at birth because of his bloodline. He is portrayed therein as a new and improved Moses, similarly escaping the King's death decree by fleeing to Egypt as an infant, going into the wilderness for 40 days (symbolic of Moses' 40 years), and descending from a mountain with his beatitudes, just as Moses descended from a mountain with the Ten Commandments.

In the *Gospel of Luke*, on the other hand, probably written shortly after *Matthew*, but to a Gentile audience, Jesus is divine *en vitro*, through immaculate conception, "**Do not be afraid Mary for you have found favor with God. And now you will conceive in your womb and bear a son, and you will name him Jesus. He will be great, and will be called the Son of the Most High, and the Lord God will give him the throne of his ancestor David.**"[3] The significance here is that the first Roman Emperor, Augustus (*the Exalted*), was officially deified in 14 CE, and, as Luke portrays Jesus, was looked upon as both human and divine. He was hugely popular among his people because he ended a hundred years of civil war and established the *Pax Romana*, a peace that lasted over 200 years, not to mention his establishment of a fairly honest government, a sound economy, a better infrastructure (including roads, buildings, bridges, and

---

[1] Mark 1:10-11.

[2] Matthew 1:1.

[3] Luke 1:30-33.

aqueducts), a postal service, free trade, art and literature, and the successful expansion of the Empire. His people felt, "Providence... by producing Augustus [has sent] us and our descendents a Savior who has put an end to war and established all things..."[4] Thus, to compete with the Emperor, *Luke* makes Jesus sound a lot like Augustus. The Immaculate Conception, in particular, is comparable to the belief the Emperor was fathered by Apollo who impregnated his mother while she slept. Quite simply, if Jesus' divinity was going to be accepted among the Romans, he had to have been divinely conceived.

By the time we get to the *Gospel of John*, written during the early part of the Second Century, sometime after 100 CE, Jesus has ascended from being Christ at baptism, to Christ at birth, to Christ at conception, to Christ before creation itself. **"In the beginning was the Word, and the Word was with God, and the Word was God. He was in the beginning with God... And the Word became flesh and dwelt among us..."**[5] It is apparent, given the evolution of the Gospel story over time, that the further we are removed from the historical Jesus, the higher our Christology. In other words, Jesus has become less human and more divine over time. One of the earliest works in the Christian Testament, *Philippians*, written prior to any of the Gospels, doesn't elevate Jesus to divine status until his death; **"...and he became obedient to the point of death—even death on a cross. Therefore God also highly exalted him and gave him the name that is above every name."**[6]

Evolving Christology

100 CE	*John, X@Creation*	**Divine**
90 CE	*Luke, X@Conception*	↑
85 CE	*Matthew, X@Birth*	
65 CE	*Mark, X@Baptism*	↓
61 CE	*Philippians, X@Death*	**Human**

---

[4] www.pbs.org/wgbh/pages/frontline/shows/religion/portrait/religions.html.
[5] John 1:1-2, 14.
[6] Philippians 2:8-9.

A similar progression also holds true concerning the stories of Jesus' resurrection, in that they become more complex over time. The earliest of these, in *Mark*, originally ends with **"Mary Magdalene, Mary the mother of James, and Salome"** simply discovering his empty tomb. It is a novel way to end such a tale, as if to metaphorically suggest that Jesus' life continues on in some way, but only in a figurative sense. There are no post-resurrection Jesus sightings in the original ending of *Mark* at 16:8; **"So they went out and fled from the tombs, for terror and amazement had seized them; and they said nothing to anyone, for they were afraid."** About 300 years later another verse was added to the ending, contradicting the original by claiming the women told Peter, and that Jesus himself sent his followers to proclaim his message throughout the world. A longer ending, probably composed in the 2nd century CE, was also added to it (vs. 9–20), taking motifs from the other Gospels that include several post-resurrection sightings and an ascension account. But, again, these additions came centuries after *Mark* was first written, and are an obvious attempt to update the original account, most likely to avoid continuing controversy about why the first Gospel doesn't mention any post-resurrection appearances or the ascension to begin with.

The next Gospel, *Matthew*, includes Jesus' post-resurrection appearance to his followers, but does not include an ascension story, "And remember, I am with you always, to the end of the age."[7] The problem with him being with us until "the end of the age," of course, is the question, *then where is he?* If he's still here, why doesn't he continue to show himself? *Luke* helps us solve this puzzle by being the first to add a story of ascension. Jesus went to be with the gods, just as Augustus had done; **"While he was blessing them, he withdrew from them and was carried up to heaven."**[8] The more simple explanation, however, representing an earlier view, was that Jesus' resurrection was purely spiritual. Those who saw him encountered him in a visionary or spiritual sense, the way Paul encountered him on the road to Damascus, as a bright light.

---

[7] Matthew 28:20.
[8] Luke 24:51.

At this point, then, the story had evolved from being metaphorical to being spiritual. But over time even the spiritual explanation wasn't enough for those Christians who began taking the resurrection more literally. They started arguing over whether or not it was spiritual or physical. The *Gospel of John* attempts to settle the dispute by including a fictional tale in which "doubting Thomas" actually feels the scars from Jesus' crucifixion, thus proving it was a bodily resurrection. It may have also been necessary to promote a physical resurrection versus a spiritual resurrection in light of the ancient Jewish disbelief in any sort of afterlife. For them life ended entirely at the grave (*Sheol*, in Hebrew) and could be continued on only through one's descendents (which also explains why they often held heirs accountable for the sins of their fathers, "**punishing children for the iniquity of parents, to the third and fourth generation...**"[9]). Thus, for the Jew, who did not separate body from soul — breath from spirit — resurrection necessitates restoration of the physical body, as in Ezekiel's vision of a valley of dry bones being restored to life, "**I will open your graves, and cause you to come up.**"[10]

Evolving Resurrection Motif

100 CE	*John: Physical*	**Divine**
90 CE	*Luke: Divine*	↑
85 CE	*Matthew: Spiritual*	↓
65 CE	*Mark: Metaphorical*	**Human**

Unfortunately these incongruities aren't limited to the various Gospel accounts of Jesus' birth and resurrection. All four Gospels, in fact, show a heavy Pauline bias against Jesus' original Disciples. This makes sense given that Paul was already a strong influence in the Christian movement long before any of the Gospels were written, and because he lived at odds with Jesus' disciples, particularly with James and Peter, its original leaders. The Gospel writers generally portrayed Jesus' Disciples as bumbling, cowardly, selfish clods who never understand what

---

[9] Exodus 20:5.
[10] Ezekiel 37:12.

Jesus was really all about. Take a look at the following inventory from *Matthew* alone:

- In wake of a terrible storm at sea, Jesus rebukes his Disciples for being afraid, "Why are you afraid, you of little faith?" [8:26]
- They respond with confusion, "**What sort of man is this, that even the winds and seas obey him?**" [8:27]
- Peter sinks for lack of faith while Jesus walks on water. [14:28-33]
- Peter rebukes Jesus for prophesying his execution, to which Jesus responds, "Get behind me, Satan!" [16:22-23]
- At the Transfiguration, Jesus disciples fall to the ground in fear. [17:6]
- Jesus tells his Disciples they were unable to cast out a particular demon "because of your little faith." [17:20]
- The Disciples selfishly argue among themselves for a chance at greatness by seeking to sit at Jesus right hand. [20:20-28]
- They fall asleep at his hour of arrest. [26:45]
- Peter denies knowing him three times. [26:69-75]
- Some of them doubt his resurrection, even after seeing him alive. [28:17]

In addition to poking quite a lot fun at Peter, in particular, *Matthew* says nothing at all about James, who, according to *Acts*, immediately emerged as the movement's leader after Jesus' execution. Is this oversight an intentional omission by the redactor for the purpose of writing Paul's chief critic and competitor almost completely out of the picture? Making him seem insignificant? The other Gospels treat James, Peter, and the rest of the Disciples similarly. By the time we get to *Acts*, the sequel to *Luke*'s Gospel, the befuddled Disciples stand out in harsh contrast to the depiction of Paul as a wise, commanding, and serious contender for the leadership of the Christian church.

It is certain, given they were all Jewish, that Jesus' initial followers saw him only as a man. Jews who believed in the coming Messiah (*Christos* in Greek) looked only for a man who would successfully restore Israel's greatness, not a demigod. Indeed, it would have been unconceivable, in light of Hebrew law, especially the prohibition against idolatry, for any Jew to worship a man. To do so would be blasphemy! "We see, thus," as Erich Fromm concluded, "that the concept of Jesus held by the early community was that he was a man chosen by God and elevated by him as a 'messiah,' and later as 'Son of God.'"[11] It was only through the Hellenism of Paul, more Roman than Jewish (if he was truly Jewish at all), who spread his own fabrication of "Christianity" to the Gentile world, that Christians eventually became less Jewish and were able to accept a paradigm allowing them to believe in the human incarnation of God, just as the Roman Emperor was worshipped and revered by his subjects as a god on Earth. In the end, the first followers of Jesus, the Nazarenes (a Jewish sect different from other Jews only in that they continued to validate Jesus' Messiahship regardless of his death and obvious failure to restore the kingdom), were overrun by the growing number of Gentile Christians, which likely forced them from their community in Jerusalem into the wilderness and eventual oblivion. As Fromm contends, "They were no longer Jews with the belief, held more passionately than by any other people, in a messianic time soon to come. They were, rather, Greeks, Romans, Syrians, and Gauls—in short, members of all the nations of the Roman Empire."[12]

It's obvious in reading Paul's writings that he regarded Jesus' life and teachings with little significance. At one point he even admits that he intentionally ignores anything prior to Jesus' death, "**I decided to know nothing among you except Christ and him crucified.**"[13] Thus, he purposely writes only of his invented demigod in symbolic terms of his own esoteric beliefs. In other words, Paul found no reason to discuss Jesus the man. He concerned himself only with this divinity he named "Christ." This is so, even though Paul tried to legitimize his beliefs by claiming to be Jewish, a claim, given his Hellenistic tendencies, that simply

---

[11] Fromm, Erich, *The Dogma of Christ*, A Fawcett Premier Book, Holt, Rinehart and Winston, Inc., 1955, 1963, Printed in U.S., July 1973, p. 51.
[12] Ibid. p. 60f.
[13] I Corinthians 2:2.

doesn't stand up against the most basic scrutiny. In his book, *The Mythmaker: Paul and the Invention of Christianity*, Talmudic scholar, Hyam Maccoby explains that Paul's use of the term "Christ" itself, rather than "Messiah," was unprecedented, and that his frequent phrase, "being in Christ," would have made no sense to a Jew. "Apart from the implied elevation of Jesus to divine status, this concept involves a relationship to the Divine that is alien to Judaism, in which the autonomy of the individual human personality is respected and guaranteed."[14] Such a term, however, would have made sense to those involved in the Greek culture's mystery cults. Maccoby goes on to point out that Paul's frequent references to Jesus as "Lord," a term reserved only in substitution for the unspeakable name of their God, "would have seemed to any Pharisee or other Jew sheer blasphemy,"[15] although, again, not at all bothersome to those Hellenists involved in the mystery cults.

This would explain why the Ebionites, a sect of Jewish "Christians," regarded Paul as an imposter who perverted the teachings of Jesus. It is possible the word "Ebionites," which means "poor men," was a nickname given to the *Nazarenes*, the name of Jesus' original followers, after the encroachment of Christian Gentiles forced them from their homes in Jerusalem. Whatever their origin, it is the Ebionites alone who have left us with the only account that can truly explain the bizarre Pauline phenomenon. Again, as Maccoby explains, "the Nazarenes or Ebionites held fast to their original beliefs which we find mentioned again and again in our Christian sources: that Jesus was a human being, born by natural process from Joseph and Mary; that he was given prophetic powers by God; that we was an observant Jew, loyal to the Torah, which he did not abrogate and which was, therefore, still fully valid: and that his message has been distorted and perverted by Paul, whose visions were deluded, and who falsely represented Jesus as having abrogated the Torah."[16] Although their writings, likely destroyed by the Catholic

---

[14] Maccoby, Hyam, *The Mythmaker: Paul and the Invention of Christianity*, HarperCollins, 1986, Barnes & Noble, Inc., 1998, New York, NY, p. 63.
[15] Ibid.
[16] Ibid. p. 176.

Church, have not survived, we do know from the writings of various Church fathers and historians, albeit with a negative bias, that the Ebionites were adamant that Paul was not Jewish, but the son of two Gentiles, and that he tried dismally to convert to Judaism, only to wind up a henchman for the High Priest before a conversion experience that led him to create a new hybrid religion that combined Judaism with his own Hellenistic worldview.

Nevertheless, by the time the Gospels were written, Paul had prevailed and Jesus' Jewish followers, including James, Peter, and the other Disciples, were regarded with scorn and ridicule. *The Book of Acts* describes Paul's first encounter with Jesus' Disciples by saying, **"they were all afraid of him,"**[17] suggesting, perhaps, his superiority over them. The pro-Pauline author also includes a vision of Peter's in which a divine voice tells him to eat various animals Jews considered ritually unclean, something Peter, like any Jew, would have found intolerable, yet something Paul advocated for throughout his writings. **"Everything is permissible,"**[18] he said, a position that made it much easier to win Gentile converts to Christ than if they had to first convert to Judaism, including becoming circumcised and adopting a strict Jewish diet. Thus, in *Acts*, the **"circumcised believers who had come with Peter were astonished that the gift of the Holy Spirit had been poured out even on the Gentiles."**[19] Still, the author of *Acts* doesn't portray the differences between the Disciples and Paul to be nearly as extreme as Paul himself does. In *Galatians*, for example, he boasts, **"When Peter came to Antioch, I opposed him to his face, because he was in the wrong."**[20]—Wrong, according to Paul, for refusing to eat with uncircumcised Gentiles. And in *Romans*, Paul goes so far as to say, **"We maintain that a man is justified by faith apart from observing the law,"**[21] a position in direct conflict with James'

---

[17] Acts 9:26.
[18] I Corinthians 10:23.
[19] Acts 10:45.
[20] Galatians 2:11.
[21] Romans 3:28.

statement that "**a person is justified by what he does and not by faith alone**."[22]

In the end it turns out that James, Jesus' true successor, along with all his other original followers, were no match for Paul and his growing army of Gentile converts. The self-proclaimed apostle successfully managed to subordinate the life and teachings of Jesus the man to the inflated demigod he named *Christos*. But Pauline religion, to this day, has never been able to completely eliminate the regressive attraction many hold for the historical Jesus. The debate over whether or not Jesus was a man or a god continued among "Christians" for hundreds of years after Paul, right up until the Roman Emperor Constantine converted to Christianity and made it an official State religion. It was shortly thereafter, in 325 CE, he organized a meeting of Church bishops in Nicaea and asked them to settle the matter once and for all by declaring that Jesus and God were of one substance (*homoousia*). The *Nicene Creed*, as it became called, paved the way for eventually making it illegal (*heresy*) to promote the idea that Jesus was not God.

Heretics were no match for Roman tyranny or the Holy Roman Church. For nearly a thousand years, during the Dark Ages, nobody dared again suggest that Jesus might have been a mere mortal, at least not out loud. But as soon as things lightened up a little, especially after the invention of the printing press made the Bible accessible to more readers, questions regarding Jesus' divinity were immediately resurrected. Michael Servetus, in particular, a 15th century Spanish theology student, was surprised, upon reading it for himself, to discover the word *trinity*, essentially invented by the Counsel of Nicaea, didn't appear anywhere in the Christian Scriptures. Excited about his discovery, and feeling certain everyone would enjoy being likewise informed, he wrote, *On the Errors of the Trinity*, laying the groundwork for the anti-Trinitarian doctrine known as *Unitarianism*—the idea that Jesus was a man, not God. Unfortunately other reformers didn't care for Servetus' opinion, including John Calvin who declared him a heretic and hunted him for many years until he was captured, tried,

---

[22] James 2:24.

and condemned, "to be bound and taken to Champel and there attached to a stake and burned with [his] book to ashes."[23]

Tragically, many others throughout Christian history have also been persecuted and tormented because they did not or could not acknowledge Jesus' divinity. Some of them must have longed, sometimes pleaded, to have their Christian tormentors themselves embrace his humanitarian teachings about loving, forgiving, and sharing with others. Of course, this is precisely why it's preferable to many to seek out the Christ of faith rather than Jesus the man. *Believing* in Christ leaves little need to actually *follow* Jesus. Just as Paul ignored Jesus' life and teachings, those who merely embrace an exalted Christology have little reason to follow Jesus' difficult example of poverty, selflessness, nonviolence, and courage to stand against oppressive and unjust forces. Faith *in* Christ has far too long superseded the faith *of* Jesus. This book is an endeavor to correct this grievous mistake, and to dig beneath the layers of mounting Christology that have evolved over time in order to understand the best we can the true essence of this *man* named Jesus.

---

[23] Howe, Charles A., *For Faith and Freedom*, Skinner House Books, Boston, MA, 1997, p. 39.

CHAPTER II

Jesus Was Political

"The chief priests, the scribes, and elders came to him and said, 'By what authority are you doing these things?'"

Jesus was a liberal, and if he were alive today in the U.S. he would most certainly vote Democrat! Then again, his staunch refusal to participate in unjust systems may preclude him from voting at all, but if he were to vote, given the limitations of our two-party system, his values would leave him no choice but to vote Democrat, and all true followers of Jesus ought to feel morally compelled to do the same! This may not have always been true, and may change in the future should other viable political parties emerge, or should Republican and Democratic values reverse as they have in the past. But given the GOP's current platform generally favoring laws against abortion, flag burning, *habeas corpus*, marriage equality, the separation of Church and State, the environment, and welfare, and those supporting corporate greed, an elitist economy, capital punishment, war, torture, and imprisonment without due process, it seems impossible, given his teachings, that anyone professing the name of Jesus could vote Republican!

Some would wrongly have us accept, however, that Jesus wasn't political at all, but concerned himself only with "spiritual" matters. But if the Gospels share anything in common at all, it is their depiction of Jesus as a man actively speaking and teaching against the establishment of his day. William R. Herzog begins his insightful book, *Parables as Subversive Speech*, by stating, "The parables of Jesus have long been revered as earthly stories with heavenly meanings. They have been viewed in this way because Jesus was thought to be a teacher of spiritual truth and divine wisdom. However, this view of Jesus stands in some tension with the account of his final trial and execution."[1]

This is so because the Romans did not execute people for teaching others to be "heavenly minded." If anything, this would have served the oppressive Roman government well by making those they exploited more docile and accepting of their difficult circumstances, and less likely to revolt. Again, as Fromm puts it, "religion serves merely to make it easier for the masses to resign themselves to the many frustrations that reality presents."[2] Indeed, as a purely spiritual teacher, Jesus would have been acting as an agent of the State and would have been encouraged, not crucified, by the authorities for doing so. As John Dominic Crossan and Jonathan L. Reed explain in *Excavating Jesus*, "crucifixion was not the punishment of citizens and aristocrats, but of slaves and servants, peasants and bandits."[3] Since it is clear Jesus was none of these, he could only have been put to death for being politically dangerous. As Herzog concludes, "One clear implication of this study is that Jesus' ministry was concerned with political and economic issues. Matters of justice were not peripheral to a spiritual gospel but were at the heart of his proclamation and practice."[4] Theologian Walter Wink puts it more concisely; "Almost every sentence Jesus uttered was an indictment of the Domination System or the disclosure of an alternative to it."[5]

Jesus' political activism and philosophy, which, again, ought already be most obvious and go without saying, will, nevertheless, be spelled out as this book proceeds. For now, however, it should be enough to begin with a closer look at a couple of his parables in light of the sociopolitical system of his day. In his story concerning *Laborers in a Vineyard*, for example,

---

[1] Herzog , William R., *Parables as Subversive Speech: Jesus as Pedagogue of the Oppressed*, Westminster/John Knox Press, Louisville, KY, 1994, p. 9.

[2] Fromm, *The Dogma of Christ*, ibid., p. 26f.

[3] Crossan, John Dominic & Reed, Jonathan L., *Excavating Jesus*, Harper Collins, New York, NY, 2001, p. 245.

[4] Herzog, ibid. p. 264.

[5] Wink, Walter, *The Powers that Be*, A Galilee Book published by Doubleday, New York, NY, 1998, p. 64.

Jesus tells of a landowner who begins his day by hiring workers to work in his vineyard, agreeing to pay them a single denarius for a day's labor. But three hours later he goes out and hires additional workers to help, also agreeing to pay them a denarius. As the story proceeds the landowner continues to hire new workers every three hours right up until the end of the day, agreeing to pay each the same amount. Needless to say, those hired early in the morning are a bit perturbed at the end of the day when they witness the landowner paying the same wages to those who have worked far less than them. To this the landowner responds, "Friend, I am doing you no wrong. Did you not agree with me for a denarius? Take what is yours and go your way. I wish to give to this last man the same as to you. Is it not lawful for me to do what I wish with my own things? Or is your eye evil because I am good?"[6]

Although the meat of this story is probably original to Jesus, passed down through oral tradition until a gospel writer finally recorded it decades after his death, it is most unlikely that it was originally accompanied by an interpretation. Nevertheless, the unknown author of *Matthew* takes it upon himself to interpret the story by adding what may be another of Jesus' authentic sayings to its close, "So the last will be first, and the first will be last. For many are called, but few are chosen."[7] A brief look at the sociopolitical circumstances of Jesus' day makes the original meaning of both the *parable* and the *saying* clear, and, ultimately vindicates the redactor's decision to link them together.

In his agrarian society, Jesus would have been well aware that the "first" had everything and the "last" had nothing. Keep in mind most the wealth in an agrarian society is tied up in agriculture, that is, in what is produced from the land. Thus, at the very top of the society were the rulers who, in Herzog's words, "viewed themselves as the rightful owners of all the lands and assets of the state, which they could confiscate and redistribute as they pleased."[8] Beneath the ruler was the ruling class, an elite group representing, much like today, 1 to 2 percent of the

---

[6] Matthew 20:13-15.

[7] Matthew 20:16.

[8] Herzog, ibid. p. 59.

population who used their political positions to accumulate even greater wealth, "because," as Herzog says, "everything was for sale, including justice, favors, offices, and influence."[9] So Jesus lived at a time when, as Crossan puts it, "1 to 2 percent of the population took 50 to 65 percent of the agricultural productivity."[10]

Retainers made up the next 5 to 7 percent of the population. This was a group that served the ruling elite by collecting payment from peasants. They were made up of priests who upheld the system through religious rhetoric; the military, which upheld it by force; and scribes, who were able to keep account of what the peasantry owed. Although the retainer class did not earn large salaries, they were able to tack on additional charges to the peasantry, which they kept for themselves. Some also hoped in the unlikely possibility they might eventually end up in the ruling class themselves. Because peasants had little or no opportunity to associate with the elite, most their hostility was projected upon their go-betweens in the retainer class.

With the exception of a small number of peddlers and merchants who provided a few luxury items to the elite, and the nearly impoverished artisans who crafted those items, most the population was made up of peasants. Whether or not they owned the land they worked on was unimportant since the ruling class took almost everything they produced. The elites considered them, "as little more than animals whose energy was needed to produce the wealth that the land generated."[11] Hence, the peasants were allowed to keep "the barest minimum needed for subsistence,"[12] and, as was typical of most ancient societies, those among the working class were also looked down upon simply because they worked. For the Jews of Jesus' day, especially, work was considered divine retribution; **"cursed is the ground because of you; in toil you shall eat of it all the days of your life**."[13] This

---

[9] Ibid. p. 61.

[10] Crossan, John Dominic, *The Birth of Christianity*, HarperCollins, New York, NY, 1998, p. 154.

[11] Herzog, Ibid. p. 64.

[12] Ibid.

[13] Genesis 3:17.

gave the ruling class divine license to exploit those who labored in the fields by so heavily taxing the fruit of their efforts that they could hardly survive. These unfortunate peasants accounted for about 70 percent of the population.

Lower still, however, were those unfortunate folks who held jobs considered religiously unclean and degrading. These were those, according to Gerhard Lenski, who "had only their bodies and animal energies to sell and who were forced to accept occupations which quickly destroyed them."[14] Because they were considered "obnoxious and offensive,"[15] they were "either herded into urban ghettos or segregated from the population."[16] Translator Stephen Mitchell makes a good argument that Jesus himself was among this class, having been born without a father in a patriarchal society that revered Abraham as the father of their nation, awaited a messianic king from the lineage of David, and worshipped a God it considered the Father of the Hebrew children. According to Jewish law, "**No bastard shall enter the assembly of YHVH, even to the tenth generation**."[17] Mitchell says the Hebrew word for "bastard," *mamzer,* was considered among the worst of insults; "*Mamzerim* were among those called the 'excrement of the community,'"[18] and, therefore, had few rights or opportunities, other than to engage in menial labor.

Perhaps this is why Jesus understood the plight of the outcast so well, and why he went around referring to himself as both the "son of God" and the "son of Man," in shear defiance of his culture's prejudice against him and others like him. It's as if he were saying, "I am a child of God, and, like it or not, I'm a legitimate part of the human race and you have an obligation to treat me and others like me with worth and dignity!" If this bastard child grew up to be a carpenter, as reported, he would have, at best, been a member of the artisan class. Again, as Herzog

---

[14] Lenski, Gerhard E., *Power and Privilege: A Theory of Social Stratification*, McGraw-Hill, New York, NY, 1966, p. 281.

[15] Ibid. p. 280.

[16] Herzog, ibid., p. 65.

[17] Deuteronomy 23:3.

[18] Mitchell, Stephen, *The Gospel According to Jesus*, HarperCollins, New York, NY, 1991, p. 25.

reminds us, "Aristocrats viewed all manual labor as degrading, and they considered those who engaged in it as inferior creatures, little better than slaves. As a result, artisans lived on the edge of destitution."[19] Perhaps few interpretations better explain Jesus' extraordinary compassion and devotion to those who have been marginalized by society. "What more powerful way could there have been for Jesus to become one with all the outcasts and despised of the earth than to be born illegitimate?" Mitchell asks, "Taking on this particular incarnation would mean experiencing, in his own body, at the most vulnerable time of human life, the most intense shame, wretchedness, and separation, so that he could eventually include and invite everyone into the kingdom of God."[20]

Finally, at the very bottom of society, varying, at times, from 5 to 15 percent of the population, were the *expendables*. These belonged to what was essentially the homeless and jobless class, the members of which spent most of their short lives begging in the streets, as prostitutes, thieves, or hiring out as day laborers during harvest time. It was this class Jesus used as examples in his parable of the laborers in the vineyard, a class "largely composed of the excess children of peasant households who could afford to pass their inheritance to only one child, usually the eldest son; the holdings of these peasants were too small to support more children."[21] Often, members of this class were forced to join gangs of young bandits, enabling them to survive until they were eventually hunted down, captured, and mercilessly killed, liked many of those labeled "terrorists" are nowadays. In any case, one's life expectancy after joining the ranks of the expendables was no greater than seven years, and the peasantry, artisans, merchants and outcasts always teetered on the verge of becoming expendable.

This unjust and oppressive stratification naturally created a great deal of hostility between the upper and lower classes. Those among the ruling class despised those they exploited in order to justify their feelings of superiority and, ultimately, to preserve the

---

[19] Herzog, ibid., p. 63.
[20] Mitchell, ibid., p. 28.
[21] Herzog, ibid. p. 88.

status quo, considering them little more than animals. Rabbi Jochanan ben Saccai, for example, head of the Sanhedrin (the Jewish Government) around 70 CE, wrote, "One may tear a common person to pieces like a fish... One who gives his daughter to a common person in marriage virtually shackles her before a lion, for just as a lion tears and devours his victim without shame, so does a common person who sleeps brutally and shamelessly with her."[22] Another from among Israel's ancient ruling class, Rabbi Eliezer expressed his prejudice and fear thusly, "If the common people did not need us for economic reasons, they would long ago have slain us."[23] This idea that the lower classes depend upon their oppressors for economic purposes, and are dangerous brutes who must be carefully managed, shows the degree of denial and self-righteousness necessary for the ruling elite to prosper themselves. Though those they exploited during Jesus' day often misplaced their anger on the available representatives of the ruling elite, rather than on the invisible rulers themselves, it would be a mistake to presume they were completely blind to the rudimentary causes of their miserable circumstances.

The "common" people—the *Am Ha-aretz*, literally meaning, "land folk," or "people of the land"—did not take kindly to having the produce of their labor so heavily taxed that they didn't have enough left to survive on. In 4 BCE, around the time of Jesus' birth, for instance, circumstances became so bad the masses revolted against paying Roman taxes and tributes. After squashing the rebellion by killing thousands of the demonstrators, the Romans further retaliated by crucifying two thousand Jewish political prisoners at once. A few years later, infuriated members of the Am Ha-aretz began organizing into popular militant political reform sects known as *Zealots*, who often used terroristic methods to thwart their oppressors. It was from among the ranks of these Zealots that most Jews turned in search of a messiah who would defeat their oppressors and restore Israel to its Davidic glory. As Erich Fromm explains, "They were the masses of the uneducated poor, the proletariat of Jerusalem, and the peasants in the country who, because of increasing political and economic

---

[22] Fromm, *The Dogma of Christ*, ibid., p. 35.
[23] Ibid.

oppression and because of social restriction and contempt, increasingly felt the urge to change existing conditions."[24] In brief, "They longed for a happy time for themselves, and also harbored hate and revenge against both their own rulers and the Romans."[25]

In light of this unjust social stratus and the general mood of anger and resentment it fostered, it's difficult to interpret the parable at hand as a mere spiritual metaphor, and the rich landowner as a symbol of Israel's compassionate God. Given their circumstances and the political climate of the day, no one in Jesus' original audience would have made such an association. This seems particularly true in light of the Hebrew Decalogue which begins, "**I am the Lord your God, who brought you out of the land of Egypt, out of the house of slavery. Have no other gods before me.**"[26] We are not to follow anything that doesn't liberate us! It seems certain, then, those in his original audience would have associated such a wealthy figure with the oppressive ruling class keeping them in servitude, misery, and abject poverty, and would have surely empathized with the laborers in the story, and admired their daring and improbable confrontation with this corrupt ruler. Again, at the time the retainer class acted as a go-between, a buffer, between the ruling elite and everyone else, making it nearly impossible for most people to ever encounter a member of the ruling class, let alone speak with and dare look one of such elevated status in the eye. Rather, they would have been culturally conditioned, through the same honor/shame code that still exists in the Middle East today, to gaze downward in silence in the presence of a social superior, never looking up, eye-to-eye, as an equal, let alone daring, as our parabolic laborers do, to give a member of the ruling elite the proverbial "evil eye." As in other parables, however, Jesus rectifies this injustice by telling a story in which the members of the underclass, in this case, the "least" of all, the expendables, are in direct contact with the ruling elite. This gives singular meaning to the oft-repeated phrase, "the first will be last and the last will be first." By fictitiously and vicariously allowing members of his

---

[24] Ibid., p. 42.
[25] Ibid.
[26] Exodus 20:2-3.

25

audience to deal directly with the ruling class, Jesus enables them to more clearly understand the sociopolitical dynamics behind their own undesirable circumstances, possibly motivating them, through righteous indignation, to finally take a stand against such injustice, even as he does by telling this political parable. Perhaps the best way to make this point, then, and to fully understand its political thrust, is to compare it side-by-side with the following modern retelling.

The Laborers in the Vineyard [Matt. 20:1-16]	*The Workers and the Tycoon*
For the kingdom of heaven is like a landowner who went out early in the morning to hire laborers for his vineyard.	What has become of God's beautiful creation? It's like a wealthy tycoon who needs workers for an expensive construction project. So he drives his brand new company pickup truck into the inner city, to a corner near a convenience store where a large group of mostly poor African American and Latino men have gathered, making themselves available for whoever might want to hire them for the day. The
Now when he had agreed with the laborers for a denarius a day, he sent them into his vineyard.	wealthy tycoon informs the group that he's willing to pay fifty bucks cash for a hard day's work. The men closest to the truck practically
And he went out about the third hour and saw others standing idle in the marketplace, and said to them, "You also go into the vineyard, and whatever is right I will give you." And they went.	leap into the bed, and the tycoon hauls them off to his construction site.
Again he went out about the sixth and the ninth hour, and did likewise. And about the eleventh hour he went out and found others standing idle, and said to them, "Why have you been standing here idle all day?" They said to him,	Around lunch time he realizes the project isn't progressing as fast as he'd like, so he drives back to the inner city street corner and picks up a few more workers who've been standing there since morning. Then, a few hours later, he goes back for another load. Finally, just before quitting time, he tells all the men to keep

"Because no one hired us."

He said to them, "You also go into the vineyard and whatever is right you will receive." So when evening had come, the owner of the vineyard said to his steward, "Call the laborers and give them their wages, beginning with the last to the first." And when those came who were hired about the eleventh hour, they each received a denarius. But when the first came, they supposed that they would receive more; and they likewise received each a denarius. And when they had received it, they murmured against the landowner, saying, "These last men have worked only one hour, and you made them equal to us who have borne the burden and the heat of the day."

But he answered one of them, "Friend, I am doing you no wrong. Did you not agree with me for a denarius? Take what is yours and go your way. I wish to give to this last man the same as to you. It is not lawful for me to do what I wish with my own things? Or is your eye evil because I am good?"

So the last will be first, and the first will be last. For many are called, but few are chosen.

working until he returns. An hour later he returns with even more workers from the street corner. All the men he hires end up working until well after dark.

Finally the tycoon instructs his foreman to begin paying the workers, starting with those he hired last, giving each man fifty dollars. When he gets to the men hired early in the morning they naturally expect a little more, but when they receive the same as everyone else, they begin grumbling, "This isn't fair. We worked all day long for you, nearly breaking our backs in the heat of the day, and you insult us by giving us the same pay as these guys who've only worked a few hours."

"Hey pal," the rich tycoon responds, "I'm not doing anything wrong. I told you I'd pay you fifty bucks, and that's all I'm paying you, just like you agreed. Besides, you all look alike to me, why shouldn't I treat you the same? It's my money and I have the right to spend it anyway I want. I'm not breaking any laws am I? Why give me the evil eye?"

One of these days, those who think they're big shots are going to get knocked down to size, because everyone is expected to do what's right, but few ever do.

In this contemporary reversion we can more easily see that the "landowner" hardly represents a just and loving God. On the contrary, his bigotry, arrogance, and cruelty is so overt that we have little choice but to recognize just how corrupt and cruel the entire sociopolitical system is, because, as he points out, he is acting within the law, a position he maliciously exploits by intentionally and sadistically making those who worked the longest and hardest watch as he pays the others the same amount first. But speaking overtly against such corruption and injustice in Jesus' day was dangerous, to say the least. So, many dissidents learned to speak in code, perhaps by pseudonymously attributing a seditious work to a dead but renowned author. Much of the literature attributed to the prophet Isaiah, for example, in *Isaiah*, was written long after he died, perhaps by students who considered themselves of his ilk. *The Revelation to John*, at the end of the Christian Scriptures, is likewise pseudonymously attributed to Jesus' disciple named John (as is the *Gospel of John*, for that matter), and regularly uses the code name, "Babylon," in place of "Rome," and the number 666, which numerologically spells *Nero Caesar*, as a symbolic reference to his return as Emperor Domitian, a particularly ruthless dictator who persecuted the Christians during the time at least part of the work is thought to have been composed. There is also the well-known *Pseudepigrapha* (meaning, "falsely inscribed"), which includes a compilation of works falsely attributed to the likes of Adam and Eve, Enoch, and Abraham, among others. It is unlikely the authors of these works were trying to intentionally mislead their readers into thinking they were actually written by their namesakes. Rather, they were, first and foremost, protecting their anonymity to avoid retribution from the authorities, and, secondly, hoped to entice fans of the personages after whom these works were named.

There was, therefore, nothing particularly unusual in Jesus' day about using code language to make a politically dangerous point. Since Jesus appears not to have been a writer, he would only have *spoken* in code, using parables, as we have already seen, and clever clichés, to make his seditious points. Indeed, it seems to me, many of his stories may have been the ancient equivalent of modern political satire. "Satire" comes from the Greek *satyrs*, referring to those somewhat lewd mythological figures that often went around with erections. Satire is funny for the same reason "dirty jokes," are funny, because it presents a shock to the system by revealing something unexpected or obscene that's not supposed to be "brought up" in polite society. The word *komos*, itself, from which we get the word "comedy," etymologically means, "to reveal." Humor, like exhibitionism, reveals something that's otherwise unseen, which is why it's often shocking and why we can't help but laugh or blush in response. When speaking of the Greek garden god, *Priapus*, for example, Thomas Moore explains he "is the spoiler of all that looks dignified in human life."[27] Priapus, a rather unattractive fellow with a constant erection, was often used as a scarecrow in Greek gardens. This is really the point of obscene humor, to scare away "all kinds of winged spirits — our lofty thoughts, our airy ideas, our flighty opinions, and our otherworldly aspirations."[28]

It is likely then, as a political dissident, that Jesus would have used humor through his satirical stories to reveal certain political realities in a way that wouldn't immediately lead to his arrest and execution. His satire, in particular, seems to have represented his attempt to "reveal" those members of the ruling elite who had become all but invisible in a system that shielded them from those they exploited. A good example, found in all three of the synoptic gospels, regards *The Parable of the Wicked Tenants*, which I prefer to call, *The Parable of the Absentee Landlord*:

> There once was a landowner who planted a vineyard, put a fence around it, dug a wine press, and built a watchtower. Then he leased it to tenants and went to another country.[29]

A purely spiritual retrospect expects us, once again, to accept this "landowner" as a metaphor for God, perhaps acting in the role of Creator. But, for all the reasons mentioned before and then some, those who were being exploited by such people,

---

[27] Moore, Thomas, *The Soul of Sex*, HarperCollins Publishers, New York, NY, 1998, p. 118.
[28] Ibid., p. 120.
[29] Matthew 21:33.

leaving them with barely enough to survive, would not have viewed them so kindly. On the contrary, the fact that this man was a landowner probably meant he had violated the Tenth Commandment, **"You shall not covet your neighbor's house; you shall not covet your neighbor's wife or his male servant or his female servant or his ox or his donkey or anything that belongs to your neighbor."**[30] As already noted, the ruling class "viewed themselves as the rightful owners of all the lands and assets of the state, which they could confiscate and redistribute as they pleased."[31] In short, the landowner in this story is most likely to have come into its possession through unscrupulous means.

The unjust confiscation of ancestral lands became a problem long before Jesus was born. Many of the Hebrew prophets complained almost incessantly about it and the poverty it caused. Isaiah protested, for instance, **"'It is you who have devoured the vineyard; the plunder of the poor is in your houses. What do you mean by crushing my people and grinding the face of the poor?' Declares the Lord God of hosts."**[32] Micah, similarly, grumbled, **"they covet fields, and seize them; houses, and take them away, they oppress householder and house, people and their inheritance,"**[33] and **"Hear now you *heads* of Jacob and *rulers* of the house of Israel, is it not for you to know justice? You who hate the good and love the evil, who tear the skin off my people, and the flesh off their bones; who eat the flesh of my people, flay their skin off them, break their bones in pieces, and chop them up like meat in a kettle, like flesh in a caldron."**[34] Likewise, the prophet Amos complained, **"I know how many are your transgressions, and how great are your sins—you who afflict the righteous, who take a bribe, and push aside the needy at the gate."**[35] The prophets began protesting unjust land appropriation after egalitarian tribal life fell sway to the sort of centralized government that made such

---

[30] Exodus 20:17.
[31] Herzog, ibid., p. 59 .
[32] Isaiah 3:14-15.
[33] Micah 2:2.
[34] Micah 3:2-3.
[35] Amos 5:12.

exploitation possible. According to Anthony Ceresko, it was under these circumstances that the ruling elite "presumed that land was the property of the king (along with members of the ruling class), who distributed parcels of it to his subjects and who could, and did, demand payment of rent and who could, and did, expropriate the land and evict its tenants at will."[36] Prior to this system of government, the land was viewed solely as belonging to God, and was passed from generation to generation among families who were expected to both benefit from and care for it. "Under the recently imposed statist model," however, "the perpetual right of the family to its patrimonial inheritance had no standing... Failures in the mutual aid system forced individuals to go into debt, mortgage their ancestral lands, and eventually lose them."[37] Landowner = God? Doubtful! Given the Jewish idea of sin as "separation," Jesus sets this story up by letting his audience know, covertly, that this landowner is a particularly "sinful" man who separates others from their ancestral lands, then separates himself from others by building fences, towers, and, finally, moving to another country altogether to operate as an absentee landlord, the ancient equivalent of many modern day corporate shareholders and stockholders.

> When the harvest time had come, he sent his slaves to the tenants to collect his produce.[38]

This line appears to be Jesus' attempt to set the record straight regarding who is actually responsible for the difficult circumstances of his listeners. Because the landlord, like other members of the ruling elite, operated from a distance, he was effectively invisible to those he exploited—*out of sight, out of mind!* So, instead of correctly blaming the 1 or 2 percent of the population taking most the resources for themselves, those who were being exploited tended to project their aggression onto their go-betweens, members of the retainer class, those bureaucrats

---

[36] Ceresko, Anthony, *Introduction to the Old Testament*, Orbis Books, Maryknoll, NY, 1992, p. 160.

[37] Ibid., p. 161.

[38] Matthew 21:34.

who, often out of desperation, felt forced to participate in an unjust system in order to survive. "They were functionaries who implemented the policies of the elites," explains Herzog, "...The rewards available at the highest level of the bureaucracy were lucrative, but the price paid by bureaucrats for doing their work, at any level of the system, was also high, because bureaucratic retainers absorbed the hostility directed toward the invisible elites."[39] But here Jesus, who was often criticized for associating with such bureaucrats, does not refer to those who have come to take the tenants' harvest as "publicans" or "tax collectors," but as "slaves," intimating that they have no choice in the matter either— that they too are victims of a corrupt system created by the greed of a few. It should always be remembered that Jesus, who stood staunchly against the exploitative system of his day, also championed the plight of the "tax collectors," those desperate folks sent as go-betweens to do the dirty work of the ruling elite.

> But the tenants seized his slaves and beat one,
> killed another, and stoned another.[40]

Here Jesus suggests that those in his audience too often misplaced their aggression on those who didn't deserve it, on those who were also slaves to the system. This might be done in a spontaneous act of frustration (beating one), or by grossly violating the commandment, "**You shall not kill**," (killing one), or by justifying such action by punishing them according to the law (stoning another). This is also the point where this tragedy takes a comic turn. Any "tenant" hearing this story may have had murderous thoughts against those sent to exploit them, but they would not have acted on such thoughts for fear of being arrested and executed. Imagine their reaction, then, when Jesus delivers the next line:

> Again he sent other slaves, more than the first;
> and they treated them in the same way.[41]

---

[39] Herzog, ibid. , p. 61.
[40] Matthew 21:35.
[41] Matthew 21:36.

I imagine a few in the audience, tenant farmers themselves, chuckling in astonishment. "Lucky break!" one of them says.

"Yeah," another chimes in, "Those guys should have been dead meat."

"What landowner would be dumb enough to give them a second chance?" Another says, with a chuckle.

"He's really going to be pissed now!"

They must have laughed out loud when, instead of telling them the authorities were at last sent to arrest the tenants, Jesus continued:

> Finally he sent his son to them, saying, "They will respect my son." But when the tenants saw the son, they said to themselves, "This is the heir; come, let us kill him and get his inheritance." So they seized him, threw him out of the vineyard, and killed him.[42]

Once again this absentee landlord proves to be so out of touch with what's going on, so separate from the land and the people he exploits, that he simply cannot understand the consequences of his greed. He cannot comprehend the hostility generated among those who have been marginalized by the corrupt system through which he is benefiting. He doesn't know that what he's doing is wrong, that it hurts others, because he's blocked out the world with his privacy fence, elevated himself above others in his watchtower, and distanced himself from the lives of those he exploits. And, in the end, like King Midas, whose greed for gold brings about the death of his own children, this man's absenteeism, his separation, his "sin," expressed as ignorance, leads to the death of his own son. Desperate people are prone to do desperate things, and those whose greed causes desperation among others, in any age, ought to understand the potential consequences. To remove ourselves from the hurt we cause others may ease our consciences, but it does not ease the suffering we help create.

---

[42] Matthew 21:37-39.

This is probably where the original parable ends, even though each of the synoptic writers goes on to explain its meaning retrospective of Jesus' death, as if it were meant to refer to his own rejection and execution. It is clear, however, like any human being, Jesus could not have predicted the circumstances of his death, and, as we have seen, he spoke in code in an attempt and expectation of staying alive. Viewing this story in light of the political circumstance of his own day, rather than two thousand years of Christian hindsight, suggests he was using satire to caricaturize the ruling elite as greedy, distant, out of touch buffoons who, though invisible, ought to be viewed as the real source of exploitation, not those who must unfortunately represent their interests in order to make a living. Taking out our anger against those beyond reach by reaching for those nearby—going home and "kicking the dog" as it were—only perpetuates injustice and is sure to doom us all! Perhaps the best way to grasp the impact this story would have had on its original audience, however, is to simply offer another modern retelling:

Parable of the Absentee Landlord [Matt. 21:33-39]	*Parable of the Clueless Billionaire*
There once was a landowner who planted a vineyard, put a fence around it, dug a wine press, and built a watchtower. Then he leased it to tenants and went to another country.	Once this guy invented a microchip, started a company, and became one of the richest men on the planet. He then hired lots of people to work for him while he stayed up in his top floor office. He hired supervisors to make sure the rest of his workers were doing their jobs.
When the harvest time had come, he sent his slaves to the tenants to collect his produce.	
But the tenants seized his slaves and beat one, killed another, and stoned another.	Some disgruntled employees told one supervisor to "fuck off," threw one out the window, and sued another. So the billionaire hired even more supervisors, who ended up being treated worse than the first bunch.
Again he sent other slaves, more than the first; and they treated them in the same way.	Finally he says to himself, "Surely they'll love my boy, he's such a

Finally he sent his son to them, saying, "They will respect my son." But when the tenants saw the son, they said to themselves, "This is the heir; come, let us kill him and get his inheritance." So they seized him, threw him out of the vineyard, and killed him.	great kid!" But as soon as he showed up, they said, "This guy's gonna end up just like his daddy. Let's rob him." So they dragged him to the parking lot, took his wallet, and ended up killing him.

By telling seditious parables like these, Jesus, often satirically, tried to expose the causes underlying the many social, economic, and political injustices of his day. Since it was unlikely most of those being exploited would ever have the real opportunity to confront the invisible elite responsible for their harsh circumstances, he allowed them to do so, vicariously, through his many mutinous stories. His *Parable of the Rich Man and Lazarus*, in which a rich man suffering in Hell begs for a drink of water from a poor man he had exploited in life, further develops Jesus' theme concerning the impossible chasm between the elite and those they disenfranchise. The *Parable of the Unforgiving Servant*, in which a man, desperate to pay his debts, takes his frustration out on those who owe him money, illustrates the perpetual injustices stemming from "trickle-down economics." *The Parable of the Talents* pertains to those who are constantly under pressure to increase the profits of their superiors, and exposes the plight of those who don't. There's also his *Parable of the Unjust Judge*, about a destitute widow who must fight for justice from a man who expects a bribe. Stories like these abound in the Gospels. It is difficult to accept that Jesus would have so habitually alluded to examples of corruption, greed, exploitation, and injustice, merely to make some esoteric or otherworldly point! He was clearly political—a fact, that ended up costing him his life. The only real question for us today regards the true nature of his politics. Did he represent the conservative ideas of fundamentalist Christianity that twist his teachings to prop up the exploitative system he died fighting against? Or were his values more progressive? It is the aim of this book to show that he was decidedly liberal and, if he were around today, given the limited choices, he would, undoubtedly, vote accordingly!

CHAPTER III

Jesus Was a Situation Ethicist

"I ask you, is it lawful to do good or harm on the Sabbath, to save life or to destroy it?"

The whole of moral philosophy can be summarized by one question; *should we do the right thing or the best thing?* How you answer this question determines whether or not you favor *deontological ethics*, focusing on means, or *teleological ethics*, concerned more with outcomes. It may seem a simple question, but it's not always so easy to answer. Around the turn of the 19th century, for example, a form of this question was posed during a meeting of Kentucky's Long Run Baptist Association, causing a dispute and eventual split in its founding church. The argument began during an association gathering when someone raised a hypothetical question concerning whether or not it would be right or wrong to tell a lie in order to protect a child hiding from an Indian raiding party. Apparently the gathering took place on the burial site of Abraham Lincoln's grandfather who had been killed in just such a raid—the same raid that also came close to claiming the life of his son, future father of the President. Church members disagreed so sharply over the issue that the association had to become involved by declaring those who would tell the truth regardless of the consequences, the legitimate Long Run Baptist Church. The others left to form another church about twenty miles away. Although they named themselves the Flat Rock Baptist Church, they were, for many years, referred to as the "lying Baptists."

The "legitimate" Baptists, who would not lie to save a life, represent the *deontological* position that it's always necessary to do the "right" thing, regardless of the consequences. The root of this word, *ontos*, comes from the Greek word for "is," suggesting a morality that considers "right" and "wrong" as entities in and of themselves. In the case of the Long Run Baptists, for example, it is always intrinsically right to tell the truth and always intrinsically wrong to lie. The "lying Baptists," on the other hand, demonstrate the *teleological* perspective, which stems from the Greek word, *telos*, meaning, "end." Teleological ethics suggest morality is based on the end results of our actions, not on the actions themselves, looking toward the *best* possible outcome. *Utilitarianism*, for example, positing that morality ought to be based on that which brings about *the greatest good for the greatest number of people*, falls into this camp. Whereas the *Divine Command Theory*, also called, *Theological Volunteerism*, positing that certain "divinely inspired" rules, like the Decalogue (Ten Commandments) must be obeyed in all circumstances, is an example of a deontological ethic. In brief, deontology suggests *the means justify the ends*, and teleology suggests *the ends justify the means*.

In our litigious culture, we have all been taught that the "ends never justify the means," that "ignorance of the law is no excuse," but, as my college philosophy professor use to ask, "If the ends don't justify the means, what does?" This is not unlike Jesus' question to those who criticized him for healing on the Sabbath. "Is it lawful to do good or harm on the Sabbath, to save life or to destroy it?"[1] Clearly he was more concerned with the consequences of his actions than with obeying the strict letter of the law, making him, in effect, a teleological ethicist. Unlike the Utilitarians, however, Jesus seems to have concerned himself as much with the needs of individuals as he did the masses. Like Gandhi, who said, "I do not believe in the doctrine of the greatest good of the greatest number. It means in its nakedness that in order to achieve the supposed good of 51 percent the interest of 49 percent may be, or rather, should be sacrificed,"[2] Jesus' morality did not accept the notion of "collateral damage," that the needs of the many outweigh the needs of the few, or the one. Although he was followed by crowds, ministered to whole cities, and worked to feed the hungry multitudes, the Gospels primarily describe his care and concern for individuals. "Which of you," he asked, "having a hundred sheep and losing one of them, does not leave the ninety-nine in the wilderness and go after the one that is lost

---

[1] Luke 6:9.

[2] Gandhi, *All Men are Brothers*, ed., Krishna Kripalani, Continuum Publishing Corp., New York, NY, 1980, p. 131.

until he finds it?"[3] This ethical perspective led to his teaching that we serve God most, not by obeying strict commandments, but by feeding someone who is hungry and thirsty, clothing someone who is naked, caring for someone who is sick, and visiting someone in prison. He did not challenge us to love our neighbors, pluralistically, but to, singularly, "love your neighbor as yourself."[4]

He approached each person, each situation, openly, without any preconceived rules or overarching notions dictating his response. His only governing predisposition was his principle of love. "'You shall love the Lord your God with all your heart, and with all your soul, and with all your mind.' This is the greatest and first commandment. And the second is like it: 'You shall love your neighbor as yourself.'" He then concludes, "On these two commandments hang all the law and the prophets."[5] In doing so, he summarizes and subjugates the entire Jewish Torah (the Written Law) and the writings of the Prophets (those believed to have spoken on behalf of God) to the authority of love. He was, therefore, willing, as we have seen, to violate the law if doing so brought about a more loving outcome. "The Sabbath was made for humankind," he said, "and not humankind for the Sabbath."[6]

By promoting and placing love above all else, Jesus seems to have been more a situation ethicist than anything else. *Situation Ethics* was coined in 1966 with the publication of Joseph Fletcher's controversial book by the same name. "The situationist," he writes, "enters into every decision-making situation fully armed with the ethical maxims of his community and its heritage, and he treats them with respect as illuminator of his problems. Just the same he is prepared in any situation to compromise them or set them aside *in the situation* if love seems better served by doing so."[7] In this spirit, although he was willing

---

[3] Luke 15:4.
[4] Matthew 22:39.
[5] Matthew 22:37-40.
[6] Mark 2:27.
[7] Fletcher, Joseph, *Situation Ethics*, The Westminster Press, Philadelphia, PA, 1966, p. 26.

to violate the law when necessary, Jesus was not an anarchist. "Do not think that I have come to abolish the law or the prophets," he said, "I have come not to abolish but to fulfill."[8]

Situation Ethics seems to exist somewhere between what Fletcher calls *legalism* and *antinomianism*. The former, he writes, "enters into every decision making situation encumbered with a whole apparatus of prefabricated rules and regulations,"[9] compared to its extreme opposite approach, the latter, through which, in his words, "one enters into the decision-making situation armed with no principles or maxims whatsoever, to say nothing of rules."[10] The former can be extremely heartless and unforgiving, while the latter can be reactive and inconsistent. Situation Ethics, on the other hand, may be willing to forgo the law if the circumstances so require, but it always enters into a situation with love as its predicate. Indeed, if there is anything deontological about Situation Ethics at all, it is this notion that, as Fletcher purports, "Only one 'thing' is intrinsically good, namely, love; nothing else at all."[11] This is not unlike what Augustine surmised in saying, "Love with care, then do what you want."[12] Entering each situation with love as our highest goal eliminates the need for external law and supersedes every law. Paul Tillich, who said, "The law of love is the ultimate law because it is the negation of law," went on to suggest that it satisfies both the antinomian and legalistic tendency because, "love can never become fanatical in a fight for the absolute, or cynical under the impact of the relative."[13]

Jesus' middle way, then, Situation Ethics, has both a profound respect for the law through its determination to obey, not the letter, but the heart of the law; and a ready willingness to disregard the law under circumstances wherein it might prove detrimental to the health and wellbeing of others. Yet, even though Fletcher based this ethic largely on the teachings of Jesus,

---

[8] Matthew 5:17.
[9] Fletcher, ibid., p. 18.
[10] Ibid. p. 22.
[11] Ibid. p. 57.
[12] Ibid. p. 13.
[13] Tillich, Paul, *Systematic Theology*, Vol. I, 1951, p. 152.

and presents them from a decidedly Christian perspective, the controversy it's created among Christians is no less divisive than the ethical dilemma that split the Long Run Baptist Church so long ago. Unfortunately, and almost inexplicably, many Christians today seem more interested in posting the Decalogue in public courthouses than with predicating their behavior on love. These would, as such, have great problems with Fletcher's claim, "that none of the Ten Commandments represents a normative principle for human conduct which is intrinsically valid or universally obliging regardless of the circumstances."[14] During a 1971 debate, John Warwick Montgomery, a professor at Trinity Evangelical Divinity School, responded, "the biblical revelation constitutes a transcendent word from God establishing ethical values once for all... Situations are not only judged by absolute principles in this life; they will be so judged in the next."[15] Even so, after Fletcher asked him the very question that split Long Run, Montgomery was forced to admit, "If, concretely, I were put in the position that you described of either informing a killer as to where a child was hidden or lying about it, it's conceivable that I would have to lie. But if I did so, I would be unable to justify this ethically... In Christian terminology, I would have committed a sin, which should drive me to the Cross for forgiveness."[16]

Montgomery's hypothetical response is reminiscent of Huck Finn's fictional response to the moral dilemma presented him when considering whether or not he ought to help his friend Jim escape slavery. He knew, according to the law, that it would be a great sin to effectively steal another person's "property," and that it was utterly wrong, according to Southern convention, to help a slave go free, "and if I was ever to see anybody from that town again," he thought to himself, "I'd be ready to get down and lick his boots for shame."[17] After first deciding not to help his friend, shirking his duty toward love in favor of convention, Huck seeks justification by turning, of all things, to religion. "I felt so

---

[14] Fletcher & Montgomery, *Situation Ethics*, Bethany House Publishers, Minneapolis, MN, 1972, p. 13.

[15] Ibid., p. 44 & 45.

[16] Ibid., p. 51.

[17] Ibid.

good and all washed clean of sin for the first time I had ever felt so in my life, and I knowed I could pray now."[18] But, like Montgomery, who, in the end, would lie to save a child's life, then rush to the "Cross" for forgiveness, Huck's higher moral conscience doesn't allow the law to fully suppress his instinct for love. Thus, regarding the letter he'd written to expose Jim's whereabouts, he says, "I took it up, and held it in my hand, I was a-trembling, because I'd got to decide, forever, betwixt two things, and I knowed it. I studied a minute, sort of holding my breath, and then says to myself: 'All right, then, I'll go to hell...'"[19] In disregarding the law for love, Huck decides to do what he knows in his head to be wrong, in order to do what in his heart he knows is best. The only difference between this and genuine Situation Ethics is that a true situation ethicist, unlike Huck or Montgomery, is free to do what he or she thinks is best without experiencing residual feelings of shame and remorse for doing what others consider wrong. Like Jesus, the true situation ethicist consciously makes a moral decision without apology. "So the Son of Man is lord even of the Sabbath,"[20] he boasts.

Joseph Fletcher's Six Propositions of Situation Ethics

1.   Only one 'thing' is intrinsically good; namely love, and nothing else.
2.   The ruling norm of Christian decision is love: nothing else.
3.   Love and justice are the same, for justice is love distributed, nothing else.
4.   Love wills the neighbor's good whether we like him or not.
5.   Only the end justifies the means; nothing else.
6.   Love's decisions are made situationally, not prescriptively.

How odd, in light of all this, that so many Christians today prefer the Decalogue, along with many other selective Levitical taboos, over Jesus' ethic of love, especially in light even of Paul, the true founder of Christianity, who said relentlessly that Christ

---

[18] Twain, Mark, *The Adventures of Huckleberry Finn*, Bantam Books, New York, NY, 1884, 1986, p. 206.
[19] Ibid.
[20] Mark 2:28.

came to free them from the law. A bit of a situation ethicist himself, Paul said, "'**All things are lawful,' but not all things are beneficial. 'All things are lawful,' but not all things build up.**"[21] This being the case, he goes on to suggest the principle of love ought always be the deciding factor, "**Do not seek your own advantage, but that of the other.**"[22] Yet vast numbers of Christians today are theological volunteerists who seek to force what they perceive as divine commands on the whole of society, which is quite contrary to the teachings of both Paul and Jesus (not to mention contrary to the ideas of freedom and Democracy). Perhaps this is so, however, because this fundamental ethical question—*should we do the right thing or the best thing*—is one of life's great perennial questions that can never be wholly answered. Thus, it remains a primary struggle within each of us, whatever our religion might be. We know it precedes Fletcher and Montgomery, the "legitimate Baptists" and the "lying Baptists," and the first Christians who argued over how much of the Jewish Law Gentile converts were expected to follow.

Even Jesus' Jewish forbears did not always agree concerning the nature of morality, despite having the Law of Moses, and, later, the Words of the Prophets, to help guide them. Indeed, many of the Prophets arose in response to a strict deontological interpretation of the Torah that emphasized ritual, but had little concern for people. *Amos* says, for example, "**Take away from me the noise of your songs; I will not listen to the melody of your harps. But let justice roll down like waters, and righteousness like an ever-flowing stream.**"[23] *Micah* asks, rhetorically, "**With what shall I come before the Lord, and bow myself before God on high? Shall I come before him with burnt offerings, with calves a year old? ...with thousands of rams... thousands of rivers of oil? Shall I give my firstborn for my transgression, the fruit of my body for the sin of my soul?**[24] The prophet then responds, teleologically, "**He has told you, O mortal, what is good; and what does the Lord require**

---

[21] I Corinthians 10:23.
[22] I Corinthians 10:24.
[23] Amos 5:23-24.
[24] Micah 6:6-7.

43

of you but to do justice, and to love kindness, and to walk
humbly with your God?"[25] In *Mark*, Jesus himself quotes one
such prophet, "Isaiah prophesied rightly about you hypocrites,
as it is written, 'This people honors me with their lips, but
their hearts are far from me; in vain they worship me,
teaching human precepts as doctrines.'"[26] What all of these
perspectives share in common is the teleological vantage, that the
ends justify the means, that rules and rituals are only so good as
the outcomes they produce, and these outcomes must be sought
through the predicate of love, expressed as compassion for others
and justice for all.

But, like most societies, the ancient Jews were a divided
people, a loosely bound confederation of tribes (the, so called,
"Twelve Tribes of Israel), comprised of economic refugees,
including *Hebrews* (mercenaries) and, perhaps, a few escaped
slaves (the Moses group), who banded together to share their hard
earned resources, and to protect each other from invaders and
pillagers. They never managed to achieve unanimity concerning
how they should be governed, and eventually split entirely into
two kingdoms, the Israelites in the North, and the Judeans in the
South. Even so, their many stories have come to us as one story
presented in the Hebrew Scriptures, which, as you might imagine,
is replete with divergent positions on a variety of topics, including,
morality. It would be a mistake, therefore, to presume all who fell
under the "Jewish" umbrella, shared the same opinion about the
Torah, including the Ten Commandments. Just as we continue to
wrestle with the perennial moral dilemma today, it's reasonable to
presume they too wondered if, at times, their laws proved too rigid
and unforgiving in matters of the heart.

This seems to be precisely what Ezekiel was getting at
when he prophesied, "**I will give them one heart and put a new
spirit within them; I will remove the heart of stone from their
flesh and give them a heart of flesh, so that they may follow my
statutes and keep my ordinances and obey them. Then they
shall be my people, and I will be their God.**"[27] Ezekiel, like

---

[25] Micah 6:8.
[26] Mark 7:6-7.
[27] Ezekiel 11:19-20.

Jesus, felt so strongly that the law of the heart supersedes the law of stone tablets that he later reiterates this same message, "**A new heart I will give you, and a new spirit I will put within you; and I will remove from your body the heart of stone and give you a heart of flesh. I will put my spirit within you, and make you follow my statutes and be careful to observe my ordinances.**"[28] Jesus, like so many of the prophets, understood that love must predicate all laws, that it is the first law, the law above all laws—love of God, love of neighbor, "On these two commandments hang all the law and the prophets."

Sadly, the Fall/Redemption theology indicative of most Christians creates much disdain for and mistrust of the "flesh." On occasion, for example, when Christians inquire about my Unitarian Universalist faith and discover I don't "preach" solely from the Bible, they ask, "Upon what authority do you base your beliefs?" When I explain that I ultimately trust the authority of my own heart, of what I feel to be right within the core of my own being, they usually respond by saying something like, "If we all did so, if we all did whatever we feel is right, the world would be full of Adolph Hitlers." After noting that Hitler, who said, "by defending myself against the Jew, I am fighting for the work of the Lord,"[29] was a Christian Biblicist who based his anti-Semitic views on the Bible, I go on to point out that Jesus, by contrast, taught us to look inwardly, into our hearts, toward the law of love. True, he did say, as has already been pointed out, "Do not think that I have come to abolish the law or the prophets. I have come not to abolish but to fulfill." But he goes on to explain that in fulfilling the law, we must do more than simply obey it to the letter, we must get at its heart, which is always compassion and justice. "For I tell you, unless your righteousness exceeds that of the scribes and Pharisees, you will never enter the kingdom of heaven."[30] He explains what it means to exceed the righteousness of these puritanical legalists by presenting a series of antitheses to the Jewish law. Whereas the law forbids murder,

---

[28] Ezekiel 36:26.
[29] Hitler, Adolph, *Mein Kampf*, Ralph Mannheim, ed., Mariner Books, New York, NY, 1999, p. 562.
[30] Matthew 5:20.

adultery, swearing falsely, and permits "eye for eye" justice, and hatred for one's enemies; Jesus presses further, into the heart of the law, by suggesting we can't even get angry with others, or lust, or swear at all, or seek retribution of any kind against those who injure us, and teaches that we must love even our enemies, "For if you love those who love you, what reward do you have?"[31]

Though it may sound too hedonistic for many to accept, Jesus relied upon his "heart of flesh" to inform him morally. Still, those who fear and disdain the body's natural inclinations, hold with contempt the ideas of philosophers like Epicurus, who said, "we recognize pleasure as the first good innate in us, and from pleasure we begin every act of choice and avoidance, and to pleasure we return again."[32] It's true that those who don't develop past the moral and psychological awareness of a toddler are likely to seek only their own most basic and immediate pleasures, regardless of, and sometimes in conflict with, the needs of those around them. But once we mature beyond such ethical egoism, and learn that to get along in the world we must make certain concessions—that we must to take turns, share, and play by the rules—then we cease to act purely in our own interests. Some of us, like Fletcher, Huck Finn, and, inevitably, even Montgomery, come to realize there is an even higher morality at work than society's rules, mores, and conventions can express. These, as we have seen, would go so far as to violate the law in the name of love, should the situation demand it. In other words, pleasure is not limited to the immature whims of a child who desires only immediate gratification. There are more noble pleasures and principles at work in the human heart. As Epicurus said, "For it is not continuous drinkings and revelings, nor the satisfaction of lusts, nor the enjoyment of fish and other luxuries of the wealthy table, which produces a pleasant life, but sober reasoning, searching out of motives of all choice and avoidance, and banishing mere opinions, to which are due the greatest disturbance of the spirit."[33] It is a sign of great immaturity, of moral and

---

[31] Matthew 5:46.

[32] Stumpf, Samuel E., *Philosophy, History and Problems*, 3rd ed., McGraw-Hill Book Company, New York, NY 1971, 1983, p. 108.

[33] Ibid.

cognitive delinquency, to presume *pleasure* is confined purely to self-gratification and physiological interests. Truth, wisdom, faith, justice, peace, freedom, equality, compassion, friendship, and love, are eminently more pleasurable than merely feeding our *id*. We are fundamentally social creatures, which means we take as much pleasure in the health and happiness of those around us as we do our own.

Even so, there is something to be said for our primitive instinctive impulses and drives. Sensuality, as we shall explore more fully in Chapter XI, is the primary, if not only way we experience the Divine. We see God, through God's handiwork, through Creation, in the awe and wonder of the beauty that surrounds us. The Hebrew Scriptures refer to this experience as *Hokmah*, translated as "Wisdom." Creation, the sensual world, is Wisdom. It is the realm to which we turn to find God most clearly. **"Therefore nothing defiled gains entrance into her. For she is the reflection of the working of God, and an image of his goodness."**[34] Our instinctive appetites, from this perspective, represent our instinct for the Divine. Pleasure is born of our desire to know God. As we naturally mature, therefore, as we have evolved to do, beyond our childish worldview, developing a healthy attitude of mutuality and kindness toward others, there is no need to mistrust our physiological impulses. With love as our predicate, passion is tempered always by compassion, and rage by courage.

Mistrust of the body, fear of our desires, stem, ultimately, from those who mistrust and fear their own urges because they themselves have not matured beyond the ability to seek only their own self-interests. This undeveloped mindset understands pleasure only as, "If it feels good, do it," because it has not grown to fully appreciate the presence of others in the world. Like the preschooler stamping his or her feet saying, "give me, give me, I want, I want," such a mindset, especially demonstrated by an adult, becomes heartless and, sometimes, dangerous, and rightly cannot be trusted. But as we develop and begin to value others, as love takes over, the pleasure principle moves beyond the id, and comes to understand, as Fletcher did, that, "Love and justice are

[34] Wisdom of Solomon 7:25-26.

the same, for justice is love distributed;"[35] that what we want for ourselves, we must seek also for others. If we take pleasure in having adequate food, water, clothing, shelter, health, and security, then, morally speaking, love obligates us to make certain these same pleasures are available to everyone. Jesus expressed this, of course, with his own affirmative version of the universal *Golden Rule*, **"Do unto others as you would have them do unto you."**[36] Indeed, this golden rule of thumb is so basic to the human heart that it's expressed in virtually every religious tradition. Confucius said, "Do not do to others what you would not like yourself."[37] Buddhism teaches, "Hurt not others in ways that you yourself would find hurtful."[38] Hinduism says, "This is the sum of duty; do naught unto others what you would not have them do to you."[39] In Islam it is said, "No one of you is a believer until he desires for his brother that which he desires for himself."[40] Taoism states similarly, "Regard your neighbor's gain as your gain, and your neighbor's loss as your own loss."[41] And the Talmud, from Jesus' own tradition, says, "What is hateful to you, do not do to your fellows," and goes on, like Jesus, to suggest, "This is the entire Law; all the rest is commentary."[42]

Thus, the Golden Rule is really the pleasure principle evolved enough to include the needs of others in its desires. It is what the Psalmist referred to in singing, **"The law of their God is in their hearts,"**[43] and the meaning of Ezekiel's saying, **"I will put my spirit within you, and make you follow my statutes and be careful to observe my ordinances."** Stone tablets can never supersede the heart of flesh God gives each of us, reminding us, most naturally, what is good and what is required—to seek goodness for others. Jesus' tradition claims that each of us is

---

[35] Fletcher, ibid., p. 87.

[36] Luke 6:31.

[37] Analects 12:2.

[38] Udana-Varga 5,1.

[39] Mhabharata 5, 1517.

[40] Sunnah.

[41] Tai Shang Kan Yin P'ien.

[42] Talmud, Shabbat 3id.

[43] Psalms 37:31.

made in the image and likeness of God, and that it is only when we remain separate from others that our desires become self-serving, destructive, and lewd. Motivated by love, however, by the heart center, we act upon God's spirit within us, upon the Holy Spirit hovering over and permeating all beings.

God has sown goodness.
No child is born evil.
We are all called to holiness.
The values that God has sown in the human heart
and the present-day people esteem so highly
are not rare gems;
>   *they are things that appear continually.*
Why then is there so much evil?
Because the evil inclinations of the human heart
have corrupted people, and they need purification.
The original, pristine human vocation is goodness.
We have all been born for goodness:
>   *no one is born with inclinations to kidnap,*
>   *no one is born with inclinations to be a criminal,*
>   *no one is born to be a torturer,*
>   *no one is born to be a murderer.*
We have all been born to be good,
>   *to love one another,*
>   *to understand one another.*

— Oscar Romero[44]

---

[44] Romero, Oscar, *The Violence of Love*, Orbis Books, Maryknoll, NY, 1987, 2007, p. 65f.

CHAPTER IV

Jesus Was Pro-Choice

"I came that they may have life, and have it abundantly."

It is particularly difficult to comprehend why Christian fundamentalists protest abortion and stem cell research with such ferocity, ostensibly because they value the "sanctity" of life, yet are usually vocal proponents of war. Stems cells and people who don't exist yet, the "unborn," are sacred, but those who have actually been born seem to be on their own! Thirty years after Roe v. Wade, for instance, which gave women reproductive freedom, the now deceased fundamentalist preacher, Jerry Falwell, complained, "Today, many doctors and political defenders of abortion have become wealthy on the slaughter of blameless victims; but they will forever have the blood of the unborn on their hands."[1] Yet in response to the estimated deaths of somewhere between 160,000 and 600,000 "blameless" Iraqi civilians, victims of an unwarranted oil war that's made billions for corporate war profiteers like AEGIS, Bechtel, Lockheed Martin, and, the now infamous, Halliburton, he simply said, "President Bush declared war in Iraq to defend innocent people. This is a worthy pursuit."[2] In his absurd article, *God is Pro-War*, he attempted to explain how "peaceful" Christians can condone such a war by managing to ignore everything Jesus actually said and, instead, points us to the symbolic *Book of Revelation*'s vulgar depiction of "Christ" with a "sharp sword" hanging out of his mouth. He then spins the sixth commandment by claiming it only instructs us not to "murder," and, in his words, "there's a difference between killing and

---

[1] www.juntosociety.com/guest/falwell/jf_tyoa010303.html, November 29, 2006.
[2] http://worldnetdaily.com/news/article.asp?ARTICLE_ID=36859, *God is Pro-War*, posted January 31, 2004.

murdering,"[3] ludicrously implying that it's okay to kill people as long as we don't murder them.

Christian extremism, which seeks to force its inane beliefs and hateful ways onto everyone else, is obviously more interested in the unborn than the born. Fundamentalist televangelist, Pat Robertson, who categorically states, "Abortion is murder," argues, "One of the things we must protect from the moment of conception to the moment of natural death is the life of people."[4] It's hard to imagine this is the same man who made international headlines by openly calling for the assassination of duly elected Venezuelan President Hugo Chavez during an August 2005 television broadcast of his *700 Club*; "You know, I don't know about this doctrine of assassination, but if he thinks we're trying to assassinate him, I think that we really ought to go ahead and do it. It's a whole lot cheaper than starting a war... We have the ability to take him out, and I think the time has come that we exercise that ability. We don't need another $200 billion war to get rid of one, you know, strong-arm dictator. It's a whole lot easier to have some of the covert operatives do the job and then get it over with." It is unimaginable that anyone with even a superficial knowledge of Jesus' life and teachings could make such a claim, let alone somebody like Robertson who professes to be a Christian leader and scholar.

Another prominent antiabortion extremist once daringly exclaimed, "You have a responsibility to protect your neighbor's life, and to *use force if necessary* to do so. In an effort to suppress this truth, you may mix my blood with the blood of the unborn, and those who have fought to defend the oppressed. However, truth and righteousness will prevail. May God help you to protect

---

[3] Ibid.

[4] Hill, Paul, *Defending the Defenseless*, August 2003, from a revised paper in an anthology in The Current Controversy Series: *The Abortion Controversy*, Greenhaven Press, 2001, found at www.armyofgod.com/PHill_ShortShot.html, December 1, 2006.

the unborn as you would want to be protected."[5] This was the closing statement given by Paul Hill during his capital murder trial, the former Presbyterian minister who was executed in Florida in 2003 for the shooting deaths of Dr. John Britton and his bodyguard, retired Air Force Lt. Col. James H. Barrett, along with the merciless wounding of Britton's wife outside an abortion clinic. Hill went to his death claiming these murders (Or were they merely "killings?") were an act of Christian love. "I realized that a large number of very important things would be accomplished by my shooting another abortionist in Pensacola..." he wrote, unapologetically, after the killing spree, "But most importantly, I realized that this would uphold the truth of the Gospel at the precise point of Satan's attack (the abortionist's knife)."[6] He later described how he felt after his arrest, "Soon I was alone in a large one-man cell, and could direct all my praise and thanks to the Lord. I repeatedly sang a song commonly used at rescues. The first stanza is, 'Our God is an awesome God'; He most certainly is. The only way to handle the pain of being separated from my family was to continually rejoice in the Lord for all that He had done."[7] We must wonder how radical extremists like Hill, Robertson, and Falwell can possibly justify murder or "killing" in the Lord's name.

This doesn't mean abortion isn't terrible. It is! It's a horrible choice to face, let alone to make, and the thought of terminating a human life, even at its earliest stages, seems diabolical! There can be little disagreement about this even among those of us who believe continuing a pregnancy ought to be a woman's choice. The fetal heart develops and begins beating after 21 days, usually before a mother even knows she's pregnant. Like it or not, liberal or not, it's true, abortion stops a beating heart! A responsible society should, therefore, make every compassionate effort to prevent abortion!

[1b] Ibid.

[6] Ibid.

[7] Ibid.

But compassion means recognizing that such a difficult decision is never black and white. Such mercilessly rigid thinking, indicative of all religious extremists, is a sure sign of psychological immaturity and moral underdevelopment. The pioneering work of developmental psychologist Jean Piaget, in fact, suggests several similarities between the thought processes of fundamentalists and preschool children. Neither, for instance, makes an "effort to stick to one opinion on any given subject."[8] This means, in brief, that fundamentalists, like young children, appear to contradict themselves, which is precisely why extremists like Falwell, Robertson, and Hill can simultaneously be anti-abortion and pro-war. "It is not that they adopt opinions that are self-contradictory, but they adopt opinions successively, which, if they compared would contradict each other; and they forget the points of view which they previously adopted."[9]

The self-contradiction common among both fundamentalists and young children demonstrates a mind that hasn't yet developed the capacity for connecting the dots. "Each distortion arises from inability to make relations mentally."[10] As a result, such a mind has no problem grasping absolute concepts like, "hot" and "cold," or "good" and "bad," but has difficulty understanding what is meant by "hotter," or "colder," or "better" and "worse." In short, fundamentalists, like preschoolers, can't intellectually cope with shades of grey. They don't comprehend the relationships between ideas and events. "Bigger" and "smaller" can only be understood in relation to something else, whereas, "A child uses 'big' and 'small' without confusion, since they imply one single comparison..."[11] This was the same black-and-white inconsistent reasoning demonstrated by George W. Bush when thrice vetoing stem cell research on the grounds that "all human life is sacred,"

---

[8] Beard, Ruth M., *An Outline of Piaget's Developmental Psychology*, A Mentor Book, Basic Books, Inc., New York, NY, 1972, p. 76.
[9] Ibid.
[10] Ibid., p. 78.
[11] Ibid.

yet maintaining the highest criminal execution record of any governor in Texas history, and while waging an unnecessary war that has cost hundreds of thousands of innocent lives in the Middle East.

A third mindset also common among fundamentalists and children seems to be that both "are aware of rules and take them to be absolute."[12] A religious extremist understands "good" and "evil" as unyielding, regardless of relative circumstances, but is unable to make a distinction between the "lesser of two evils." Abortion, for example, may never be a "good" choice to make, but it may be the "best" choice one can make given the situation. But for the fundamentalist, like a small child, something that is "bad" is always bad in every circumstance. Because they can't think in relative terms, they can't easily comprehend how something considered bad might be the best choice in some cases, which is why the etymological root in the word "bad" is the same as in "better" and "best." Sometimes *bad* is *best*! The unknown author of the mystical, *Cloud of Unknowing*, spoke somewhat humorously of Christians who think so simplistically by saying "they have but one spiritual nostril."[13] Having two spiritual nostrils, on the other hand, enables us to "decide the good from the bad, the bad from the worse, and the good from the better before pronouncing judgment."[14] In other words, a mature mind looks at things from all directions, connecting the dots, relatively, before making ethical decisions, which, even then, may only enable us to make a choice that is less harmful than another, but harmful nonetheless.

This is why the same author, in his *Book of Privy Council*, wrote, "What is important is that you attend to your own calling and do not discuss or judge God's designs in the lives of others...

---

[12] Ibid., p. 79.
[13] Johnston, William, ed., *The Cloud of Unknowing & Book of Privy Counseling*, Doubleday, Random House, Inc., New York, NY, 1973, 1996, p. 108.
[14] Ibid.

Believe me, if you begin judging this and that about other people you will fall into error."[15] This is especially difficult for the immature fundamentalist who, again, like a little child, attributes authoritative rules and ideas to a supreme authority. The problem with this is, as Piaget explained, "the little child cannot differentiate between the impulses of his own fancy and the rules imposed on him from above."[16] Confusing one's own will with the will of God, one's own beliefs as ultimate truth, and one's own moral values as absolute, is bad enough, but, coupled with the typical authoritarian need to punish "wrongdoers," too often leads to the sort of violence advocated by Pat Robertson, justified by Jerry Falwell, and perpetrated by Paul Hill. Repelling such hypocrisy is, no doubt, at the heart of what Jesus meant when he said, "Do not judge, so that you may not be judged... Why do you see the speck in your neighbor's eye, but do not notice the log in your own eye?" [17]

Fortunately, under normal development, even second graders become relativistic in their thinking and begin to realize rules are meant to benefit people, not burden and enslave them, and must, therefore, be changed if and when they become harmful. Jesus demonstrated such ethical maturity when faced with the choice of going hungry or being criticized for violating the Sabbath law. "The Sabbath was made for people, not people for the Sabbath,"[18] he said. Is abortion a bad decision to make? Of course! But is it the worst decision to make in every circumstance? What if continuing a pregnancy threatens a woman's life? What if a sexually responsible woman is the unfortunate victim of rape? Should she be forced to put her body, mind, and soul through additional torment by continuing an unwanted pregnancy, and perhaps a lifetime of struggling to care for a child she had not wanted or prepared for? What of the

---

[15] Ibid., p. 165f.
[16] Beard, ibid., p. 80.
[17] Matthew 7:2-3.
[18] Mark 2:27.

teenage girl whose conservative parents and community, in the name of rigid "abstinence only" thinking, did not provide adequate sex education, who becomes pregnant in a moment of unrestrained curiosity and passion? Must she quit school, give up any real future she may have had, and begin working a minimum wage job for the rest of her life in order to inadequately provide for a child she didn't expect? Moreover, what is to become of all these unwanted children once they are born? What sort of life might they have, many likely to be raised by a single parent who is nearly always absent trying to make a meager living, perhaps resentful and too emotionally and psychologically immature to have gained the wisdom and patience required for child rearing?

Jesus may not have directly addressed these questions, or ever have used the word, "abortion," but we do know he was a man of great compassion who was willing to bend the rules, even the Ten Commandments, when necessary. We also know that he was far more concerned with the born than the unborn, clearly stating, "I came that they may have life, and have it abundantly."[19] Jesus addressed the quality of life, not its quantity. He understood that genuine respect for life, the rarest and greatest gift in the Universe, seeks a certain standard of living that is free of violence, poverty, bigotry and oppression. It is not enough to force more unplanned and unwanted children to be born into the world without providing them with all the love, care, security, safety, and support they will need to live an abundant and joyful life. To promote life without these qualities is to commit idolatry—biodolatry—the worship of life merely for the sake of life itself.

Jesus understood that life is not to be worshipped, that it is not the end-all-be-all, the *alpha* and the *omega*. There are some things far more important than life, things that, at times, put our lives at risk, and are worth risking our lives for. Jesus said, "Whoever wants to save his life will lose it, but whoever loses

---

[19] John10:10.

his life for me will find it,"[20] because he, of all people, knew the importance of letting life go if it means improving the overall quality and meaning of life in general. "There is no greater love than to lay down your life for your friends,"[21] he is reported to have said. All of us must eventually and inevitably die. And like all of us, Jesus would have liked to have avoided this fate—"My Father, if it is possible, let this cup pass before me,"[22]—but, according to tradition, he bravely faced his death in the name of something far more important than life—ministering to the poor, liberating the captives, healing the sick, and freeing the oppressed.[23] Yet, as Herzog explains, "It appears that Jerusalem elites collaborating with their Roman overlords executed Jesus because he was a threat to their economic and political interests."[24] There can be little doubt that Jesus loved life, all life, including his own, and would certainly have preferred not to have been so brutally executed, yet he was willing to risk everything, including his own life, in the hope of improving the quality of life for all.

In light of all this, it's difficult to comprehend the Christian fundamentalist's singular obsession with abortion, with the "unborn," when it seems to care so little about people who are actually living. The undeniable truth is that Christianity has been covertly or overtly behind much of the oppression and many of the worst atrocities in human history, and has routinely proven that it has little regard for life, human or otherwise. Shortly after Emperor Constantine made Christianity the official State religion in ancient Rome, for instance, the often brutal and unrelenting persecution of the *pagani* (rural farmers with earth-centered beliefs) began, which included the destruction of their temples and outlawing their worship under penalty of death. From then on, outlawing unorthodox beliefs became standard operating

---

[20] Matthew 16:25.
[21] John 15:13.
[22] Matthew 26:39.
[23] Luke 4:18.
[24] Herzog, ibid., p. 9.

procedure for the Christian powers-that-be, as did naming those who held illegal beliefs "heretics," a word that simply means, "able to choose." Christianity's persecution of those who *chose* different beliefs continued for hundreds of years during various bloody crusades against those outside its domain, and the torture and execution of those within it through horrific Inquisitions.

Sadly, words cannot express the individual terror and unfathomable suffering endured by the millions who fell victim to Christian brutality during these Crusades and Inquisitions. The terrible stories of these events are replete with tales of people by the tens of thousands being mercilessly dismembered, losing eyes, ears, tongues, hands and entire limbs, before being beaten to death or burned alive. Others had their bones crushed and their flesh pulled from their bodies while their mouths were stuffed with rags to dampen the sound of their agonizing screams. Some were dragged behind horses and used as target practice, while others were killed in their beds, or hung, or, including a basket full of babies, thrown into rivers to drown. When the Spanish first arrived in the "New World" they often baptized indigenous babies and children to save their souls, then immediately smashed their heads against rocks to prevent them from growing up and losing their salvation by sinning. This, they claimed, was an act of Christian love! Others thought nothing of selling the children of "heretics" and "heathens" into slavery. Indeed, Christendom has historically perpetuated and justified slavery based on various passages found in the Hebrew and Christian scriptures.

There is, disturbingly, much more that can be recounted concerning Christianity's unrelenting and continuing crimes against the very "life" it purports to value so highly when discussing abortion; from its medieval and Salem witch-hunts, to its anti-Semitic theology, to its subordination of women, to its condemnation of scientists like Copernicus, Galileo, and Darwin, to its exploitation of indigenous peoples by missionaries, to its continued war of hate against gays and lesbians. In many cases it has not even tried to guise its hatred and cruelty, but has, on the contrary, used the blood of its victims as a stern warning to all *heretics* who might dare think for themselves. This was the case in the city of Münster in 1535 when tens of thousands of Anabaptists were drowned, beheaded, or burned to death. After they were horribly tortured and executed, the bodies of some of their leaders were placed in a cage suspended from a church rafter where they hung for more than 350 years. Talk about evidence that demands a verdict! As a movement, Christianity has littered history with the bloody corpses of innocents, without shame or remorse, and would, no doubt, do so again in this country were it not for the fragile civil laws protecting Americans from religious persecution—something the Christian Taliban is trying hard to change.

During the night of December 2, 1577, the famous Spanish mystic, San Juan de la Cruz, was pulled from his bed by his own Carmelite brethren who severely flogged him, then locked him in a small lavatory where he remained for nine-months, in the sweltering heat of summer, and the subfreezing Toledo winter, with only a carpet on the floor to cover himself. The few scraps of bread and occasional sardines he was given to eat caused dysentery, and, with no change of clothes, his body became devoured with lice. On Fridays he was made to kneel at the table of his keepers who forced him to eat his bread and water like a dog. "Look at him, brothers," the prior mocked, "this miserable wretched little friar, scarcely good enough to be a convent porter! He seeks to reform others when what he needs is to reform himself. Now bare your shoulders: it is on them that we will write the rules of the new reform."[25] Each of the friars then took turns whipping him with a cane, scarring him for what was left of his short life. His blood soaked clothes matted into his broken flesh and his untreated wounds became infested with maggots. Somehow he eventually managed to escape these horrific circumstances, only to die of illness a short time later, in part,

---

[25] Brenan, Gerald, *St. John of the Cross: His Life and Poetry*, Cambridge University Press, London, 1973, p. 31.

because a jealous and vengeful prior refused him medical treatment.

San Juan's story, and untold millions like it, makes Christianity's opposition to abortion based on the "sanctity of life," a farciful joke! Clearly there is something else going on here, some other reason Christian extremists pretend to care so much for the unborn and stem cells, in the irrefutable wake of a 2000 year old record of violence and oppression against the living! In plain psychological terms, this blatant contradiction can only be seen as *compensation*, an ego defense mechanism that enables us to avoid failure in one area by overemphasizing another. In other words, all this talk of abortion is a mere smokescreen fundamentalist Christians unconsciously hope will make them appear to love life, and, for that matter, to follow the teachings of Jesus, in light of an otherwise dismal record. Only this can explain why after nearly two terms of conservative rule during the Bush Administration, in all three branches of the U.S. government, abortion remains legal. The truth is fundamentalists want abortion to remain legal as much, if not more, than anyone else, because without it they would have no mechanism of deceiving themselves and others about their deliberate rejection of Jesus' life honoring teachings of love and nonviolence. This would also explain why they are as against proper sex education, contraception, and planned parenthood, as they are abortion. Why oppose the only real methods proven to reduce abortion rates if they're so dead against it?

The fact that they use *compensation* so transparently isn't a surprise coming from a group stuck at the earliest phase of moral and psychological development. *Fixation* is the psychological term used to describe those who cease to mature by remaining so stuck, (or fixed) at a premature stage. It is not surprising because those who use one such defense mechanism are likely to use several. Some that are likely to play a role regarding this hypocritical abortion obsession include; *Deflection*, the attempt to redirect attention to others; *Dissociation*, the compartmentalizing, or splitting off, one group of ideas from another, creating a bizarre inconsistency. In other words, in order to deflect criticism away from Christianity's two thousand year history of violence and oppression against the born, it collectively feigns concern for life by obsessing about the unborn; *Isolation*, the splitting of emotions from thoughts, so that, in this case, one claims, intellectually, to value life, yet acts without empathy toward the lives it persecutes and destroys; *Omnipotence*, coping with external stresses by assuming one is superior to others and has the right to control them—like passing laws that deny women reproductive rights; *Projection*, blaming one's own thoughts and feelings (i.e., disregard for life), on others; along with *Projective Identification*, condemning someone else's behavior by behaving similarly (i.e., killing someone for killing someone); and, *Reaction Formation*, going to opposite extremes to overcompensate for undesirable behavior, in this case, by leading a crusade against abortion, protecting the unborn, while demonstrating a long history of antisocial, if not sociopathic, behavior toward almost everyone else.

Jesus, of course, was a highly evolved ethical being who demonstrated a level of psychological maturity far beyond such ego defenses, beyond the extremist, inconsistent, judgmental, ignorant, arrogant, authoritarian, and punitive mindset so typical of fundamentalism. He did not demonstrate the developmental delinquency characteristic of those who have, oddly enough, absconded with the moral high ground in his name. Putting people before policies (and politics), Jesus would have considered the abortion issue as he did all else, with compassion and openness, realizing, like all highly developed minds, things are never black and white. The Apostle Paul wrote, **"When I was a child, I talked like a child, I thought like a child, I reasoned like a child. When I became a man, I put childish ways behind me."**[26] It is time all Christians put away childish things—

---

[26] I Corinthians 13:11.

extremism, intolerance, selfishness, hatred, and denial—and truly begin emulating the life and teachings of the man they have so long professed to revere. If all the Christians in the world were to do so, truly living as if life, all life, is a sacred gift from God, then all people and all creatures would understand what Jesus meant when he said, "Heaven is among you."

CHAPTER V

Jesus was Pro-Life

"'Lord, if my brother sins against me, how often should I forgive him? As many as seven times?' Jesus said to him, 'Not seven times, but, I tell you, seventy-seven times.'"

It's hard to fathom how anyone professing to follow Jesus can support capital punishment, if for no other reason than because Jesus himself was a victim of the death penalty. What is surprising, however, is that opinion polls indicate fundamentalist Christians don't support it anymore than most Americans (about 73 percent, according to a 1998 poll).[1] Race and geography, rather than religion, seem to be the determining factors in how many of us view capital punishment. According to Unnever and Cullen's research article, *Christian Fundamentalism and Support for Capital Punishment*, "individuals who opposed the death penalty were more likely to be African American and born outside the United States and that those who supported capital punishment tended to be politically conservative and native southerners."[2] This should not be surprising given the fact that a disproportionate number of African Americans are incarcerated and on Death Row. What seems unexpected, however, is that conservative Christians, in general, aren't outraged by our penal system's continued use of capital punishment given their obsessive rhetoric about saving the unborn, and the political and legal extremities to which they'll go to prevent family members from disconnecting brain-dead relatives from artificial life support systems, all in the name of "sacred life."

---

[1] Cullen, Francis T., & Unnever, James D., "Christian Fundamentalism and Support for Capital Punishment," *Journal of Research in Crime Delinquency*, 2006; 43; p. 176.

[2] Ibid. p. 185f.

While they're not out there advocating for the death penalty, their silence and complacency about it seems entirely inconsistent with a religion that's supposed to be rooted in compassion and forgiveness. As Martin Luther King understood, "A time comes when silence is betrayal." Its silence regarding capital punishment may be due to fundamentalism's commitment to the doctrine of *original sin*, combined with its pre-conventional (childish morality) devotion to a punitive-father-god, which, together, supersede higher ethical (post-conventional) principles like compassion and forgiveness. In brief, if everyone is born a sinner, then everyone deserves to be punished. For what, in the end, is the death penalty compared to the eternal fires of Hell that all of us deserve?

Interestingly, research also suggests that the stronger an individual's religious practice, the less likely he or she is to support the death penalty,[3] which leaves Unnever and Cullen wondering why other researchers haven't "fully explored the relationships among being a Christian fundamentalist having a strong religious practice and support for the death penalty."[4] In other words, if those who put their faith into practice tend to be against capital punishment, why are so many fundamentalists in support of it? To me the logical answer seems quite clear— fundamentalists don't practice their religion!

This may be difficult to grasp considering the argument that fundamentalists are among the most religious people in the world. Although this may be true to some degree, we must make the distinction between *orthodoxy* and *orthopraxy*. The word "orthodox" combines the Latin words *ortho*, meaning "straight," (as in the orthodontist who straightens teeth), with the word *doxa*, meaning "teaching," (as in doxology). In short, *orthodoxy* simply means "straight teaching." *Orthopraxy*, on the other hand, combines *ortho* with *praxi*, the Latin word for "practice," thus referring to "straight-practice." Fundamentalists are orthodox,

---

[3] Ibid., p. 185.
[4] Ibid.

meaning they concern themselves mostly with holding and expressing the right beliefs, and not so much with their behavior—orthopraxi. They tend to relate better to the orthodox Apostle Paul, who said, **"We know that a person is not justified by the works of the law but through faith in Jesus Christ,"** [5] than with the orthopraxy of James, who argued to the contrary, **"faith without works is dead."**[6] In brief, fundamentalists are dogmatic, not pragmatic, and, therefore, don't concern themselves as much with demonstrating the forgiveness and compassion modeled by Jesus as they do with simply holding the right ideas about him; namely, that **"whosoever *believeth* in him shall not perish but have everlasting life."**[7]

Again, according to Unnever and Cullen's research, "individuals who had a harsh hierarchal image of God were more likely and those who were compassionate were less likely to support the death penalty."[8] This finding may seem somewhat obvious, but what is confusing is that the same results indicate that those who tested highest in the areas of forgiveness and compassion were also Biblical literalists.[9] These findings may seem a bit confusing, but a closer look at the questions used for determining them indicate they may only prove, again, that fundamentalists *believe* in compassion and forgiveness, but say nothing about how they put them into *practice*. Although the survey questions about forgiveness did pertain to a superficial rating about how often they forgive themselves and others, the single question about compassion asked outright, on a scale from 1 to 4, whether they strongly *agree* or *disagree* with the statement, "I feel a deep sense of responsibility for reducing pain and suffering in the world."[10] Thus, the results simply measure whether

---

[5] Galatians 2:16.
[6] James 2:26.
[7] John 3:16.
[8] Cullen & Unnever, ibid., p. 185.
[9] Ibid.. p. 184f.
[10] Ibid., p. 177.

or not those questioned believe in compassion, perhaps to the point where they have genuine feelings of obligation to those who suffer, but prove nothing about how they demonstrate compassion. Yet compassion is not a belief that we agree or disagree with; it's something we act upon!

It does not seem possible for any of us, let alone, and especially, those who profess to follow a man who was himself a victim of capital punishment, to merely pay lip service to compassion and forgiveness in light of all the injustices associated with the executions of criminals. During its history the U.S. has legally executed more than 13,000 people, and continues to execute an average of 1 to 2 prisoners each week. Ninety percent of those executed are too poor to afford a lawyer, and, again, a disproportionate number of them are of minority status. 74 percent of the federal death penalty cases between 1995 and 2000 involved minority defendants, and more than 80 percent of Federal death row prisoners were African American or Hispanic. Furthermore, since DNA testing has come onto the scene, more than a hundred Death Row inmates have been proven innocent, suggesting many more are probably innocent, and, even worse, an untold number of innocents have already been executed.

Obviously it doesn't take a great deal of theological training to know what Jesus would have to say about all of this if he were alive today. During his lifetime many people ascribed to the Hebrew maxim, "an eye for an eye," which meant those found guilty of murder could be legally stoned to death, but it also meant those convicted of lesser infractions should not be disproportionately punished. "An eye for an eye" means, "let the punishment fit the crime." Don't take a whole head for an eye, or the life of a peasant too poor to pay his taxes, or of a hungry orphan who must steal to survive, or of a woman accused of prostitution because she has been raped and victimized by men who refuse to take responsibility for their own actions.

Unfortunately, at the time, "an eye for an eye," was just that, a maxim. It did not reflect Hebrew law, which allowed execution by stoning for a number of offenses we would certainly consider minor. It was a compassionate saying expressed by those in Jesus' day who opposed the death penalty. If they had cars at the time, "an eye for an eye," would have been a bumper sticker displayed by those opposing capital punishment. But for Jesus it didn't go far enough. "You have heard that it was said, 'an eye for an eye and a tooth for a tooth,'" he told his followers, "but I say to you, do not resist an evildoer. But if anyone strikes you on the right cheek, turn the other also."[11] Jesus taught the opposite of revenge—he taught forgiveness, and compassion. "You have heard it said, 'You shall love your neighbor and hate your enemy.' But I say to you, Love your enemies and pray for those who persecute you..."[12] For if you forgive others their trespasses, your heavenly Father will also forgive you."[13] Elsewhere, when Peter asks, "**Lord, if another member of the church sins against me, how often should I forgive? As many as seven times?**" Jesus is reported to have responded, "Not seven times, but, I tell you, seventy-seven times."[14] For the Jews, seven is a holy number symbolizing completion, just as Yahweh rested on the seventh day after creating the world. Thus, many Jews took the letter of the law literally and thought they were required to generously forgive wrongdoers just seven times before unloading God's full fury on them. But Jesus, as always, tried to get at the heart of the law, not by eliminating it, but making it even more difficult to observe, in this case, by saying, "seventy-seven times," which is another way of saying you must never stop extending forgiveness.

Jesus' position about capital punishment was, no doubt, born of his deep compassion for others, but must also have been in direct response to the horrific abuses of power he witnessed by the Roman authorities. According to the ancient historian, Josephus,

[11] Matthew 5:38.
[12] Matthew 5:43.
[13] Matthew 6:15.
[14] Matthew 18: 21.

the Romans crucified thousands of people near Jerusalem during Jesus' life, and sometimes conducted mass executions, involving as many as five-hundred crucifixions a day.[15] And, just as today, in which capital punishment is mostly reserved for poor minorities, in Jesus' day, as you will recall, "crucifixion was not the punishment of citizens and aristocrats, but of slaves and servants, peasants and bandits."[16] One can only imagine the overwhelming grief experienced by somebody with the compassion of Jesus upon witnessing firsthand thousands of crosses holding the remains of legally executed criminals left to rot and be picked apart by birds and dogs, perhaps seeing and hearing the agony of those in the excruciating final throws of death, and the overbearing stench that was all that lingered of those whose only true crime was poverty. Jesus also experienced the personal loss of his mentor, John the Baptist, who was legally beheaded. And finally, as we all know, Jesus himself received the death penalty for being a public nuisance.

The decision to emphasize crucified Christ rather than the life affirming teachings of Jesus the man reflects Christianity's more necrophilous orientation. Historically speaking, this "love of the dead" has been part of the Christian tradition since its inception when its founder admitted, "**I decided to know nothing among you except Christ and him crucified.**"[17] The result, especially 2000 years later, as we have seen, has been its focus upon people who don't yet live and those who have died, the unborn and the afterlife. The first Christians, in fact, held most of their meetings in cemeteries and catacombs, partly to hideout from the authorities, but mostly to include their dead in their rituals, whom they fully expected to be raised at the imminent return of Christ. As historian, David Chidester explains, "Christians met at

---

[15] Crossan, John Dominic, & Reed, Jonathan L., *Excavating Jesus*, HarperCollins, New York, NY, 2001, p. 246.
[16] Ibid., p. 245.
[17] I Corinthians 2:2.

the cemetery for special religious activities that renewed relations with the dead;"[18]

> Assembling at the burial site, they shared a meal of fish, bread, cakes, and wine. As part of the ritual, they poured a libation of wine over the tomb, inviting the deceased to share in the enjoyment of the meal. By eating and drinking with the dead these Christians reaffirmed bonds of kinship and community that could not be broken by death. More than a memorial ritual, therefore, the *refrigerium* was an occasion for speaking with the dead, for offering prayers or requesting assistance, in ways that suggested the continuity of a relationship. The ritual meal in the cemetery was devoted not merely to the memory of the deceased friends and relatives, but to their ongoing presence in social life."[19]

Christians have a long history of relating to the dead, at least, as much as to the living, and eventually, especially during the 3rd century, they became obsessed with dying as martyrs themselves. Having been persecuted and outlawed to varying degrees since Nero blamed them for the fires of Rome in 64 CE, they came, it seems, not only to accept, but to embrace their plight by seeking out martyrdom to prove their faith. "First the martyr achieved instant salvation by imitating the model of sacrificial suffering, torture, and death established by Jesus Christ... Second, in the process of imitating Jesus Christ, the martyr also set a model to be followed by other Christians who sought redemption in the face of adversity."[20] Perhaps this necrophilous orientation is summarized best in the words of Vibia Perpetua, a 3rd century

---

[18] Chidester, David. *Christianity: A Global History*, HaperCollins Publishers, New York, NY, 2000, p. 72.
[19] Ibid., p. 72f.
[20] Ibid., p. 78.

martyr who, upon her baptism, said, "The Spirit told me I should seek nothing from the water other than the suffering flesh."[21]

This obsession with death and suffering, this worship of a crucified figure, further explains the moral rigor mortis typical of most fundamentalists. "To the necrophilous person justice means correct division, and they are willing to kill or die for the sake of what they call justice," Erich Fromm once explained, "'Law and order' for them are idols—everything that threatens law and order is felt as a satanic attack against their supreme values."[22] In light of this rigid unforgiving attitude, then, it's easy to understand why Christian fundamentalists tend to ignore the plight of criminals put to death for breaking the law. They cannot grasp, as Meister Eckhart did, that "compassion means justice," not punishment. As a situation ethicist, by contrast, Jesus, who said, "Let the dead bury the dead,"[23] understood that "justice is love distributed;" and is, therefore, not something we bring people to, but something we bring to people.

As this work proceeds we will more fully explore Jesus' *biophilous*—life affirming—teachings. For now, however, it should be clear to any who look even superficially at his life, where he must have stood regarding capital punishment. Not only because he was a person of great compassion who witnessed thousands of his own people unjustly executed, but also because he was a victim of the death penalty himself. Yet it does seem promising, at least, that even though they don't overtly oppose the death penalty, most fundamentalists today are simply uninterested in the issue. Unlike their obsession with abortion and right-to-life cases, capital punishment doesn't seem to be on their collective radar screen of concerns. Thus, it seems possible, given their orthodox beliefs about the value of life, it may not take a great deal of persuasion to get fundamentalist Christians, as a whole, to

---

[21] Ibid., p. 79.
[22] Fromm Erich, *The Heart of Man*, Harper Colophon Edition, Harper & Row, New York, NY, 1980, copyright, 1964, p. 41.
[23] Matthew 8:22.

begin including prisoners in their right-to-life campaign, in their *orthopraxy*. In the end, we might hope, our collective instinct toward the value of life will come to reflect our actions, and, bringing an end to the injustice of capital punishment, may be a cause that leads conservatives and progressives to set aside our differences and unite, truly, as "one people under God." Until then, "let those who have not erred, cast the first stone."

CHAPTER VI

Jesus was a Draft Dodger

*"Put your sword back in its place; for all who live by the
sword will perish by the sword."*

A few weeks before Christmas 2003, I attended an interfaith breakfast during which Gandhi's grandson, Arun Gandhi, gave the keynote address. He began by telling about the summer his parents sent him to stay with his famous grandfather in India. He was twelve years old at the time, living in South Africa, where he'd had a run in with a gang of white youth who beat him up for being "too black." A short time later he was assaulted by a group of black youth for being "too white." How desperate and lonely he must have felt, especially at an age when chum relations become so vital to the development of one's self worth and sense of identity. Needless to say, Arun was angry. "When I told grandfather about the beatings," he recounted, "he listened intently as he put his arms around me in a gesture of love and comfort. 'I can understand your anger,' he said. 'But do you know that anger is like electricity? It can be powerful, as powerful and destructive as electricity. Anger is the same. If you don't harness your anger, then it will also destroy and kill.'" But Grandpa Gandhi wasn't judging his grandson's anger in the least. When he put his arms around him, he accepted him unconditionally, loving everything about him, including his rage. "Anger is the beginning of justice," he said, "anger is necessary."

This notion immediately began having a profound effect on my psyche. Until then, I suppose, I had been judging my own rage, and was probably even a little afraid of it. But the thought that it might somehow be essential to my work in social justice began to break through this false paradigm on the deepest of levels. A few weeks after hearing Arun's lecture I had a dream in which Gandhi came to teach me about anger. He told me there are four ways to express anger. The first of these is the one we're all most familiar with, *explosive anger*. It's what happens when we suddenly blow up, reacting violently and aggressively. On an individual level, he explained, it might mean giving someone the finger while we're caught in traffic, or cussing at someone before we've had time to think about the consequences, or getting into a fist-fight, or, at its worse, it might lead to murder. On a collective level, explosive anger happens when we literally go to war and shoot or drop bombs on each other.

"The second kind of anger," he continued, "is *implosive anger*." This kind of anger is expressed collectively when we cause structures, like old buildings, to collapse inwardly so that they don't cause damage to the other structures around them. Although it might be an effective means of demolition, implosions can be extremely dangerous. In fact, as you may know, implosion is part of the process in creating nuclear explosions, along with creating stars, and was ultimately responsible for the explosion that caused the Big Bang. Sometimes holding anger in can end up causing an even bigger explosion! This is why implosive anger is especially detrimental to individuals, because it makes us direct all of it inwardly at ourselves, either because external pressures force us to contain it, or because we're afraid of hurting those around us. It's analogous to diving so deeply into the ocean that the water pressure eventually crushes us. Thus, implosive anger is often responsible for feelings of depression along with all self-destructive behaviors, including suicide.

The third type of angry expression, according to my nocturnal visitor, is *subversive anger*. It's expressed collectively by terrorists, like suicide bombers, who don't stick around long enough to take responsibility for their violent actions. It also includes those perpetrators of murder-suicides, especially mass murderers like those responsible for the massacres at Columbine High School in 1999, and more recently at Virginia Tech. On a personal level, subversive anger is expressed through passive aggressive behaviors like being stubborn, uncooperative, procrastinating, or by communicating indirectly to those we're angry at by talking to a third party, hoping someone else might do something about an issue we're uncomfortable dealing with ourselves—a form of communication known as *triangulation*.

But the only authentic, meaningful, and productive expression of anger is what my dream-Gandhi called "*nonviolent direct action*." As with the other kinds of anger, he went on to explain how we might express this in both a personal and collective fashion. All of us know how well it works on a collective level given what Gandhi himself managed to accomplish in liberating India, and what Martin Luther King, Jr. was able to accomplish for civil rights through his use of nonviolence. But on an individual level, nonviolent direct action means confronting those we feel have treated us wrongly in an open and honest manner—not by calling them names or fighting with them; not by becoming depressed or hurt because of their actions; and not by talking about them behind their backs. To be direct and honest, though non-threatening, in this way, is an act of love motivated, paradoxically, by rage.

It was after this profound dream experience that I was able to more clearly articulate what had been stewing in my mind ever since hearing Arun Gandhi's lecture—anger is necessary, anger is positive, anger motivates nonviolence, without anger we will never have peace and justice. As difficult as this seeming paradox might be to grasp, it makes sense when we actually look at the etymology of the word *courage*. It's a combination of the Latin word for "heart," *cor*, and *rabies*, meaning "madness," or "fury." In other words, courage is the madness of the heart! It's angry love, or, perhaps better put, anger that's been loved—anger transformed by the power of love. "Anger is like a howling baby," Thich Nhat Hanh, another nonviolent activist, tells us, "The baby needs his mother to embrace him. You are the mother for your baby, your anger... Just embracing your anger, just breathing in and breathing out, that is good enough. The baby will feel relief right away."[1] If we don't love our anger in this way, guiding it and nourishing it with the heart, it remains immature and can only express itself in destructive ways, through explosion, implosion, and subversion. In loving it, however, it matures into full-grown courage and gives us the strength to do big things. I once heard theologian Matthew Fox even explain that *rage* is also the root of the word *large*. Courage, the rage of the heart, makes us bigger! It empowers us to do big things, like Dr. Seuss' Grinch whose heart grows three sizes upon discovering the true meaning of Christmas. Gandhi and King accomplished big things because they had big hearts, courage, and they had courage because they were angry.

Jesus must have been angry too. We know this, not because he was explosive, but because he was nonviolent, exemplified by his numerous sayings; "Turn the other cheek... Love your Enemies... Do not exchange evil for evil... Do good to those who harm you... Put away your sword... Those who live by the sword will die by the sword." As theologian Walter Wink surmises, "Jesus, in short, abhors both passivity and violence. He articulates, out of the history of his own people's struggles, a way by which evil can be opposed without being mirrored, the oppressor resisted without being emulated, and the enemy neutralized without being destroyed."[2] Despite his unequivocal teachings about non-violence, Christians throughout history, as already noted, have somehow managed to justify violence against others. Often such justification hinges upon the convenient misinterpretation of a few scriptures, or by the invention of a Church doctrine that circumvents Jesus' actual teachings.

The most common event cited to justify violence, however, regards Jesus' outburst in the Temple when he turned

---

[1] Hanh, Thich Nhat, *Anger*, Riverhead Books, New York, NY, 2001, p. 27f.

[2] Wink, Walter, *The Powers that Be*, A Galilee Book published by Doubleday, New York, NY, 1998, p. 111.

over the tables of a few merchants. Admittedly, this occasion, which led to his arrest and execution, was more explosive than was usual for Jesus, but it can hardly be construed as violent. Nobody was hurt. It was a harmless, albeit untypical, act of disgust directed toward a corrupt system that had allowed this holy place to become a center of greed and exploitation. Dr. King once defended the violence of the summer riots of 1967 in this same way. "This blood-lust interpretation ignores one of the most striking features of the city riots," he explained, "...the violence, to a certain degree, was focused against property rather than against people."[3] He goes on to explain that most the injuries that did occur were caused by police and military officials trying to protect private property. In the same way, the only person who was injured by Jesus' action was himself. Like the rioters of 1967, he was lashing out against a society that used much of its resources to protect the private property of relatively few people, while so many others were left hung out to dry by an unjust and exploitative system.

Another verse some Christians like to use to prove Jesus was violent is *Mark* 3:5, regarding his response to a few puritanical Pharisees, **"He looked around at them with anger."** Again, we've already established that Jesus was necessarily angry. All true rabble-rousers are, for, again, "anger is the beginning of justice." But anger isn't the equivalent of violence. *Looking* at others with anger isn't that same as pummeling them. Then, of course, there is Jesus' saying, "I have not come to bring peace but a sword."[4] Clearly this was but a figure of speech reflecting the radical nature of Jesus' teachings. He understood that his ideas would not be accepted by everyone, and, without a doubt, would create divisions, even among some members of the same family. "...one's foes will be members of one's own household,"[5] he

---

[3] King, Martin Luther, *A Testament of Hope*, Washington, James, ed., HarperCollins, New York, NY, 1986, 1981, p. 648f.

[4] Matthew 10:34.

[5] Matthew 10:36.

said. This is the only logical way to reconcile this statement with his many indisputable teachings about compassion and nonviolence.

Jesus' early followers understood this and refused to fight, often at great peril to themselves. One of the characteristics contributing to their persecution by the Roman authorities was their refusal to serve in the military, even if it meant their own execution. Hippolytus, a second century Christian leader, writing about admission into the faith, said:

> A gladiator or trainer of gladiators, or a huntsman (in wild-beast shows) or anyone connected with the shows, or a public official in charge of gladiatorial exhibitions must desist or be rejected. A soldier of the civil authority must be taught not to kill men and to refuse to do so if he is commanded, and to refuse to take an oath; if he is unwilling to comply, he must be rejected. A military commander or civic magistrate that wears the purple must resign or be rejected. If a catechumen or a believer seeks to become a soldier, they must be rejected, for they have despised God.[6]

This prohibition against violence didn't change for more than three hundred years, until Constantine made it possible for Christianity to become the official State religion. In *A History of Christianity*, Owen Chadwick explains, "The early church had not liked its member to fight in armies. When all society was supposed to be Christian, that rule could no longer apply, because someone had to defend society."[7] In addition, because all soldiers were state employees, they had to be Christians, which meant the days of Christian pacifism were over. Two hundred years later Augustine took things as step further by arguing that it is one's

---

[6] Fromm, *The Dogma of Christ*, ibid., p. 59
[7] Chadwick, Owen, *A History of Christianity*, St. Martin's Press, New York, NY, 1995, p. 197.

duty to defend one's neighbors by any means necessary, even if it might not be permissible for Christians to defend themselves. "With that deft stroke," Walter Wink laments, "Augustine opened the door to the just-war theory, the military defense of the Roman Empire, and the use of torture and capital punishment. Following his lead, Christians have ever since been justifying wars fought for nothing more than national interest as 'just.'"[8]

Early Christians understood, like Jesus, that it is not possible to bring people to justice, it is only possible to bring justice to people. In the end violence never works! It may bring some short-term satisfaction—a false sense of personal empowerment, or temporary control of scarce resources—but it always leads only to more violence, more destruction, more hatred, and more injustice. Walter Wink further illustrates this by pointing out that the casualties in the 16th century amounted to 1.6 million people. Just one century later that number inverted to 6.1 million people. In the 1700's it rose again to 7 million people. By the 19th century it nearly tripled to 19.4 million people. And by the end of the 20th century, with all our modern knowledge and technology, we succeeded in killing a staggering 109 million people with our mechanisms of war.[9] And now, at the start of yet another new millennium, millions around the world have already lost their lives to war. In all ages, nearly half of those killed have been civilians, a percentage that has exponentially increased only during recent decades. Violence simply does not work. It never has, it never will, and Jesus knew it!

Nonviolence, on the other hand, has proven to be extremely successful during those rare occasions it has been used in human history. On January 26, 1930, for example, Gandhi signed India's Declaration of Independence, then made his historic march to the Dandi to make salt in protest of a law prohibiting its sale and production by anyone other than the British government. This was especially outrageous considering this important mineral

---

[8] Wink, Walter, ibid., p. 99.
[9] Wink, ibid., p. 137.

was naturally abundant in India, and diabolically oppressive considering people in hot humid regions need to continually replenish the salt they lose from sweating. Even though it took another 17 years, Gandhi's march proved successful because he was able to drive the British occupiers from his homeland without resorting to violence. Sure there were plenty of bumps and bruises along the way, but nothing compared to the violence of, say, Vietnam, during which well over a million people were killed in a war that lasted 11 years; or to World War II, a six year war, during which more than sixty million people lost their lives worldwide.

It took quite a bit longer, more than 70 years, for the nonviolent women's suffrage movement to finally win American women the right to vote in 1920. But many would consider this time well spent in light of the relatively brief Civil War that cost the lives of more than 600,000 soldiers alone. Similarly, if America's Civil Rights movement made its greatest advances between 1955, when Rosa Parks refused to give up her bus seat to a white man, and 1968, with the passage of the Civil Rights Bill, then we must agree, Dr. King's nonviolent response to discrimination was a huge success, even though it ultimately cost him his own life. Unfortunately, nonviolent action does often evoke violent retaliation from those oppressive regimes it challenges, but the death toll is usually a mere fraction of that which results from warfare. The peaceful Dr. King once lamented, "I have been arrested five times and put in Alabama jails. My home has been bombed twice. A day seldom goes by that my family and I are not the recipients of threats of death. I have been the victim of a near-fatal stabbing. So in a real sense I have been battered by the storms of persecution."[10] Yes, there is violence and grave risk associated with nonviolent action, but far less than otherwise if, at least, one side in a conflict understands what Jesus meant by, "Love your enemies... do good to those who persecute you... turn the other cheek."

---

[10] King, ibid., p. 41.

Despite the terrible violence and injustice often inflicted against nonviolent activists, we must admit that nonviolence is a far more powerful and practical force for good than war and violence. Nonviolence works! Again, as Walter Wink reminds us, "In 1989 alone, thirteen nations comprising 1.7 billion people—over thirty-two percent of humanity—experienced nonviolent revolutions."[11] He is referring, of course, to the mostly nonviolent spread of democracy throughout Eastern Europe that ended the Cold War. It may not have been as successful in China where, that same year, hundreds, perhaps thousands, of peaceful demonstrators were massacred in Tiananmen Square. Still, who can forget the almost archetypal image of that unknown Chinese rebel standing down a squad of military tanks? It's an image that has come to epitomize the power of nonviolent action!

In fact, nonviolence works so well, it is often a shock to the system, particularly to the social system of domination and violence that has typified human interaction since ancient times. Around 1975, for instance, at the "end" of the Vietnam War, many Americans were in shock, and probably felt a little afraid, because their faith in this ancient paradigm that says, "violence will save us," had been so badly shaken. The first thing they had to cope with in light of Vietnam, despite romanticizing previous wars, was the startling realization that violence can fail. Perhaps more

---

[11] Wink, ibid., p. 117.

importantly, directly on the heels of the successful nonviolent Civil Rights movement, Americans witnessed thousands of peaceful protestors help facilitate an end to the war. So, for the first time, many had to admit that nonviolence is a practical and powerfully effective solution to conflict.

Fortunately for them, filmmaker Steven Spielberg came to the rescue that year with his surprising box office hit, *Jaws*. Surely this low-budget horror flick, with such poor special effects that most the fake shark footage ended up on the cutting room floor, would have been a complete flop were it not the perfect medicine for what was ailing many Americans. The story of a small town police chief restoring order to his community by killing a gigantic shark was the perfect catharsis amidst the years of chaos culminating in 1975. Thousands of young people had been killed in war; thousands more were demonstrating in the streets; some were being killed in those streets by the very police officers sworn to protect them; many people saw TV coverage of the North Vietnamese taking over Saigon and U.S. officials airlifted to safety, despite years wasted on war; school integration through busing had begun only a few months earlier; women were demanding to be treated as equals; and President Nixon had only just recently resigned from office after a national scandal. The country was in chaos, and many Americans were feeling insecure and afraid. They needed to be reassured that the world wasn't really broken, that their collective story wasn't a lie—violence had to be redeemed! So they went in droves to watch goodly Chief Brody restore peace to his utopian seaside town by destroying a deadly menace from the deep.

This explanation for the film's success isn't too farfetched when we consider it in light of the ancient dominator myth that humans have collectively maintained for thousands of years. *Jaws* is essentially a modern retelling of the ancient Babylonian story of Marduk and Tiamat. Tiamat was a monstrous chaos goddess who lived in the sea. Other Babylonian gods were terrified of her because they never knew when she might rise from its depths to wreck havoc. In an act of desperation they sought help from Marduk, a typical storm god, or hammer god (much like Yahweh, Indra, Zeus, and Thor, respectively, of the Jewish, Hindu, Greek, and Nordic traditions). Marduk agreed to help, but only if the other gods would put him in charge of things, which, under such duress, they gladly obliged. In the end Marduk defeats Tiamat by causing her to swallow a hurricane then shooting her with his arrow, causing her to explode. He then used her remains to reorder the universe, creating the heavens, the Earth, and all creatures. Thus Marduk uses violence to restore order. Likewise, in *Jaws*, it's Chief Brody's job to restore order by destroying his own version of Tiamat, a giant great-white shark. And he does so in exactly the same manner as Marduk, by placing an air tank in her mouth and blowing it up with his pistol. No more shark, no more chaos, order is restored.

The similarity between these two stories is not coincidental. On the contrary, this formula—hero restores order by violently destroying chaos—is the basis of almost every story told from ancient times until now. This common story, which Walter Wink calls "The Myth of Redemptive Violence," is, in his words, "the real myth of the modern world. It, and not Judaism or Christianity or Islam, is the dominant religion in our society today."[12] We see and hear it being retold everywhere everyday, not only in John Wayne, Clint Eastwood, and Arnold Schwarzenegger movies, as we might expect, but also in common children's stories. How many such stories culminate in violence? Disney films like *Aladdin*, *The Lion King*, *Beauty and the Beast*, end the same as *Jaws* and *Marduk*, with the hero winning a violent battle over the enemy. Although Wink admits this is not true of all children's stories, it is the norm. "Examples would include the Teenage Mutant Ninja Turtles, the X-Men, Transformers, the Fantastic Four, Silver Surfer, Ice Man, the Superman Family, Captain America, the Lone Ranger and Tonto, Batman and Robin,

---

[12] Ibid., p. 42.

Road Runner and Wile E. Coyote, and Tom and Jerry."[13] Given this list, it's obvious that neither Wink nor I are very current on children's programming, but I'm confidant things haven't changed much since we were kids.

Indeed, my favorite retelling of the Myth of Redemptive Violence comes from the classic television series starring Don Adams as secret agent Maxwell Smart in *Get Smart*. Wink points out that the "good guys," Smart and his partner, agent 99, work for an organization called CONTROL in an effort to thwart the evil plans of an organization called CHAOS. It doesn't get any plainer than that! During the show's last episode, first aired in 1970 (during the midst of the Vietnam War), the series' villain is finally defeated once and for all after a cigarette blows up in his mouth and forces him to his doom off the edge of a cliff. Smart would have referred to this as "the old exploding cigarette trick," which, as we have seen, is at least as old as Marduk's defeat over Tiamat, and used also to defeat the shark in *Jaws*. After this final blow to CHAOS, 99 remarks, "You know, Max, sometimes I think we're no better than they are, the way we murder and kill and destroy people." And so the series ends with Smart's nonchalant but poignant response, "Why 99, you know we have to murder and kill and destroy in order to preserve everything that's good in the world."

Unfortunately the Myth of Redemptive Violence isn't restricted to the world of entertainment. More often, it has been, and is being, lived out among us. Today we may not be afraid of sea monsters, or sharks, or even communists, but we're still afraid of whatever the enemy is we've conjured in our imaginations to help us perpetuate this age-old paradigm so we can feel safe in an otherwise chaotic world. So, as creatures of habit, we thoughtlessly repeat this tragic tale, believing it is really violence, not Jesus, that will save us. Today we're trying to blow up terrorists because they "hate our freedom." Who knows who it

---

[13] Ibid., p. 43.

might be tomorrow, or ten years, or a generation from now? One thing is for certain, as long as we continue to reenact this myth, there must always be another enemy to destroy. Even though violence never really works, we'll keep on trying, hoping, someday, things might end up like they do in the movies, with a happy ending.

If, as biologist Richard Dawkins suggests, ideas behave a lot like genes in the way they become dominant among human beings, often suppressing less prominent ideological traits in the process, then the Myth of Redemptive Violence has certainly become a dominant characteristic in the idea pool. But just as certain recessive genes lie dormant behind the scenes, sometimes showing up unexpectedly, there are also recessive ideas that the dominator myth cannot completely stamp out. One of these, "memes," as Dawkins calls them, is the principle of *nonviolence*. Although it has remained recessive for thousands of years, it still crops up now and again in certain individuals, like Gandhi, King, and Jesus, not to mention Leo Tolstoy, Clara Barton, Ralph Waldo Emerson, Henry David Thoreau, Susan B. Anthony, Albert Schweitzer, Dorothy Day, Mother Jones, Philip and Daniel Berrigan, the Dalai Lama, Thomas Merton, Father Oscar Romero, Julia "Butterfly" Hill, Nelson Mandela, Desmond Tutu, Father Roy Bourgeois, John Lennon, Cindy Sheehan, etc., etc., and the countless millions who have followed figures like these throughout history to help bring about justice and liberty through nonviolence.

In Hindu mythology this recessive meme is represented by a young three-headed acetic created to take over the throne of Indra. With the first head he studies the sacred texts, with the second he nourishes himself, and with the third he appreciates all that is. Indra, a typical hammer god, prone to using force and violence to make things happen, feels threatened by the gentle, pious, and humble acetic because his power is increasing and he seems destined to one day absorb the entire universe. So Indra decides to destroy his nemesis, first by exposing him, unsuccessfully, to carnal temptation. When this fails, however, Indra resorts to his usual habit—violence—and strikes him down with a thunderbolt. But even in death his body continues to radiate light. Indra orders a passing woodsman to cut off his heads, out of which burst a flurry of birds that fly off in all directions.

Hammer gods like Indra, Yahweh, Zeus, Thor, and Marduk, might better be referred to as *pioneer gods* because they are often revered by the pioneers struggling to survive in harsh new lands against the unpredictable and, sometimes, dangerous forces of nature. Before finding their way, around 1500 BCE, to what would become India, for example, the ancient Aryans, as they are called, were a peaceful people who farmed their lands, had no ambition to conquer new territory, and revered all life because they believed the Divine was present in all things. But as they slowly migrated from the Caucasian steppes of southern Russia, into a harsher climate, it became increasingly difficult for them to grow food and maintain livestock. The threat of drought was of particular concern in the hot arid conditions many found themselves in. Getting their basic physiological needs met became their primary concern and left them uninterested in relating to the divine presence in all things. They began elevating the importance of Indra, once a minor warrior-god in a larger pantheon, because he could use his hammer to break open the stubborn clouds and force them to release their showers of blessing upon the people. Focusing most of their worship on this warrior-god made these once gentle people more violent themselves, especially once they domesticated horses and turned their slow ox-driven carts into fast war-chariots. As Karen Armstrong points out, "With their superior weapons, they could conduct lightning raids on neighboring settlements and steal cattle and crops."[14] These raiders justified such violence and exploitation by believing they were only imitating Indra who road about the heavens making war and

---

[14] Armstrong, Karen, *The Great Transformation*, Alfred A. Knopf, New York, NY, 2006, p. 7.

taking what he wants. "Heroes with noble horses, fain for battle, selected warriors call on me in combat. I, bountiful Indra, excite the conflict, I stir the dust, Lord of surpassing vigour!"[15] So, in the name of their religion, "They killed, plundered, and pillaged, terrorizing the more conservative Aryans, who were bewildered, frightened, and entirely disoriented, feeling that their lives had been turned upside down."[16] And so these very same people who once recognized God in all things, lived peacefully together, and conjured stories about gentle ascetics, allowed their nonviolent memes to become regressive, and came, instead, to embrace the dominator Myth of Redemptive Violence.

But the good news is that the regressive story of nonviolence cannot be completely stamped out. Returning to our myth, when the ascetic's heads were cut off, his ideas flew forth in all direction like a flock of birds, migrating to new places, transporting the seeds of wisdom and peace, and landing wherever they may. The principle of nonviolence, threatening Indra's throne, cannot be killed, and may, someday, become the dominant meme that truly does absorb the entire universe. This has certainly been true of India, Gandhi's homeland. Indeed, it can be argued that Gandhi's passion for nonviolence, *ahimsa*, was part of his genetic as well as his memetic inheritance. For beginning in the 9th century BCE things began to take a turn in India. The people were feeling more settled and at home; their economy was becoming more agrarian; raiding parties fell out of fashion; and, perhaps most importantly, they stopped believing in violence and returned to asceticism. Even their religious rituals were reformed to ban all semblances of violence, including animal sacrifices. By the 5th century BCE *ahimsa* had become the basis of their way of life, the dominant meme, and they returned to a way of life that strived to see the Divine in all things. As Armstrong puts it, "All beings shared the same nature, therefore, and must be treated with the same courtesy and respect that we would wish to receive

---

[15] Ibid.
[16] Ibid.

ourselves."[17] In the end, even Indra abandons the path of violence, humbling himself as a student of the great teacher, Prajapati, to become an ascetic seeking his own *atman*, his own true self, through the practice of *ahimsa*, becoming like the peaceful ascetic he once murdered.

Somewhere along the line the ideas about nonviolence so dominant in Jesus' teachings also took a recess. But that doesn't mean they're not still around, waiting to become dominant, to absorb the entire world. Jesus was among those rare individuals who manifested this recessive instinct for the power of life. Although his talents as a wonder worker, like everything else about him, were greatly exaggerated over time, the Gospels portray him as a peaceful man who used his gifts to heal and restore life. It's not always easy he admitted, "For the gate is narrow and the road is hard that leads to life, and there are few who find it."[18] Still, he believed in the principle of life, not death—in nonviolence, not war—and he tried to better the lives of all he encountered by embracing them, encouraging them, and striving to establish a society that would offer abundant life for all.

---

[17] Ibid., p. 241
[18] Matthew 7:13.

CHAPTER VII

Jesus Was Civilly Disobedient

"He entered the house of God, when Abiathar was high priest, and ate the bread of the Presence, which is not lawful for any but the priests to eat, and gave some to his companions."

Not long ago, during our walk together on a cooler than usual summer morning, my spouse and I passed by a Methodist church advertising a forthcoming "Patriots Service" on July 4th — "Weird," I thought. It's always peculiar to me how so many Christians paradigmatically presume that being faithful includes unwavering devotion to one's country, especially Christians here in the U.S. It's peculiar because there seems to be little Biblical basis for this belief, except for the often ill-cited Jesus saying, "Render unto Caesar what is Caesar's..."[1] At best, however, taking this verse out of context in this way should lead only to the erroneous conclusion that Jesus was advocating that we should all pay our taxes, not, as many presume, that God expects us to obey our government under most, if not all, circumstances, especially when it means violating Jesus' more obvious teachings. Of course, there are other verses that can also be taken to an extreme to make the same point. Some take verses like *Romans* 13:1, which says, **"Let every person be subject to the governing authorities; for there is no authority except from God, and those authorities that exist have been instituted by God,"** and *I Timothy* 2:1-2, **"I urge that supplications, prayers, intercessions, and thanksgivings be made for everyone, for kings and all who are in high positions, so that we may lead a quiet and peaceable life in all godliness and dignity,"** as proof enough that it is our divine obligation to submit to governing authorities. But praying for others doesn't also mean we're supposed to submit to them, anymore than respecting authority means we're supposed to quietly follow orders when the

---

[1] Matthew 22:21.

establishment is unjust. Even fundamentalist "theologians," like Bible Professor Wayne Grudem recognize "that human government, like all the other blessings of common grace that God gives, can be used either for good or evil purposes."[2]

Despite Grudem's pre-conventional (childish/black & white) understanding of morality, indicative of fundamentalism in general, few of us can deny that governments sometimes do "bad" things. In such cases a puritanical understanding of these misconstrued verses can lead too easily to compliance and complacency in the wake of grave injustices perpetrated by civil authorities. Nevertheless, ever since 313 CE when Constantine officially recognized Christianity, and later, in 381 CE, when emperor Theodosius I made it the only legally recognized religion, the Church and State have had good reason to work hand in hand. As Historian David Chidester explains, "After Constantine's edict, they began to redefine the position of Christianity in the empire as both a religious and a political force... In the process, the Roman Empire became a Christian Empire."[3] As such, it only made sense for the Church to encourage loyalty and obedience to the State, given that both were essentially one and the same.

The problem with having a government so infused with ideology is that improper beliefs rather than improper behaviors, *dogma* rather than *pragma*, faith rather than works, become *primo facto*. Under these circumstances, ideas themselves can be construed as dangerous and become outlawed. Just as there are government agents today on the lookout for terrorists, the Holy Roman Empire once appointed government agents to hunt down and destroy those who held illegal ideas—inquisitors on the hunt for heretics. Keep in mind, once again, the word "heretic" comes from the Greek word *hairetikos*, which simply means "able to choose." Heretics are those who "choose" their own ideas rather than blindly embrace Government/Church doctrine. *Heresy* is another word for "Freedom."

In a free society it seems unthinkable that citizens might be arrested, imprisoned, or executed because they hold "illegal"

---

[2] Grudem, Wayne, *Bible Doctrine*, Zondervan, Grand Rapids, MI, 1999, p. 276.
[3] Chidester, David, ibid,, p. 91f.

ideas, but this is precisely the danger when ideological institutions get mixed up with governing institutions. Democracy is supposed to encourage free thought and freedom of expression, while protecting those with minority opinions from the oppressive tendencies of its majority. In a true democracy everyone benefits equally and shares the same privileges and protections under the law despite their differences. Unfortunately, *Democracy* and *Freedom* are themselves high ideals that we seem to have great difficulty living up to. In his classic work, *Escape From Freedom*, Erich Fromm suggests people are innately afraid of genuine freedom because it may lead to the personal experience of feeling isolated and alone. I dare say we may also fear the freedom of others for the same reason, because they may choose (heresy) to abandon us, ideologically or otherwise. In either case, instead of seeking to live free in a genuinely free society, we undermine freedom and democracy by gravitating toward institutions, groups, and popular ideas. "As a matter of fact," Fromm writes, "in watching the phenomenon of human decisions [heresy], one is struck by the extent to which people are mistaken in taking as 'their' decision what in effect is submission to convention, duty, or simple pressure. It almost seems that 'original' decision is a comparatively rare phenomenon in a society which supposedly makes individual decision the cornerstone of its existence."[4] The truth seems to be that most of us don't really want freedom because we'd rather feel like we belong. So we end up taking on the hoard mentality as if it were our own, and often feel self-righteous and justified in poking fun of and otherwise oppressing those who don't. We want to fit in, but too often, in the process, cease to be able to differentiate our own authentic thoughts, feelings, and desires from those of the collective. Seeking, in this way, to reestablish those primary bonds we lose through the normal process of individuation, we seek inclusion by embracing the ideas, emotions, and will of the masses. "But these new bonds do not constitute real union with the real world. [One] pays for the new security by giving up the integrity of [one's] self."[5] Sharing a

---

[4] Fromm Erich, *Escape from Freedom*, Avon Books, New York, NY, 1941, 1966, p. 225.
[5] Ibid., p. 263.

common religion is, of course, the most usual means of establishing this false sense of genuine connection to others. Using religion for this purpose truly does make it the "opiate of the masses" that Karl Marx spoke of. It becomes little more than a painkiller, numbing us to our feelings of being isolated and alone. The film *V for Vendetta*, based on the 1980's graphic novel, depicts a fascist society bound together by the shared dictum, "Strength through Unity, Unity through Faith." Fear of freedom almost inevitably ushers us toward fascism, often by promoting a common "faith."

Despite the erroneous and ludicrous modern myth that says the United States was founded as a "Christian Nation," the fact is, the early framers of our society knew all too well this threat of religious exploitation, and attempted to protect freedom by instituting the separation of Church and State. John Adams, who said, "This would be the best of all possible worlds, if there were no religion in it,"[6] ratified the Treaty of Tripoli, which states emphatically, "the government of the United States of America is not in any sense founded on the Christian religion."[7] Thomas Jefferson thought Christianity was based on Plato, not Jesus, and went so far as to write, "The doctrines which flowed from the lips of Jesus himself are within the comprehension of a child; but thousands of volumes have not yet explained the Platonisms engrafted on them; and for this obvious reason that nonsense can never be explained."[8] James Madison wrote, "Religious bondage shackles and debilitates the mind and unfits it for every noble enterprise."[9] Ethan Allen did not dispute being called "a deist," being conscious, in his words, "that I am no Christian."[10] Finally, regarding religions in general, Thomas Paine said, "I disbelieve

---

[6] Peabody, James, ed., *A Biography of His Own*, p. 403.

[7] Treaty of Tripoli (Treaty of Peace & Friendship), 1796, Article XI.

[8] Brodie, Fawn M, *Thomas Jefferson, an Intimate History*, Norton and Co., Inc., New York, NY 1974, p. 453.

[9] Moore, Virginia, *The Madisons*, McGrall-Hill Co., New York, NY, 1979, p. 43.

[10] Koch, G. Adolph, *Religion in the American Enlightenment*, Thomas Crowell Co., New York, NY, 1968, p. 352.

them all.[11] It was such beliefs about religion that led our founders to write the First Amendment; *"Congress shall make no law respecting an establishment of religion, or prohibiting the free exercise thereof..."*

Unfortunately, as Reinhold Niebuhr put it, "Myth is not history, it's truer than history." Nowadays Christian extremists are ignoring the principles upon which our country was founded in order to replace what remains of our experimental democracy with a fascist theocracy. In his book, *A New Reformation*, controversial theologian Matthew Fox writes, "I am so upset by the hijacking of the name of Jesus and the beauty of Christ consciousness, that I am not reliable as a spokesperson for their [fundamentalists] version of Christianity."[12] So in a chapter entitled, "Fundamentalists in Their Own Words," he let's them speak for themselves. Here's what he reports some of them have said about separation of Church and State:

> *"There is no such thing as separation of church and state in the Constitution. It is a lie of the Left and we are not going to take it anymore."* —**Pat Robertson**, Televangelist

> *"The Constitution does not guarantee separation of church and state."* —**Tom Delay**, Former House Majority Leader

> *"There is no such thing as separation of church and state. It is merely a figment of the imagination of infidels."* —**W.A. Criswell**, Baptist Minister

> *"There should be absolutely no separation of church and state in America."* —**David Baron**, President, Wallbuilders

---

[11] Paine, Thomas, *The Age of Reason*, Pormetheus Books, Buffalo, NY, 1984, p. 9.

[12] Fox, Matthew, *A New Reformation*, Wisdom University Press, Oakland, CA, 2005, p. 23.

"We were here first, this is our government. They stole it. And we're coming to take it back... After the Christian majority takes control, pluralism will be seen as immoral and evil and the state will not permit anybody the right to practice evil." —**Oliver North**, Conservative Political Commentator

"We see the outlines of a new social order... the state will no longer be separated from the church." —**Yves DePont**, Fundamentalist Catholic

Unfortunately these sorts of remarks reflect only a sampling of the same sentiments shared by many freedom haters who are consciously or unconsciously guising a fascist agenda in religious jargon. If, by "hijacking" the name of Jesus and Christ Consciousness, Matthew Fox means the Christian Taliban is misrepresenting the teachings of Jesus in order to feign moral superiority, he cannot be more correct! It seems clear that Jesus held little interest in maintaining the status quo. Clearly he was a radical who approached his religious tradition in a fresh and vibrant manner even though his unconventional positions sometimes incurred the wrath of more traditional authorities and contributed to his eventual execution.

It has already been pointed out, for instance, that Jesus gave a radical reinterpretation of the Sabbath Law when he and his disciples were criticized for gathering food on the "State" mandated day of rest. "The Sabbath was made for humankind, not humankind for the Sabbath,"[13] he responded. The Markan Gospel goes on to indicate he was later questioned by the authorities for healing a man on the Sabbath. "Is it lawful to do good or to do harm on the Sabbath," he responded, "to save a life or to kill?"[14] This particular story says Jesus became so angry with the authorities that he boldly defied the law right in front of them, asking the man to "Stretch out your hand," so he could

---

[13] Mark 2:27.
[14] Mark 3:4.

perform the healing in their very presence.[15] Such defiance is, naturally, the very meaning of *Civil Disobedience*. As Henry David Thoreau wrote in his pamphlet by that same title, "It is not desirable to cultivate a respect for the law, so much as for the right." Jesus, like Thoreau, was a man who understood that rules and authorities exist to benefit people. But when they interfere with that purpose and create hardship and injustice, it becomes necessary to violate the rules and disobey the authorities. Again, as Thoreau put it, "Law never made men a whit more just; and, by means of their respect for it, even the well-disposed are daily made the agents of injustice."

Unlike Thoreau, however, who seemed, at times, to favor anarchy, "That government is best which governs not at all," Jesus asked his followers to look into the heart of the law, "Do not think that I have come to abolish the law or the prophets; I have come not to abolish but to fulfill."[16] As noted in Chapter III, he was not satisfied with those who merely obeyed the letter of the law if they did not fulfill its intent. "You have heard that it was said to those of ancient times, 'You shall not murder'; and 'whoever murders shall be liable to judgment.' But I say to you that if you are angry with a brother or sister, you will be liable to judgment; and if you insult a brother or sister, you will be liable to the council; and if you say, 'You fool,' you will be liable to the hell of fire."[17] The letter of the law says it is enough that we do not kill each other, but the principle behind the law is that we should all learn to love each other, if not emotively, at least through our actions. It is not enough, for instance, to restrain from murder if we're part of an unjust system that diminishes the quality of life for others by causing them to lack their needs, suffer, or be oppressed.

By juxtaposing "You have heard it said" with "But I say to you," Jesus is also blatantly affirming the superiority of his own personal opinion over that of the written law. Here he would

---

[15] Contemporary scholars agree the historical Jesus likely did conduct a healing ministry, although the miraculous cures described in the gospels are most assuredly exaggerated.

[16] Matthew 5:17.

[17] Matthew 5:21-22

agree with Thoreau's statement, "The only obligation which I have a right to assume is to do at any time what I think right." Clearly Jesus was operating here at the highest level of moral development, what developmental psychologist, Lawrence Kohlberg called the *post-conventional* level, demonstrated by the ability to transcend conventional ideas of morality, often limited to mores and laws, and adhering, instead, to universal principles like truth, compassion, and justice. While discussing post-conventional morality in his book, *Stages of Faith*, James Fowler explains that, "it is attunement to the ends for which governments are created and maintained, [its] prior-to-society perspective serves as a critical principle that can, under certain circumstances, justify civil disobedience and principled efforts to alter or overthrow unjust laws and social policies." In other words, Jesus understood governments exist "of the people, for the people, and by the people," and when their laws and customs become harmful to the people, it's time to take a different course.

Further still, by seeking out the principles specifically behind the Jewish law, Jesus was also operating at the highest level of theological development, which Fromm says, "...goes in the direction of transforming God from the figure of a father into a symbol of his principles, those of justice, truth and love. God *is* truth, God *is* justice."[18] At this level, he suggests, "God is not a person, not a thing" but the "symbol of the principle of unity behind the manifoldness of phenomena."[19] This is certainly the direction Jesus was heading by putting the principle of love above all else, including the law, and what the author of *I John*, reflecting on Jesus' teachings about loving one another, summarized so succinctly in saying, "**God is love**."[20]

Returning for a moment to the example of his unauthorized healing of a man on the Sabbath, it's noteworthy the author of *Mark* uses the specific phrase, "**he was grieved at their hardness of heart**,"[21] to explain Jesus' anger toward his

---

[18] Fromm, *The Art of Loving*, Bantam Books, Harper & Row, New York, NY, 1956, 1972, p. 58.
[19] Ibid.
[20] I John 4:16.
[21] Mark 3:5.

puritanical opponents. This term, "hardness of heart," is not one his Jewish audience would have been unfamiliar with. They would have recalled the account of Pharaoh and his people being plagued with a series of problems. First their water source becomes contaminated with blood, followed by an onslaught of frogs, swarms of flies, sick and dying livestock, a breakout of boils, destructive storms, locusts, darkness, and the mysterious death of their children. Believing these plagues might be punishment for enslaving the Hebrews, the Pharaoh promises to let his captives go free each time a new plague occurs. But when it comes right down to it, **"the heart of the Pharaoh was hardened, and he would not let the Israelites go."**[22]

This *hardening of the heart* refers, then, to an unwillingness to bend, to be flexible, to change, even when our ways are destroying us and/or others. As noted earlier, *Ezekiel* refers to this same sort of legalistic "arterial sclerosis" in stating, **"I will remove from you your heart of stone and give you a heart of flesh."**[23] Again, the heart of stone, representing the written law—stone tablets—is hard and inflexible, ontological, always to be obeyed in every circumstance regardless of the outcome. The heart of flesh, by contrast, is teleological, focusing on outcomes, and must always defer, like Jesus, to love. It was his heart of flesh, his inclination toward the pleasure principle, that most informed him morally, summarized by his rendition of the universal Golden Rule, "Do unto others as you would have them do unto you." It was from this perspective of love that he was so readily willing to disobey the civil authorities and their stone-cold laws in favor of his own humanitarian principles. "This is the entire law," the Talmud tells us, "all the rest is commentary!"[24] It appears Jesus skimmed over the commentary and got right to the heart of the matter.

Tragically, it was his penchant for superseding the law, for civil disobedience, that also got him killed. In his book, *Jesus, Justice and the Reign of God*, William R. Herzog explains that in agrarian societies like Jesus', "Ancient temples served a crucial

---

[22] Exodus 9:35.
[23] Ezekiel 36:26.
[24] Shabbat 3id.

function in making... economic exploitation possible."[25] This is so, he continues, because, "In the ancient world, there was no separation of church and state. Temples reflected the interests of the rulers and articulated their ideologies. Indeed, temples were embedded in the political systems of which they were a part."[26] Hence, the ruling elite were able to exploit the larger population, acquiring their surplus produce through taxation and tithing by convincing the peasant class (70 percent of the population) its compliance was a religious duty. Given his radical, non-compliant character, Jesus would have seen through this ruse and, because of his passionate and compassionate nature, would have been motivated to do something about it. That "something" came in the form of a prophetic demonstration during which he symbolically "cleansed" the Temple by turning over the tables of a few "moneychangers," emblematic of the exploitative temple system in general. Shortly thereafter he was arrested and executed for this act of civil disobedience.

---

[25] Herzog, William R., *Jesus, Justice and the Reign of God*, ibid., p. 112f.
[26] Ibid., p. 113.

97

CHAPTER VIII

Jesus Was a Member of the Liberal Media

*"Then Jesus asked him, 'What is your name?' He replied,
'My name is Legion; for we are many.'"*

Jesus may not have been an actual reporter given that there weren't any newspapers or other media outlets around in his day. Yet, as an itinerant preacher, he was in the information business, such as it was, and spent the last years of his life traveling throughout the land delivering his version of what he called the "good news" by letting folks know "the time has come, the kingdom of God is at hand."[1] After his business got off the ground and he gained a small following, he was able to commission a few followers, perhaps as many as seventy, to deliver the same message, "As you go," he said, "proclaim the good news, 'The kingdom of heaven has come near.'"[2] He may have had only the one headline, limited distribution, and an imperfect delivery mechanism, to say the least, but he definitely worked to broadcast his message in whatever way he could.

But reporting the *good news* under the watchful eye of the oppressive Roman government wasn't easy, and Jesus, who, as a Jew, had few rights at best, certainly did not enjoy anything like our Bill of Rights protecting his freedom of speech—a right some of us have come to take for granted, and more than a few, it seems, have come to loathe. As noted earlier, Jesus often guised his message in parabolic language to keep from being immediately arrested for sedition. He publicized the plight of the oppressed and exposed those responsible by telling fictional stories that kept his dissident message under the radar of the authorities. "**Jesus told the crowd all these things in parables; without a parable he told them nothing.**"[3]

---

[1] Mark 1:15.
[2] Matthew 10:7.
[3] Matthew 13:34.

Rod Serling, creator of *The Twilight Zone*, is a more contemporary example of one who had to do the same thing to get his progressive message across through an otherwise impossible media. Serling, himself a victim of anti-Semitism who grew into a nonviolent, antiwar, social activist, got his start when Kraft Television Theatre produced his Emmy Award winning teleplay, *Patterns*, about corporate greed and corruption. After becoming an overnight success, he went on to win several more Emmy's for presenting poignant stories promoting his progressive views, changing the face of television drama in the process. Despite his success and popularity, however, Serling eventually grew weary of having to compromise his message to appease corporate sponsors. His teleplay, *Noon on Doomsday*, for example, loosely based on the true story of Emmett Till, the black teenager whose brutal murder in 1955 was followed by an acquittal of his white murderers by an all white jury, was dramatically altered after its sponsor, the United States Steel Company, received thousands of letters threatening a boycott. The story's victim, initially African American, was eventually turned into a nameless foreigner, the word "lynch" was removed entirely from the script, and the location was moved from the South to New England. During a 1959 interview with Mike Wallace, Serling complained, "I'm convinced they'd have gone up to Alaska or the North Pole... using Eskimos as a possible minority, except, I suppose, the costume problem was a sufficient severity not to attempt it. But it became a lukewarm, eviscerated, emasculated kind of show." The sponsors even requested that the story's homicidal killer be changed to a good American boy who just took a wrong turn.

This sort of experience is what eventually led Serling to turn from drama to science fiction. "I think it's criminal that we are not permitted to make dramatic note of the social evils that exist, of controversial themes as they are inherent in our society," he said, "I think it's ridiculous that drama, which by its very nature should make a comment on those things which effect our daily lives, is in a position, at least in terms of television, of not being able to take that stand." So he began writing *The Twilight Zone*, the three time Emmy Award winning series for which he is remembered most, that enabled him to address many of his social concerns—racism, prejudice, greed, war, and poverty—by subtly guising them as science fiction. "I don't think it far-fetched that he should have been as impressed as he was by science fiction," his friend, producer Dick Berg, later commented, "particularly because he had much on his mind politically and in terms of social conditions, and science fiction—*The Twilight Zone* specifically—gave him as much flexibility in developing those themes as he might have had anywhere else at that time."[4] Today we don't recall Serling's many award winning dramas, but we do remember, and sometimes see, the many social parables he brought forth from *The Twilight Zone*.

Obviously Jesus did not tell science fiction stories, but there was, as noted earlier, a degree of surrealism in his parables, especially in the unlikely way they brought oppressors and oppressed together (i.e., landowners and tenants, rich and poor, men and women, ruling elites and expendables). It was the improbability of these stories, and the comic relief that accompanied their absurdity, that enabled Jesus to tell them relatively safely. The authorities did not take them seriously, anymore than Serling's science fiction was, as indicated by Mike Wallace's question to him, "So you're giving up writing anything important for TV?" Had Jesus been more direct, using real characters in real situations, naming names, pointing fingers at real people and institutions, he would have been "censored" in more ways than one. Even so, like Serling, he proved to be a great storyteller whose fanciful parables have proven to be as timeless as they are entertaining and profound.

It goes without saying, then, that Jesus valued what little freedom of speech he did have, and advocated self expression for others, especially for those who his society had marginalized and left without a voice of their own. "**A demoniac was brought to him. And, when the demon had been cast out,** *the one who had been mute spoke*."[5] It ought to also go without saying that the many miraculous healings attributed to Jesus in the gospels are exaggerations—they simply could not have happened in the impossible ways reported! Yet, taken as somewhat parabolic in

---

[4] Zicree, Mark Scott, *The Twilight Zone Companion*, 2nd ed., Silman-James Press, Los Angeles, CA, 1982, 1989, p. 15.

[5] Matthew 9:32-33.

their own way, many of these accounts contain a great wealth of meaning. Touching the diseased skin of lepers, for instance, considered unclean and untouchable by the mainstream, must have healed the deep wounds of isolation and shame experienced by these social-pariahs. Similarly, opening the eyes of the blind becomes a metaphor of revealing false paradigms and showing people the truth. Enabling those who are lame to stand and walk symbolizes Jesus' desire to reinvigorate and empower those who have been beaten down. Encouraging those who have been crippled by oppression to "stretch" themselves, invites those who society has held back to expand their possibilities and seek self-fulfillment. And by opening the mouths of mutes, like this "demoniac," Jesus gave voice to those who had been silenced.

We now know, thanks to the advent of modern medicine, that many of those who were once considered to be "possessed" by demons, actually suffered from dissociative disorders like schizophrenia, or physical conditions like epilepsy. But what are we to make of those strange encounters in which Jesus communicates directly with the demons inside the possessed, like the "man of the city" told of in *Luke*?

> **For a long time he had worn no clothes, and he did not live in a house but in the tombs. When he saw Jesus, he fell down before him and shouted at the top of his voice, "What have you to do with me, Jesus, Son of the Most High God? I beg you, do not torment me"—for Jesus had commanded the unclean spirit to come out of the man. (For many times it had seized him; he was kept under guard and bound with chains and shackles, but he would break the bonds and be driven by the demon into the wilds.) Jesus then asked him, "What is your name?" He said, "Legion"; for many demons had entered him. They begged him not to order them to go back into the abyss.**

Nowadays, should we encounter such a person, we would not consider him "possessed," but might certainly consider him

101

"touched," if not stark raving mad! Indeed, given his level of rage, it's unlikely that this fellow was either epileptic or schizophrenic, but simply a madman; that is, a man filled with such anger it could not be contained. The chains and shackles used to imprison him in the city may be a metaphor of the economic and social restrictions that prevented him from making a decent living. Rather than being tormented by his own inner demons, he may have been tormented by those oppressive authorities that prevented him from expressing his frustration by shutting him up and keeping him down. Herzog points out that, "Demon possession and madness are two forms of accommodation found in colonized populations where the imperial occupier has attempted to strip away the identity of the local populace and sought to impose an alien identity on them."[6] Like comedy, sarcasm, and science fiction, madness can be a thin shield of safety in an oppressive society because none of it is taken too seriously. Thus, the authorities are more likely to "accommodate" such behavior, believing it to be non-threatening. "In these circumstances," Herzog continues, "demonic possession becomes a form of 'oblique protest' against the colonial overlord because, if he is viewed as possessed, a demoniac can express what others feel but repress."[7] Perhaps this man, whose complaints were so many he called them "legion," came to the point that he would rather be considered crazy than to repress his outrage any longer, that is to return, in his words, "into the abyss" of silence.

Moreover, those in power at the time would have had a hand in "demonizing" this unfortunate fellow in order to prevent him from being taken too seriously by others. It's the same reason conservative propagandists like Sean Hannity and Tucker Carlson have respectively called Al Gore "unhinged" and a "wild-eyed religious nut" for expressing his "inconvenient truth" about global warming. To portray him as unstable, as a madman, as a nutcase, is an effort to invalidate his message. In the same way, this "man of the city" may have been called "demon possessed" to invalidate his tirades against tyranny. "It was a form of social control," Herzog suggests, "In effect, this labeling degrades the possessed

[6] Herzog, William R., ibid., p. 209.
[7] Ibid.

'by destroying their selfhood' and denying what they have experienced and expressed in their fits of possession."[8] Thus, in exorcising their "demons," Jesus is effectively validating anything these demoniacs have to say thereafter, just as he figuratively restores speech to the man whose demon had made him mute.

The validity of this interpretation becomes even weightier when we consider that Jesus' authority to cast out demons came into question by public officials. **"It is only by Beelzebub,"** they declared, **"the prince of demons, that this fellow drives out demons."**[9] In validating what these crazy demoniacs had to say, Jesus threatened the whole system, and was himself accused of being possessed by the worst demon of all for doing so. Again, as Herzog puts it, "When unauthorized exorcists arise to address the problem, collaborators will stigmatize them by using witchcraft accusations or branding them as sorcerers."[10] Like Tucker Carlson, who once referred to Al Gore as "a bad guy" on his propagandistic "Beat the Press" segment on MSNBC, Jesus' adversaries tried to discredit his message by demonizing him. It really is one of the oldest tricks in the book! Declaring someone a demoniac in the ancient world is the modern equivalent of declaring someone insane, effectively silencing a person by rendering what he or she has to say meaningless, or, as Wallace concluded, "not important."

In short, the Orwellian media of his day, those who were authorized to say who was and wasn't officially demon possessed, who was and wasn't to be taken seriously, tried to undermine Jesus' authority by mischaracterizing him as "a bad guy," "unhinged," "a wild-eyed religious nut," "Beelzebub." They did so because they feared what might happen if his "good news" about "God's kingdom among us" should ever be taken seriously. The majority of people might have stopped relying upon the unjust system keeping them chained and shackled, and started depending on each other, sharing their resources and energies, instead of placing everything into the hands of one or two percent of the population. This is the same reason that today's corporate controlled media regularly portrays filmmaker Michael Moore,

---

[8] Ibid.
[9] Matthew 9:24.
[10] Herzog, ibid., p. 210.

who uses his medium advocating on behalf of poor Americans, as, an "anti-American propagandist," who "is unable to conceal his liberal bias, and refuses to present information in a truthful and accurate manner."[11]

Despite similar defamation, Jesus spoke his truth, often at great risk, and tried to empower others to do the same, especially those who had been officially demonized and discredited by the powers-that-be. In claiming he had no authority in these matters, that he wasn't an expert, and that he was himself a "nutcase," those threatened religious officials backing the establishment tried to reassert their own claim as the sole authority on such matters. It might be the modern equivalent of a psychiatrist having somebody brought up on charges of "practicing medicine without a license" simply for giving advice to a friend. As Herzog explains, "Necessarily, collaborators will attempt to gain control of the phenomenon by stepping into the role of authorized or official exorcists."[12] Their real concern, however, and the reason behind their malicious attempt to demonize and discredit Jesus, was to prevent him from validating the speech of those they had already effectively silenced. For once Jesus opened their mouths by *depossessing* them, what they had to say—their complaints, frustrations, and outbursts—could no longer be so easily dismissed. "The exorcised could no longer utter their protest as a form of displaced insanity; they were now accountable for what they had seen and responsible for what they said," says Herzog, "This made them politically dangerous and socially disruptive."[13]

But Jesus also understood that communication is a two-way street. In addition to defending freedom of speech for those who had been officially silenced, he attempted to open the minds and hearts of those who had been socially conditioned to turn a deaf ear to those whom the powers had deemed dangerous. Part of what happens when we hear propagandists like Sean Hannity and Tucker Carlson insulting those with whom they disagree, rather than dialoging with them maturely in the spirit of honest inquiry,

---

[11] Comment made by Sean Hannity on the Fox News Channel, June 17, 2007.
[12] Ibid., p. 209.
[13] Ibid., p. 210.

is that we presume those they are discrediting deserve such treatment. What other choice do we have when we aren't able to hear the other side, when corporate controlled media uses its unstoppable influence to present only its own elitist agenda? Jesus, by contrast, worked to bring everyone to the table, including and especially those who were considered outcasts. Like Master Ueshiba, who said, "The Way of Harmony never restrains, restricts, or shackles anything. It embraces all, and purifies everything," Jesus understood that for his community to truly usher in the Kingdom of God, people had to begin listening to each another.

In addition to socializing with outcasts, validating demoniacs, and curing those who had been crippled, broken, blinded, silenced, and beaten into submission, Jesus, as we have seen, told stories that brought the most unlikely characters together. His parable of the *Absentee Landlord*, discussed in Chapter II, as you will recall, specifically addresses just how out of touch the "first" are with the "least;" so out of touch, in fact, they are unable to recognize the anger and suffering of others caused by their own greed. Nor do they comprehend the potential danger to themselves caused by shutting people down. If the mainstream media, for example, doesn't start taking climate change seriously, while there is still time to alter the destructive course we're on, it will soon be too late for all of us (if it isn't already). In the parable, you will remember, the absentee landlord, behind his fence, high up in his tower, in a land far far away, brings injury or death to everyone he sends to deal with his angry tenants, including his own children, his own future, all because he cannot bring himself to take an honest look at the situation and listen to those he has distanced himself from with his elitist lifestyle.

There is a story in *Mark* of another man whose blindness specifically prevented him from seeing the humanity in others. "Can you see anything?" Jesus asked, "**And the man looked up and said, 'I can see people, but they look like trees walking.' Then Jesus laid his hands on his eyes again; and he looked intently and his sight was restored, and he saw everything**

clearly."[14] The point here seems to be that this man had to look "intently" before he could see people as they are. Those who are behind fences, in towers, far away, are intentionally avoiding those whose lives they destroy, so they don't have to see them as real people. True healing of such blindness can only come when those who are on top, the *first* (including the First World), turn their intention upon those on the bottom, the *least*. "So the last will be first, and the first will be last."

Along with healing the proverbial "blind eye," Jesus also tried to open the "deaf ear."

> **They brought to him one who was deaf and spoke with difficulty, and they implored him to lay his hand on him. Jesus took him aside from the crowd, by himself, and put his fingers into his ears, and after spitting, he touched his tongue with the saliva; and looking up to heaven with a deep sigh, he said to him, "Ephphatha!" that is, "Be opened!' And his ears were opened, and the impediment of his tongue was removed, and he began speaking plainly.[15]**

This is one of my favorite healing stories because it portrays Jesus in such a compassionate and human light. It begins with him taking the man aside, away from the crowd, as if not to embarrass him. Being unable to comprehend what others are saying, whether we're deaf, foreign, or simply know little of the subject matter, can be terribly isolating and awkward, especially when, in a crowd, somebody tries to help us understand by making wild and unusual physical gestures. Nobody wants to become a spectacle, especially when they don't understand what's going on. So Jesus, very thoughtfully, gets this guy alone before sticking his fingers in his ears, which is merely sign language for, "I'm going to open your ears." He then touches the man's tongue to let him know this action should also take care of his speech impediment. Then, after a deep sigh, body language for "here it comes," he

---

[14] Mark 8: 24-25.
[15] Mark 7:32-35.

says, "Be opened!" Afterward the man is able to hear and speak plainly.

As a metaphor, this incident suggests that not hearing others is an impediment to speech—that not listening is directly linked to poor communication. Dismissing those we disagree with by calling them names, for instance, is an immature form of communication rooted in an overt unwillingness to hear what others have to say. That it's happening today in the mainstream media by adults purporting to represent "fair and balanced news" is as inexcusable as it is inexplicable. Calling someone like Al Gore names, a Nobel Peace Prize winner, because we don't want to hear what he has to say makes us deaf, not clever! Leading the public to believe climate change isn't happening, or, having been finally forced to admit it is happening in the wake of undeniable heat waves, droughts, and apocalyptic storms, arguing instead that it's part of a natural cycle while intentionally suppressing scientific research proving it's caused by humans, is ignorant and irresponsible. Jesus sought to heal such deafness by commanding us to "be open!" Communication works both ways, which is why **"He makes even the deaf to hear and the mute to speak."**[16]

We see, from all of this, a picture of Jesus as a man devoted to free expression and freedom of speech who readily defied those who used their influence to silence others, including him. We must wonder, therefore, as difficult and dangerous as it was to "broadcast" in his own day, how he might react to what has happened to today's mainstream media which regularly "demonizes" those it would dismiss, and completely shuts out those stories and voices that might prove inconvenient to today's ruling elite. Our national news media, once the guardian and progenitor of free speech in our country, has become the almost exclusive tool of those wishing to propagandize their own rightwing agenda. This is so despite all the inane and unsubstantiated rhetoric about the, so called, "Liberal Media" promulgated largely by disgruntled conservative pundits during the Clinton Administration, seeking only to quail and invalidate any positive mention of a President who was actually unjustly hounded by the mass media more than any other in history. In

---

[16] Mark 7:37.

truth, the Republican Party came into possession of the national media during the Reagan Administration, long before Clinton was elected to office, and cleverly used it to publicize this absurd myth that the media is liberal.

But framing it in this way, as the "liberal media," these ultra-conservatives, not so cleverly, tried to disguise their assault upon our First Amendment Right to freedom of speech. Even in the midst of taking control of the media for themselves, they tried to discredit anything the public might hear that did not stem directly from their own reports. All of us should keep in mind that the term "liberal media" is absolutely synonymous with "free press." An attack against the liberal media is an attack against the First Amendment, pure and simple! Nevertheless, in their efforts to control the flow of information by deregulating the communications industry, they successfully created an atmosphere of mistrust regarding news in general, at least until they could get their own "fair and balanced" delivery system in place, a system that has, through competition for ratings, poisoned most of the mainstream media. In fact, soon after Reagan appointed Mark Fowler as Chairman of the Federal Communications Commission in 1981, guidelines establishing minimal amounts of non-entertainment programming were abolished; the, all-important, Fairness Doctrine, requiring broadcasters to act in the "public interest" by "covering important policy issues and providing equal time to both sides of public questions,"[17] was eliminated; and, worst of all, the number of stations permitted to be owned by a single entity has continued to expand. As Robert F. Kennedy, Jr. has noted in his important book, *Crimes Against Nature*, "The right-wing radio conglomerate Clear Channel, which in 1995 operated 40 radio stations, today owns over 1,200 stations and controls 11 percent of the market. Rupert Murdoch's News Corporation is the largest media conglomerate on the planet, one of seven media giants that own or control virtually all of the United States' 2000 TV stations, 11,000 radio stations, and 11,000 newspapers and magazines."[18] In other words, the once free press

---

[17] Kennedy, Jr., Robert F. *Crimes Against Nature*, Harper Perennial, New York, NY, 2004, 2005, p. 176.
[18] Ibid. p. 178.

has been added to the list of national resources that has come under control of the top one percent of the population, in this case, into the hands of just seven CEO's.

As a Jewish religious leader, Jesus would have come by his appreciation of free speech naturally, and, if he were alive today, would be gravely dismayed by the tight corporate and political controls that have usurped its free expression in a nation that once stood as a beacon of hope and freedom for the entire world. Jewish Rabbi's, in particular, widely held that the Oral Torah, based on the teachings of those who commented on the Scriptures, was equally as valid as the Written Torah. Because they considered this Oral Law to be just as inspired as the written word, many of their comments, once spelled out in the Talmud and Mishnah, also became part of their sacred texts. It was this basic human freedom to express oneself that allowed Jesus to oft repeat the formula, "You have heard it said... but I say to you..." Jesus valued his right to express his own ideas about things, and tried to encourage and restore such freedom to others whenever he could. If he were here today he would work to open the eyes of those whose false paradigms have caused them to dehumanize others, and blinded them to the suffering they cause in the world. He would try to open the hearts and minds of those who have turned a deaf ear to those with whom they disagree in an effort to shut them down and out. He would advocate on behalf of those the system has demonized and discredited. He would, with deep compassion, open the mouths of those who have been so marginalized they are without a voice, and those who are so without hope, they have been left speechless.

CHAPTER IX

Jesus Was a Universal Healthcare Provider

"They had come to him from every village of Galilee and Judea and from Jerusalem; and the power of the Lord was with him to heal."

Whatever else Jesus may have been, scholars widely agree that he was a healer, of sorts, who offered his services freely to everyone in need. As Robert Funk, of the *Jesus Seminar*, puts it, "The evidence is overwhelming that Jesus was regarded as a healer during his public career."[1] It is difficult, in such light, to comprehend how so many Christians today concern themselves with posting the Ten Commandments in public buildings, including prayer in public schools, and, especially, abortion, yet have little to nothing to say about the growing number of Americans without adequate healthcare. According to the National Coalition on Health Care, 47 million U.S. citizens were without health insurance as of 2005, more than 8 million of which are children. How is it that then President George W. Bush, who called Jesus his favorite "political philosopher" during a 2000 political debate, could usher in a Presidential era during which the number of uninsured increased by nearly 7 million? This is the same President who wasted hundreds of billions on his unfounded war in Iraq, yet, in 2007, vetoed a bill to provide $35 billion, spread out over five years, to help provide health coverage to 10 million children, calling it "an incremental step toward the goal of government-run healthcare." How can this be? How can anyone professing to follow Jesus turn away those who are sick, especially our nation's poorest children?

"Great crowds came to him, bringing with them the lame, the maimed, the blind, the mute and many others. They

---

[1] Funk, Robert W. & The Jesus Seminar, *The Acts of Jesus: The Search for the Authentic Deeds of Jesus*, HarperCollins, New York, NY, 1998, p. 59.

put them at this feet and he cured them."[2] There are a few reports of Jesus feeling so overwhelmed by the throngs of sick coming to him for cures that he had to seek solitude. **"In the morning, while it was still very dark, he got up and went out to a deserted place, and there he prayed.**"[3] Yet, after just a little R&R, he was always quick to resume his ministry, which included healing the sick. **"When they found him, they said, 'Everyone is searching for you.' He answered, 'Let us go on to the neighboring towns, so that I may proclaim the message there also; for that is what I came out to do.'"**[4] Today the throngs of nearly 50 million Americans needing healthcare are also overwhelming, and it follows that anyone professing to follow Doctor Jesus must recognize that part of his mission, part of what he "came out to do," was to provide healthcare to those in need—something he also expected his followers to do by instructing them to, "Cure the sick."[5] Indeed, it has been made abundantly clear that Jesus' greatest concern was for those he called the "least among us," making it impossible to imagine he would quietly tolerate our nation, which has more resources than any nation in human history, allowing nearly a fifth of its population, including 11 percent of its precious children, to live without healthcare—hardly the abundant life his good news about Heaven among us calls for! Jesus—Bush's favorite political philosopher? I think not! "You will know them by their fruits,"[6] he said.

Clearly, Jesus did not promote the kind of family values conservatives talk about, namely, families in which the father, as it's head, dominates the household from the top down, which is merely a micro-version of the patriarchal run government that exists in every dominator culture. "For I have come to set a man against his father, and a daughter against her mother, and a daughter-in-law against her mother-in-law; and one's foes will be members of one's own household."[7] Jesus wanted to disrupt

---

[2] Matthew 15:30.
[3] Mark 1:35.
[4] Mark 1:37-38.
[5] Matthew 10:8.
[6] Matthew 7:20.
[7] Matthew 10:35-36.

patriarchal hierarchy on every level—"Call no man father," he said—but this doesn't mean he didn't value families. Rather, he wanted to initiate the kingdom of God among us by fostering and encouraging egalitarian relationships between everyone, in which men, women, children, rich and poor, alike, have abundant life, including abundant health.

When I was a boy, not too long ago, growing up in a traditional nuclear family, my parents were able to modestly provide us with enough food, shelter, and clothing on a single income. Pest control wasn't glamorous work, and years of handling and breathing poison probably helped lead to my father's early demise. Yet, as a child who grew up largely in the 70's, I can still remember the days when one Working Class job per household was enough to provide for a family of six and still have enough left over for a substantial savings account. Nor was there a healthcare crisis in those days. Full benefits, including dental, were part of nearly every fulltime job. Sometimes the other parent, usually the mother in those days, would choose to take a second job, often part-time, in order to earn a little extra income for luxuries the family couldn't otherwise afford, but not as a necessity for paying everyday living expenses.

But then the other shoe dropped, Ronald Reagan was elected, and the age of "trickle-down-economics" was upon us, and with it, the dismantling of the economic and social reforms that had bolstered and sustained our nation's Middle Class since FDR's Administration in the 1930's. In 1979, for instance, our nation's top 1 percent controlled about 22 percent of its wealth. By 1992 this amount had nearly doubled to 42 percent.[8] Between 1983 and 1989, furthermore, the richest 20 percent received 99 percent of the gain in wealth (with 62 percent of that going to the richest 1 percent), while the bottom 80 percent had to share what was left of the remaining 1 percent.[9] One result of this assault on the Middle Class is that its members could no longer afford to save their money, the lower third of which had been able to save an average of 5 percent of their income since the 1960's. In 1980 this

---

[8] Wolff, Edward, N., *The American Prospect*, vol. 6, Issue 22, June 23, 1995.
[9] Ibid.

freedom dissipated and most Americans have been unable to save much, if anything, ever since. Many have tried to make up for it by creating equity in their homes, but this too peaked at 65.6 percent in 1980 and has been declining ever since. At the same time, Reagonomics enabled the average savings of the nation's top third to rise from 9.3 percent to 22.5 percent.[10]

This financial inequity, brought about by the party promoting "family values," has virtually destroyed the quality of traditional family life by forcing both parents into the workforce, leaving them with little choice but to have their children raised largely in daycare centers. In 2006, according to the U.S. Census Bureau, the number of married couple families with both husband and wife in the work force in the U.S. was 53.5 percent, up from 39.7 percent in 1979. In many cases one spouse works just to provide health benefits, while the other tries to bring in enough cash to pay the monthly bills. According to Juliet Schor's research in, *The Overworked American*, a third of our population now feels rushed and stressed everyday of their lives,[11] a majority of us get 1 to 1½ hour less sleep that we need each night,[12] and half of us report having too little time for our families,[13] all of which is leading to increased instances of child neglect, marital distress, sleep deprivation, and stress related illnesses. None of this seems in keeping with Jesus' abundant life philosophy, or with a political platform that's supposed to be based on family values. It seems there's a great discrepancy today between family values and "valuing families." Jesus, in his effort to promote the just sharing of resources and power, may have sought to disrupt the archaic idea that "Father knows best," and, "a man's home is his castle," but this was only because he wanted everyone, including women and children, to benefit from society, having a fair say and a fair share of its resources, including health benefits.

"That evening, at sundown, they brought to him all who were sick or possessed with demons. And the whole city

---

[10] Ibid.

[11] Schut, Michael, ed., *Simpler Living, Compassionate Life*, The Morehouse Group, Denver, CO, 1999, 2001, p. 35.

[12] Ibid.

[13] Ibid.

was gathered around the door."[14] Jesus provided holistic healthcare for everyone (body, mind, and soul), including, as we have seen, demoniacs, some of whom, at least, we would consider mentally ill by today's standards. Yet where is the concern, especially from those who insist ours is a "Christian Nation," over the hundreds of thousands of people with mental illnesses who have been refused adequate treatment ever since our government effectively started shutting down psychiatric hospitals in the 1980's? Since then the number of public hospital beds for the mentally ill has been reduced by nearly 70 percent. Hundreds of thousands of them, as a result, have added to the growing ranks of homeless people in this country, and thousands more are being housed in our nation's prisons. As Bernard E. Harcourt, professor of law and criminology at the University of Chicago noted in a recent article, "Over the past 40 years, the United States dismantled a colossal mental health complex and rebuilt—bed by bed—an enormous prison."[15] He goes on to point out that our Nation's "federal and state prison populations skyrocketed from under 200,000 persons in 1970 to more than 1.3 million in 2002,"[16] a number that has since increased to over 2 million, more than any other country on Earth. "I... was sick and in prison and you did not visit me," Jesus is reported to have said. **"Lord, when was it that we saw you... sick or in prison and did not take care of you? Then he answered them, 'Truly I tell you, just as you did not do it to one of the least of these, you did not do it to me.'"[17]**

In some cases, however, these demoniacs were simply those society considered "unclean" and, therefore, unworthy of its benefits. *Mark* tells us, for instance, **"Just then there was in the synagogue a man with an unclean spirit,"[18]** and later of an epileptic boy with an **"unclean spirit**.**"[19]** In addition, Jesus is

---

[14] Mark 1:32-33.
[15] Harcourt, Bernard E., "The Mentally Ill, Behind Bars," New York Times, January 15, 2007.
[16] Ibid.
[17] Mathew 25:43-45.
[18] Mark 1:23a.
[19] Mark 9:25.

reported to have "cleansed" many with leprosy, a disease that made them untouchable according to Jewish law. **"He shall remain unclean as long as he has the disease; he is unclean. He shall live alone; his dwelling shall be outside the camp."**[20] Those stigmatized with this condition were also required to dress in torn clothes so they could be easily recognized, and to shout, "Unclean, unclean," when approaching others. It was possible, upon examination by a priest, for them to be declared clean again, but only if all signs of the disease had cleared up. Yet Jesus, who, as far as we know, was not a priest, took it upon himself to do what the law gave him no right to do, give these untouchables a "clean" bill of health. **"When Jesus had come down from the mountain, great crowds followed him; and there was a leper who came to him and knelt before him, saying, 'Lord, if you choose, you can make me clean.' He stretched out his hand and *touched* him, saying, 'I do choose. Be made clean!'"**[21] Once again the author of *Matthew* illustrates Jesus' emphasis on people over laws by noting that he actually "touched" this person who society had deemed "unclean." The real point here, however, is that Jesus did not deny his services to anyone in need, especially to those whose circumstances left them without access to any other kind of healthcare.

    Job attempts to counter this association of sickness with religious impurity through his response to those "friends" who suggest his illness is a result of his own sin, **"Far be if from me to say that you are right; until I die I will not put away my integrity from me. I hold fast my righteousness, and will not let it go; my heart does not reproach me for any of my days."**[22] Unfortunately the point of *Job*, that bad things do happen to good people, remained lost on most in Jesus' day, just as it does today. Many Christians, for example, heartlessly consider AIDS to be God's curse upon homosexuals. But Jesus would not have denied compassion, care, and touch, to any in need, especially not to those the religious authorities of his own day had declared "unclean" and "cursed."

---

[20] Leviticus 13:46.

[21] Matthew 8:2-3.

[22] Job 27:5-6.

Women at the time, in particular, had a hard way to go since they were considered "unclean" for something as natural and healthy as menstruation. Again, according to the law, "**When a woman has a discharge of blood that is her regular discharge from her body, she shall be in impurity for seven days, and whoever touches her shall be unclean until the evening.**"[23] But Jesus wasn't concerned about contracting "uncleanness" when he came into contact with a woman whose ailment had caused her to bleed continuously for many years. "Take heart daughter," he said, "Your faith has made you well."[24] Jesus, who regularly included them in his companionship, much to the chagrin of others, had particular compassion regarding the plight of women. How would he feel today given that there are more than 10 million single mothers in the United States, up from just 3 million in 1970, many of whom don't have adequate health coverage for themselves or their children? According to a 2006 study by the Community Service Society in New York City, for example, 80 percent of low-income working mothers in New York don't receive employee paid health benefits, nearly half of whom didn't receive support from Medicaid or other government programs, and a third of whom reported having been unable to obtain necessary medical care for themselves or their children because they simply couldn't afford it.[25] No doubt, if Jesus were here today he would reach out to these women, touching their lives, no matter how overwhelming their numbers, in an effort to provide them the same universal healthcare he offered those who had been excluded in his own day.

Last, but not least, unless they are counted as the "least among us" that he so often advocated for, Jesus also provided healthcare to children. All three of the synoptic gospels report that he restored the health of a little girl so listless she was thought to have already died. "The child is not dead but sleeping,"[26] he reassured the child's parents, then took her by the hand and helped

---

[23] Leviticus 15:19.
[24] Matthew 9:22.
[25] CCS conducted the survey of 1,500 New York City residents between July and August of 2005.
[26] Mark 5:39.

her stand. Later on he's reported to have healed an epileptic boy whose fits were mistaken for demon possession; "**...whenever it seizes him, it dashes him down; and he foams and grinds his teeth and becomes rigid.**"[27] The boy happens to have an episode while in Jesus' presence, and, like the little girl, ends up being mistaken for dead. "**But Jesus took him by the hand and lifted him up, and he was able to stand.**"[28]

It should be obvious, as I've stated before, that the miraculous nature of Jesus' reported healings, including the impossible resurrection of these two children, are exaggerations at best. Yet most scholars believe "some vague historical remembrance lies behind"[29] these accounts. There are nineteen different cure and resuscitation accounts contained in the four Gospels, not including the reports of half a dozen exorcisms. That each of them consists of an introduction of the patient and the severity of the malady in question, followed by contact with Jesus who invokes a healing word or technique, and end with a demonstration that the patient has been cured, suggests these stories are literary conventions, not historical accounts. As such, they would have been used, like all fictional reveries, to make a larger symbolic point. As already noted in the previous chapter, opening the eyes of the blind, especially those who can't see others as human beings, and unstopping the ears of those who cannot hear, may represent Jesus' attempts to broaden the minds and hearts of others; just as opening the mouths of those who are mute, symbolizes his efforts to give voice to those who have been marginalized. In the same way, declaring clean those who the authorities had declared unclean—demoniacs (those with unclean spirits), lepers, and women with vaginal hemorrhaging—more generally suggests that Jesus regularly worked to bring those who had been ostracized back into community. Likewise, those accounts involving patients with physical malformations, like the paralytic Jesus heals by telling him "Your sins are forgiven,"[30] or

---

[27] Mark 9:18.
[28] Mark 9:27.
[29] Funk, ibid., p. 109.
[30] Mark 2:9.

the "crippled" woman who **"stood up straight,"**[31] or the man suffering from edema, commonly called "dropsy" (swelling due to excess fluid, often around the legs or heart), who Jesus healed and **"sent him on his way,"**[32] may reveal Jesus, albeit symbolically, as a man who encouraged those who felt powerless, hopeless, bent out of shape, weighted down, and heavy hearted. That these incredible stories are most certainly illustrative makes them no less meaningful than any great work of fiction, and, more importantly, seem to have grown from authentic, though originally more plausible, stories of Jesus' historical work as a caring and compassionate healer who offered universal healthcare to everyone in need.

---

[31] Luke 13:13.
[32] Luke 14:4.

CHAPTER X

Jesus Was a Communist

"You cannot serve God and wealth."

I once asked a gung-ho Christian how he could support war and claim to follow Jesus at the same time. To my surprise he didn't argue by spinning a few Biblical verses to justify his position, or by trying to overshadow Jesus' explicit pacifist teachings with some of the war stories found in the Hebrew Scriptures. Instead he quite simply admitted, "Because Jesus was perfect and we're not. We should strive to be like him, but we can never truly be like him because of our imperfection." As transparent as it is honest, this admission that *some*, at least, hold themselves to a lower standard than the one they call "Lord," is indicative of the *vertical* perspective through which many interpret and experience the Christian faith. After two thousand years of an ascending *Christology* in which Jesus has risen higher and higher toward divinity on the human/divine scale, it's no wonder many Christians have simply given up when it comes to being truly "Christ-like." *Luke*, written more than a generation after Jesus' death, says, "**While he was blessing them, he withdrew from them and was carried up into heaven. And they worshiped him...**"[1] How, then, can any mere mortal ever hope to achieve such lofty heights? With Jesus way up there and humanity way down here? The answer for many, as the man I've just mentioned admits, is that we simply can't! We're climbing Jacob's ladder. Some may be higher up on the rungs than others, but Jesus is the only one at the top. He's the "**head of the body, the church**"[2] as the author of *Colossians*[3] puts it—the divine CEO who runs the Christian corporation (*corpus*, body) from the top down.

---

[1] Luke 24:51-52.

[2] Colossians 1:18.

[3] It's widely agreed this is a pseudo-Pauline work; meaning it's attributed to Paul even though he didn't write it. Indeed, this specific verse [1:18] seems to contradict Paul's analogy of every body part being equal in *I*

A more *horizontal* approach is presented in *Matthew*, which does not include an ascension story and simply concludes with the risen Jesus saying, "And remember, I am with you always, to the end of the age."[4] This perspective keeps Jesus here on Earth, in the human realm, the realm of *pragma* (practice) not *dogma* (teachings)—in the real world, not the ideal world. Horizontally speaking, Jesus is spiritually present in our relationships with each other. "Where two or more are gathered in my name, I am there among you."[5] In the horizontal realm, the earthly pragmatic realm, Jesus is alive and present whenever people are living out his teachings among themselves. He's not way up there beyond our reach and capabilities, beyond the realm of possibility. He's not ascended to some divine throne we cannot occupy. His spirit lives in the here and now whenever we treat each other with compassion, dignity, and acceptance. "For in fact," he is reported to have said, "the kingdom of God is among you."[6]

Divine vs. Human Orientation

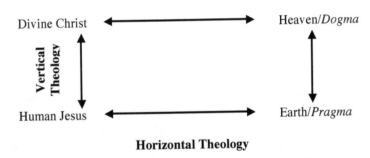

Horizontal Theology

As a human being, Jesus' example and teachings are meaningless unless they are lived out among us. But as a god he

---

Corinthians [12:12-31]. Often these deutero-Pauline works, as they're called, representing half of the Christian letters attributed to Paul, were written to subvert his authentic egalitarian teachings, especially regarding gender equality and church authority.

[4] Matthew 28:20.

[5] Matthew 18:20.

[6] Luke 17:21.

has iconic significance regardless of anything he ever actually said or did; regardless, that is, of who he really was. Given these two choices, it seems little wonder so many prefer iconic Christ over human Jesus, considering the actual teachings of the latter require real sacrifices rather than simply ascribing to a few esoteric, if not meaningless, beliefs. It's easy, after all, to merely admit we are flawed (sinners) and depend upon the blood sacrifice of God's only son for the salvation of our souls, but quite difficult to practice nonviolence, to love our enemies, to share our belongings with our neighbors, and to include outcasts and strangers among us. It requires no effort to believe in Paul's Hellenistic deity, but it demands true discipline and sacrifice to live like Jesus the man.

Jesus himself understood the difficulty of his lifestyle and once warned a would-be follower that, "Foxes have holes, and birds of the air have nests; but the Son of Man has nowhere to lay his head."[7] He had renounced everything—home, family, personal belongings, money—and instructed those who wished to be like him to do the same. As troubling as this may be to accept, especially for today's First-World-capitalist-Christians, Jesus instructed his disciples to become homeless destitute beggars. "You lack one thing," he said, "go, sell what you own, and give the money to the poor, and you will have treasure in heaven; then come, follow me."[8] The potential follower he said this to, **was shocked and went away grieving**," because, in order to follow Jesus, he had to first give up everything, including his wealth. As Charles Foster Kent noted in his classic work, *The Social Teachings of the Prophets and Jesus*, "the hot pursuit of riches was unquestionably the chief barrier that kept [people] from accepting Jesus' philosophy of living."[9]

Needless to say, those modern day proponents of the, so called, "Prosperity Gospel," who embrace great wealth as a sign of God's providence and blessing, refuse to accept poverty as a precondition for genuine Christian living. Nevertheless, Jesus' teachings on this issue seem as clear and authentic as his teachings

---

[7] Matthew 8:20.
[8] Mark 10:22.
[9] Kent, Charles Foster, *The Social Teachings of the Prophets and Jesus*, Charles Scribner & Sons, New York, NY, 1917, p. 225.

about nonviolence. Indeed, one of the tests for determining the historical authenticity of stories regarding Jesus is what we might call *inconvenient truth*. "Narrative data that might be an embarrassment to the Jesus movement," writes Robert W. Funk, "has a greater claim to historicity precisely because it survived in spite of being unfavorable to the Christian cause."[10] Scholars agree, for example, that Jesus had once been a disciple of John the Baptist. But this proved problematic in elevating Jesus' status since many would have had difficulty seeing him as greater than his master. The Gospel writers would probably have preferred to leave out any references to John whatsoever (as they did with James); a fact, however, that could not be easily omitted given that it was widely known to be true. So, instead, they worked to downplay the Baptist's significance by portraying him as "less than" his student.

Jesus is Greater than John

Matthew 3:13-15
Then Jesus came from Galilee to John at the Jordon, to be baptized by him. John would have prevented him, saying, "I need to be baptized by you, and do you come to me?" But Jesus answered him, "Let it be so for now; for it is proper for us in this way to fulfill all righteousness." Then he consented.

Mark 1:7-8
[John] proclaimed, "The one who is more powerful than I is coming after me; I am not worthy to stoop down and untie the thong on his sandals. I have baptized you with water but he will baptize you with the Holy Spirit."

Luke 3:16
John answered all of them saying, "I baptize you with water; but one who is more

---

[10] Funk, ibid., p. 35.

powerful than I is coming; I am not worthy to untie the thong of his sandals. He will baptize you with the Holy Spirit and fire."

John 1:26-27
John answered them, "I baptize with water. Among you stands one whom you do not know, the one who is coming after me; I am not worthy to untie the thong of his sandal."

Jesus' instructions on poverty have also proven to be a great inconvenience to those throughout Christian history who have used their religion for personal gain, especially by exploiting others. It is likely these teachings would have been omitted altogether were they not already well established as part of the oral tradition long before its redactors had a chance to present their own biased versions of the Jesus story. *Matthew*, tells us, for instance, that Jesus sent out his followers with these instructions, "Take no gold, or silver, or copper in your belts, no bag for your journey, or two tunics, or sandals, or a staff..."[11] *Luke* reports similarly, **"He said to them, 'Take nothing for your journey; no staff, nor bag, nor bread, nor money—not even an extra tunic.'"**[12] *Mark*, however, the earliest of the Gospels, written around 65 CE, had already tried to modify this inconvenient truth by allowing, as a bare minimum, a staff and a pair of shoes. **"He ordered them to take nothing for their journey *except a staff*; no bread, no bag, no money in their belts; but to *wear sandals* and not to put on two tunics."**[13] It appears the author of *Mark*, despite all the other warnings about wealth contained in his narrative, could not comprehend going without sandals for the protection of one's feet and a staff for protection against bandits and wild animals. Indeed, carrying a staff and wearing sandals for these reasons would have been so ordinary and obvious that one would hardly need special permission by *Mark*'s author to do so unless Jesus had actually forbidden these items in the first place.

[11] Matthew 10:9-10.
[12] Luke 9:3.
[13] Mark 6:8-9.

Nor should it go unnoticed that *Mark* only paraphrases Jesus here, unlike his Matthian and Lukan counterparts who seem to quote this saying directly as it was known to have come down from oral tradition. It goes to prove that we cannot always take the earliest reports about Jesus as the most authentic, and, more importantly, that the historical Jesus lived without a penny to his name and instructed his followers to do the same.

Indeed, *Mark*'s author seems to have struggled over this matter more than his counterparts. Although *Matthew* and *Luke* also contain versions of the story regarding the rich young ruler who goes away disappointed after Jesus instructs him to give away his riches, *Mark* gives it a somewhat personal touch by adding, **"Jesus looking upon him loved him."**[14] Perhaps this belies the author's own hope that, despite his inability to completely give up everything, at least not his sandals and staff, he might still be counted as a worthy follower. This makes sense in light of the mysterious entry, exclusive to *Mark*, added to the arrest narrative, **"A certain young man was following him, wearing nothing but a linen cloth. They caught hold of him, but he left the linen cloth and ran off naked."**[15] Can it be, by adding this element to the story, troubled by his own inability to fully obey Jesus' teachings about wealth, the author of *Mark* was vicariously obeying him via this fictitious young man, perhaps the same young man who earlier left Jesus feeling dejected, but who, in the end, gives up everything until he is left with nothing, not even the one item Jesus did allow? In any case, it seems clear the author of *Mark* altered Jesus' original saying regarding sandals and staffs because he wrestled with the idea of being completely exposed, completely naked, to the dangers and insecurity of total impoverishment.

How much easier it is for all who would follow Jesus to elevate him to divine status, making him a god compared to the rest of us, so that none can rightly be expected to actually live as he did. For the higher our Christology the less practical and possible his teachings become. Like the contemporary Christian man who supports war in spite of Jesus' teaching to the contrary,

[14] Mark 10:21.
[15] Mark 14:51-52.

and like Paul who, two-thousand years ago, wrote nothing of Jesus' life and teachings, it's so much more convenient to approach Jesus vertically as idealized Christ, than horizontally, as a human teacher with practical, though difficult, instructions.

Again, the meaning of Jesus' teachings regarding "riches" are mostly unambiguous—he was, for lack of a better term, a *communist*! Similar to Karl Marx, who said, "to each according to his need," Jesus said, "a man's life consists not in having more possessions than he needs."[16] Nevertheless, Christianity, as a whole seems to favor capitalism. This is so despite what we all know is true, that Jesus himself had no "capital" and specifically said, "Do not store up for yourselves treasures on Earth."[17] If taken literally, as so many fundamentalists are prone to do, this would mean Christians should not have savings accounts, investments, or retirement funds, or even cupboards and cabinets for that matter. But, again, a vertical understanding of the Jesus story and its meaning necessitates the hierarchical viewpoint that he is above us rather than among us. Such an understanding lends itself much more naturally toward capitalistic ideals than the actual communitarian approach Jesus advocated. Keep in mind the word *capitalism* comes from the Latin word for "head," *capitus* (from which we also get the word "cap.") So, as the "*head* of the body, the church," Jesus, exalted to Christ, becomes the *capitus munde*—the capitalist atop all others!

Vertical theology came to influence economic perspectives most directly during the 16th century, particularly in light of John Calvin's doctrine of *predestination*. This teaching, you may recall, suggests that God pre-ordained only an elect few for salvation at the beginning of time and there's nothing anyone can do to change *his* predetermined decision. Although Calvin himself may have preached against the accumulation of wealth, "For faith certainly promises itself neither longevity nor honor nor wealth in the present state,"[18] Calvinist Christians were always on the lookout for signs they were among God's chosen few,

---

[16] Luke 12:15.

[17] Matthew 6:19.

[18] Ferm, Vergilius, ed., *Classics of Protestantism*, Philosophical Library, New York, NY, 1959, p. 100.

including material prosperity. As Chidester points out, even though they could never prove salvation with absolute certainty, "these signs were all that Calvinists had to go by to determine whether or not they were being used as an instrument of God's will in the world."[19] This attitude drove Protestants to seek financial success through hard work, leading to what has become known as "the Protestant work ethic," a term coined by economist Max Weber in his, *The Protestant Ethic and the Spirit of Capitalism*. In it he explains that because Calvinists were committed as much to self-denial as to hard work, they were reluctant to spend their disposable income on "worldly" goods and pleasures. Instead they invested it in ways that proved to be even more lucrative. "By the nineteenth century," Chidester explains, "the economic system of industrial capitalism had become self-sustaining and therefore independent of the Protestant ethic that had been an integral part of its origin."[20] Even so, because capitalism is rooted in the vertical theology of Protestant Christianity, it is often presumed to be the most morally correct economic system despite the fact it violates everything Jesus actually taught on the subject!

In Chapter II, *Jesus was Political*, we looked at the exploitative economic stratum of his day in which 1 to 2 percent of the population controlled most the resources, leaving the vast majority of people barely able to survive, and many who couldn't survive at all. As Gerhard Lenski put it, "a small number of individuals enjoyed immense luxury, consuming in a single day goods and services sufficient to support large numbers of the common people for a year. At the same time a considerable portion of the population was denied the basic necessities of life and was marked out by the social system for a speedy demise."[21] This unjust economic stratum largely mirrors the capitalism of our own day, considering the richest 5 percent of the world's population "receives 82.7% of total world income, while the

---

[19] Chidester, ibid., p. 480.

[20] Ibid., p.480f.

[21] Lenski, Gerhard E., *Power and Privilege: A Theory of Social Stratification*, McGraw-Hill, New York, NY, 1966, p. 295.

poorest receives 1.4%."[22] Americans alone, accounting for only 5 percent of the world's population, consume nearly a third of its resources.[23] But what else is to be expected from a value system in which only a few are chosen to be among God's elect, while everyone else gets left out?

Yet during the time of Jesus, long before Calvin, Jews had experienced economic exploitation for more than a thousand years. They began as economic refugees from the land of Canaan, combined with bands of "outlaws" called *Khabiru* (Hebrews), and, possibly, a group of runaway Egyptian slaves (the Moses group), all of whom came together to eek out a living in the rugged hill country that is modern day Palestine. The one thing these various groups shared in common was that they had all been exploited and oppressed by the sort of unjust economic stratification previously mentioned. "Old Testament" scholar, Anthony Ceresko explains, "In the statist system, 1% to 5% of the population controlled more than half the goods produced by society, while 75% to 95% worked the land as tenants and paid heavy taxes in produce and forced labor."[24] By joining forces in the rugged hill country, "they were able to experiment and to create new economic, political, social, and religious models, often consciously the *opposite* of the hierarchically structured and socially stratified situation they had fled."[25]

While working together and sharing their sparse resources, they also began sharing their various stories until they eventually merged into the story of one people, Israel. Unfortunately, what little peace and prosperity they managed to achieve together was relatively short lived, reaching its highpoint under David, really more of a chieftain (*nagîd*) than a king, who united a loosely bound confederation of tribes by centrally locating his headquarters, and, more importantly, through the just distribution of their resources. Again, as Ceresko explains, "David did not need lavish sums of money for building projects since those he carried out were relatively modest. What revenues he did need

---

[22] Schut, ibid., p. 26.
[23] Ibid.
[24] Ceresko, Anthony R., ibid., p. 45
[25] Ibid.

came not from taxes on the surplus production of his citizens but from the incomes of the estates in the coastal plain and valleys he had acquired after his defeat of the Philistines."[26] In other words, David did not exploit his people, which was unlike every other government they'd ever encountered. David's successor, however, his son, King Solomon, quickly turned his position into a full-fledged monarchy, moving "swiftly and ruthlessly to consolidate his power and establish a firm grip on the apparatus of government,"[27] which included the assassination of challengers, including his own brother, and banishing the High Priest. Thus, their egalitarian society prospered barely a generation before Solomon's reforms doomed it to become a divided kingdom, consisting of people competing among themselves once again for its limited resources. Shortly thereafter, these disoriented tribes also began facing one oppressive foreign regime after another—the Assyrians, Babylonians, Persians, Greeks—until, by Jesus' time, it was the Romans' turn to tyrannize and exploit those who had come to be called Jews.

Thus, having been born among a people so long oppressed, it must have been difficult for Jesus to trust in any economic system, especially given the fact that the spiritual leaders of his own people, the Sadducees (priestly aristocracy), were in cahoots with the exploitative Roman authorities. As Herzog says, "the religion of the temple was always political with economic consequences, because the temple was an instrument of the policies of the ruler and the ruling class."[28] Jesus, like any Jew, would have longed to see Israel return to the good old days under King David—free of oppression and poverty—which was the crux of the Jewish hope for a future messiah (king/anointed one). As John Dominic Crossan explains, "As waves of social injustice, foreign domination, and colonial exploitation swept over Jewish territory, people imagined a future Davidic leader who would bring back the peace and glory of a bygone age hallowed by

---

[26] Ibid., p. 155f.
[27] Ibid., p. 157.
[28] Herzog, *Jesus, Justice and the Reign of God*, ibid., p. 113.

longstanding nostalgia and suffused with utopian idealism."[29] Hyam Maccoby says similarly, "the Jews all lived in hope of the coming of the Messiah, who would rescue them from the sufferings of foreign occupation and restore to them their national independence."[30]

> See, Lord, and raise up for them their king,
> the son of David, to rule over your servant Israel
> in the time known to you, O God...
> And he will have gentile nations serving under his yoke...
> There will be no unrighteousness among them in his days,
> for all shall be holy,
> and their king shall be the Lord Messiah.
>
> Psalms of Solomon [63 BCE]

Jesus may have even thought of himself as this Messiah, believing his social program, if followed, could free his people from oppression. As Maccoby points out, "Jesus was by no means the only person during this period to make a Messianic claim, and not one of these claimants was accused of blasphemy."[31] The desperate and disheartened Jews were anxious to see the messianic prophecy fulfilled, and welcomed any potential candidate. But they also maintained a healthy degree of skepticism, knowing that the proof was inevitably in the proverbial pudding. If one was truly the Messiah *he* would eventually have to restore Israel to its former greatness. Having failed to do so prior to his execution, most Jews would have shrugged their shoulders and said, "guess it wasn't this fellow Jesus." What made his first followers, the Nazarenes, unique among Jews was that they continued to believe in his messiahship even after his death. Since they were solidly Jewish, however, they would never have equated Jesus with God, which would have been blasphemous. Given that these earliest of "Christians" also understood the resurrection, at most, to be spiritual, their continued hope that Jesus could liberate Israel could

---

[29] Crossan, John Dominic, *Jesus: A Revolutionary Biography*, HarperCollins Publishers, New York, NY, 1995, p. 19.
[30] Maccoby, ibid., p. 37.
[31] Ibid.

only be linked to his practical humanitarian teachings. In other words, his spirit lived on through his teachings, and if they practiced what he preached, Jesus could still deliver Israel from oppression.

The earliest of these followers, it appears, may have gone to the greatest of extremes to put Jesus' teachings into practice, actually becoming homeless and impoverished themselves. This helps explain why some of Jesus' original Jewish followers were called Nazarenes (named after Jesus' hometown), not *Christians*, and others were called Ebionites, which means "poor men." It's possible these Jewish followers became refugees after being overwhelmed by an influx of the Gentile Christians converted *en mass* by Paul. As Maccoby suggests, "The best solution seems to be that the original name was Nazarenes, but at some point they were given the name Ebionites, as a derogatory nickname, which, however, some of them adopted with pride, since its meaning, 'poor men,' was a reminder of Jesus' saying, 'Blessed are the poor,' and also of his and James' sayings against the rich."[32] Point being; some of these earliest of Jesus' followers not only believed his social teachings could liberate them from oppression (posthumously), but that these teachings specifically meant giving up wealth, probably to the point of being homeless, "with no place to lay their heads."

It's also important to understand the Ebionites, as they came to be called, were decidedly horizontal in their thinking about Jesus. That is, they believed in him only as a "human being who came to inaugurate a new earthly age."[33] This "new age" would involve the practical application of his teachings. They also considered Paul a fraud and "regarded him as the perverter of Jesus' message and as the founder of a new religion which Jesus himself would have rejected."[34] So we see that early on there existed a tension between the horizontal views of Jesus' first followers and the vertical views presented by Paul. James, the leader of these first followers, who may have become an Ebionite himself, and whom we know was at odds with Paul, broadly

---

[32] Ibid., p 175.

[33] Ibid., p. 17.

[34] Ibid., p. 60.

argued in favor of the horizontal (human) perspective with his famous saying, **"faith without works is dead,"** and, more specifically, by saying, **"the rich will disappear like a flower in the field. For the sun rises with its scorching heat and withers the field; its flower falls, and its beauty perishes. It is the same way with the rich; in the midst of a busy life, they will wither away."**[35]

Whether or not it is true that James and other Jewish followers became "poor men," or were simply absorbed among the overwhelming number of Pauline Christians who eventually took their place, or eventually defaulted back to more traditional Judaism, it is clear the early Christians, both Jewish and Gentile, attempted to live out Jesus' economic and social teachings among themselves. The *Book of Acts* tells us quite plainly, **"All who believed were together and had all things in common; they would sell their possessions and goods and distribute the proceeds to all as any had need."** Just as there was no formal term for *capitalism* around at the time, there was no term for *communism* either. Nevertheless, the kind of community describe here was decidedly communistic. This classless community, in which there was **"no longer Jew or Greek, no longer slave or free, no longer male of female,"**[36] understood that to truly follow the example of Jesus they had to abolish private property and share their possessions in common.

They lived this way because Jesus' brand of communism, "not having more possessions than one needs," is based on his "daily bread" principle. As we have already seen, Jesus operated from a perspective of plenty, not scarcity. "I came that they may have life, and have it abundantly."[37] He understood that there ought to be plenty to go around for everyone; that the need of the many is caused only by the greed of a few. "Therefore I tell you, do not worry about you life, what you will eat or what you will drink, or about your body, what you will wear. Is not life worth more than food, and the body more than clothing?"[38] He

---

[35] James 1:9-11.
[36] Galatians 3:28.
[37] John 10:10.
[38] Matthew 6:25.

then goes on to explain that birds "neither sow nor reap nor gather into barns," yet they have plenty to eat; and flowers don't "toil and spin" yet they are clothed. "So do not worry about tomorrow, for tomorrow will bring worries of its own. Today's trouble is enough for today."[39] Once again, the vast majority of people in Jesus' day were exploited by the top (*cap*) one or two percent who overtaxed their surplus produce—literally storing it into barns—where it did little good for the poor people who actually grew it. John Dominic Crossan, who says, "A peasant is, quite simply, an *exploited* farmer," goes on to explain that, "aristocrats usually mask exploitation as reciprocity, claiming law, order, peace, and protection as returns for the peasantry's appropriated surplus. They seldom say, We are bigger and stronger than you. Therefore, we will take your surplus and prevent others from doing do. Do you have a problem with that?"[40]

Obviously Jesus did have a problem with it—a big problem! If there was anything this compassionate soul could not bare was watching others go without, especially when knowing there's plenty for everyone locked away in the coffers of a few people who have far more than they'll ever use. At one point, for example, when he comes before thousands of hungry people, he is reported to have told his disciples, "I have compassion for the crowd... because they have nothing to eat."[41] Theologian Matthew Fox reminds us that the word used for *compassion* here more literally means, "His bowels turned over."[42] Jesus simply could not stomach exploitation! Despite choosing to own nothing for himself, Jesus abhorred seeing others impoverished. Sadly, it seems to have been this gut reaction that prompted him to act so compulsively during his infamous visit to the Jewish Temple—an act of righteous indignation that led to his execution.

Such zealousness, however, was not his usual MO. He was ordinarily more thoughtful and intentional in the way he dealt

---

[39] Matthew 6:34.
[40] Crossan, John Dominic, *The Birth of Christianity*, ibid., p. 158.
[41] Mark 8:2.
[42] Fox, Matthew, *Original Blessing*, Tarcher/Putnam, New York, NY, 1983, 2000, p. 302.

with injustice, trying, primarily, to initiate socioeconomic change by getting off the economic grid himself, and by promoting alternatives through a clever public awareness campaign involving his disciples. As we have already seen, Jesus instructed them to carry his message to others, taking no more for the journey but the clothes on their backs. He further told them, "You received without payment; give without payment."[43] Whether we want to hear it or not, Jesus had contempt for money. "How hard it will be for those who are rich to enter the kingdom of God!" he exclaimed, "It's easier for a camel to go through the eye of a needle than for someone who is rich to enter the kingdom of God."[44] A horizontal (humanitarian) understanding of what he meant by this suggests, simply, that it's difficult for those who have taken more than their fair share to live in meaningful community with others. Since the kingdom of God is among us only when we live out Jesus' teachings concerning compassion and inclusion, how is it possible for those who exploit others to live in genuine community with them? This is the reason Jesus himself had no money of his own. "You cannot serve God and wealth."[45] It's why, when asked about paying taxes, he feigned complete unfamiliarity with money by asking to see a coin. "Whose head is this, and whose title?" The real point of his response, it seems, was not to comment on whether or not it is right to pay taxes, but whether or not it is right to participate in an unjust economy at all. To paraphrase him, "The economy was made for people, not people for the economy," and as soon as the economy starts hurting people it's time to try something else.

But Jesus did not abandon economics altogether. He simply modeled, encouraged, and promoted another kind of economy based on what Crossan and Reed call "reciprocal sharing" in their book, *Excavating Jesus*. Jesus instructs his disciples, for example, to exchange spiritual work (i.e., healing the sick, raising the dead, cleansing the lepers, etc., etc.) for food and shelter, because, in his words, "the laborer deserves to be

---

[43] Matthew 10:8.
[44] Mark 10:23, 25.
[45] Mark 6:24.

paid."[46] This implies reciprocity between "itinerants and householders, the destitute and the poor," Crossan and Reed explain, "But each has something to offer the other: one has spiritual gifts (healing) and the other material gifts (food to eat.)"[47] The idea of an economy based on such sharing of actual resources rather than money may have come to Jesus, in part, from his romanticization of the Davidic kingdom, of the "good ol' days," but it was most certainly inspired by his personal theology, that is, by his profound ideas about God. He often spoke of God in terms of *agape*, usually translated "to love." But, again, as Crossan and Reed remind us, "It would be better to translate it... as the much more precise term 'to share.'"[48] So the particular kind of love Jesus associated with God has to do with charity or giving. Thus, rather than saying "God is love," it might be better to understand Jesus' theology to mean, "God is sharing," among us, wherever two or more are gathered.

Needless to say, this is likely the meaning of those miracles stories regarding his feeding hungry multitudes with a few fish and loaves of bread. In *Mark*'s account it begins with just one person, a small child, willing to share his lunch, and it ends with abundance. **"They ate and they were filled; and they took up the broken pieces left over, seven baskets full."[49]** *Seven*, again, symbolizes completion and abundance. Jesus understood that if we all learn to share our resources with each other in a fair and just manner, combined with a "give us this day our daily bread" attitude, then there is always more than enough for everyone.

Extreme poverty, however, was the more likely reality for many in his day, because of an unjust economic system that prevented people from benefiting from their own productivity. Even those who could still lay claim to their ancestral lands had no claim to its produce, which was so heavily taxed by the ruling elite that there was often barely enough to subsist on. The same thing is happening nowadays to most working class Americans, not to

---

[46] Luke 10:7.
[47] Crossan & Reed, ibid., p. 124.
[48] Ibid. p. 134.
[49] Mark 8:8.

mention to our poor neighbors in the "Third World." Even those of us fortunate enough to be considered "homeowners" are usually so indebted to our mortgage companies that this term seems preposterous! A 2001 study by the U.S. Department of Housing and Urban Development and the U.S. Census Bureau reports that mortgage debt on homes rose from $1.62 trillion in 1991 to $3.48 trillion in 2001[50], making banks (especially those who own them from a distance) rich beyond measure, and "homeowners" indebted beyond reason. Perhaps it would be more accurate to call those forced to spend their entire lives slaving to pay off a 30-year-fixed-mortgage *indentured servants*!

What seems most unjust about this system, however, even more than the impossible indebtedness members of the working class must indenture themselves to, is the fact that they are not the primary benefactors of their own energies, of their own life forces! Why should a CEO be paid somewhere between 400 and 500 times more than an average worker who must struggle a lifetime to pay for something so basic and necessary as shelter for oneself and one's family? And while their salaries continue to skyrocket, the average income of the working class is declining. In 1979, the year before Reagan took office, the average income for 90 percent of Americans was $27,060. In 2005 it was $25,646, less than it was a quarter century ago.[51] It should come as no surprise, then, that the wealthiest 5 percent of Americans received 70 percent of the benefits stemming from the 2006 federal tax cuts, while 80 percent of us received less than 7 percent.[52] Ours may not be an "agrarian" society, but we are no less separated from the benefit of our own produce today than were those who labored in the fields during Jesus' day. His solution was to abandon the monetary system to the ruling elite ("Give to Caesar what is Caesar's") and begin a communitarian economy among ourselves based upon reciprocity and sharing.

---

[50] *Residential Finance Survey: 2001*, U.S. Department of Housing and Urban Development and U.S. Census Bureau, Figures IV-1, p. 17.

[51] McKibben, Bill, *Deep Economy*, Times Books, Henry Holt and Company, New York, NY, 2007, p. 11.

[52] Ibid.

It was a 2nd century Christian who wrote "**Money is the root of all evil**,"[53] a thought that is certainly in keeping with Jesus' who referred to it as "mammon,"[54] an Aramaic word that best translates, "evil master," at least in the context it was used by Jesus, "No one can serve two masters; for a slave will either hate the one and love the other, or be devoted to the one and despise the other."[55] Early Christian scholars came to take his personification of the word literally and eventually taught that *Mammon* was an actual deity, the name of a demon, or false god that plays upon human greed. There seems to be no evidence, however, for this position. The etymology of the word suggests it refers to greed or treasure obtained dishonestly. In Chapters 5 and 42 of *Ecclesiasticus*, for instance, it's translated as "goods unjustly gotten" or "ill-gotten treasure." For Jesus, it seems, money is always mammon, always "ill-gotten wealth" that, through greed, inevitably enslaves us all.

This is so, because, for him, true wealth comes from God via the abundance that is all around us—food and clothing that grows right out of the Earth, out of the Promised Land, that is given to us to care for and enjoy. But when wealth becomes associated with money instead of the produce of one's own labor, it becomes all too easy for those with the most money to exploit those who actually do all the work. Never has this been more true than today, especially since Richard Nixon did away with the Gold Standard that had been part of the global financial system since 1944. On August 15, 1971 he declared that the U.S. would no longer redeem dollars based on the value of gold, initiating a system in which, as author David Korten explains, "The dollar was now no longer anything other than a piece of high-grade paper with a number and some intricate artwork issued by the U.S. government."[56]

Historically money was gold and silver pressed into coinage with a value based directly on its size and weight. Later,

---

[53] I Timothy 6:10.

[54] Matthew 6:24.

[55] Matthew 6:24.

[56] Korten, David C., *When Corporations Rule the World*, Kumarian Press, Inc., Berrett-Koehler Publishers, New York, NY, 1995, p. 187.

to avoid carrying such weighty and tempting material about, promissory notes were issued by public officials to guarantee the amount of treasure one had stored away. These notes were the precursors of paper money. Viewing gold and silver as wealth, instead of food and clothing and shelter, was bad enough, but coming to view otherwise meaningless strips of paper as wealth, has created this system through which the wealthy elite accumulate more and more riches for themselves, and a chasm between themselves and the poor in the process. This seems to be what Jesus was getting at with his parable of *The Rich Man and Lazarus*, in which Abraham tells a rich man famous for exploiting the poor, "between you and us a great chasm has been fixed, so that those who might want to pass from here to you cannot do so, and no one can cross from there to us."[57] Money creates separation, through class and caste, and separation is sin.

Yet Jesus also understood that money holds only symbolic value so long as the vast majority of us continue to apply such meaning to it. Even when wealth was associated with actual metals, its value was only symbolic. As King Midas eventually learned, one cannot eat or drink gold. True wealth is merely having enough to provide for our basic physiological needs—food, clothing, and shelter. "Indeed your heavenly Father knows that you need all these things." Jesus said, "But strive first for the kingdom of God and his righteousness, and all these things will be given to you as well."[58] This is why the root of the word *wealth* is "well." Wealth is really just good health. It's not having more than we possibly need. Again, the reason paper money was invented was because carrying heavy metal about was too much of a burden. Having more than we need, more than our daily bread, more clothing in our closets than we can possibly wear, more boxes in our attics than we know what's in them, more clutter in our basements and garages than we have room for, becomes a weighty burden that ends up tying us down and holding us back. Wealth based on abundance, on recognizing there is plenty in this moment for all of us is liberating. But wealth based on what we have stored away in banks and barns, based on fear and greed,

---

[57] Luke 16:26.
[58] Matthew 6:32-33.

weighs down our hearts and causes us to suffer, along with those our wealth exploits. As Gandhi once said, "If I take anything that I do not need for my own immediate use, and keep it, I thieve it from somebody else."[59] And what our current monetary system takes from others is their very life force by exploiting the energies and productivity of ordinary people who must spend their lives working to help a few people become filthy rich while they are only barely getting by. As Korten puts it, "we continue to place human civilization and even the survival of our species at risk to allow a million or so people to accumulate money beyond any conceivable need."[60] Meanwhile, the other 6.9 billion of us must watch the already impossible chasm between the rich and the poor widening.

It has always been the case that those who exploit others do so by first separating them from their land, either through confiscation, exile, extortion, or by unreasonably taxing their produce, the fruit of their efforts. This was true, for instance, of those Native Americans in this country who were once forced from their lands onto government reservations where they became dependent upon the stingy benevolence of their oppressors, rather than upon what was once their noble right to sustain themselves based on their relationship with the land itself. As Chief Joseph, of the *Nez Percé*, lamented over his people's loss of the Wallowa Valley (the Land of Winding Waters) to white homesteaders, "It may never again be our home, but my father sleeps there, and I love it as I love my mother."[61] Joseph went on to lead his people in what General William Tecumseh Sherman called "one of the most extraordinary Indian wars of which there is any record."[62] Though outnumbered nearly 10 to 1, the Nez Percé continued to defeat their assailants, and the white newspapers began referring to Joseph as "the Indian Napoleon."[63] In the end, however, after

---

[59] Gandhi, *All Men are Brothers*, Kripalani, Krishna, ed., Continuum Press, New York, NY, 1982, p. 119.

[60] Korten, ibid., p. 261.

[61] Freedman, Russell, *Indian Chiefs*, Scholastic Inc., New York, NY, 1987, p. 110.

[62] Ibid., p. 98.

[63] Ibid. p. 100.

many grievous losses, Joseph and his people ended up on a reservation in Oklahoma, far away from his beloved valley. "We ought not to be forced into a country not fitted by climate to our health," he mourned, "a place where we cannot live—where the country will not let us live."[64] He died four years later, in 1900, from what his reservation doctor described as "a broken heart."[65]

Nowadays most of us don't know what it is to be separated from our ancestral lands because we never had them to begin with. We do not know the passion Joseph felt for the land when he said, "I love it as I love my mother." Yet we have been just as separated from our most basic right to be the chief benefactors of our own energies, of our own life forces. This injustice is the reason Jesus held such contempt for money, and why he refused to use it himself, and, when asked about paying taxes, had to ask for a coin and didn't even know whose face was on it. He believed, "the laborer deserves to be paid," not those who exploit them through an elitist monetary system that separates them from the full benefits of their own work.

Imagine what the world might be like today if the majority of us suddenly decided to stop ascribing symbolic value to money, and began, instead, building an economy based on Jesus' idea of reciprocal sharing, of God among us, in which there is plenty to go around for everyone. If one or two percent want to cling to their dollar bills, let them try eating them, and drinking them, and covering up with them on a cold night. And if some want to break their backs carrying gold and silver, let them. But let the rest of us see the silver in the stars and the gold in the morning sun, that we might lay claim to the rich inheritance that belongs equally and abundantly to all God's children. "Do not store up for yourselves treasures on earth, where moth and rust consume and where thieves break in and steal; but store up for yourselves treasures in heaven, where neither moth nor rust consumes and where thieves do not break in and steal. *For where your treasure is, there your heart will be also.*"[66]

---

[64] Ibid. p. 110.
[65] Ibid. p. 113.
[66] Mark 6:19-21.

139

CHAPTER XI

Jesus Was an Environmentalist

"Your will be done, on Earth as it is in Heaven."

During a November 2002 interview on CNN about the environment, Jerry Falwell, former High Priest of the status quo, scoffed, "It was global cooling 30 years ago... and it's global warming now. And neither of us will be here 100 years from now to know what it is. But I can tell you our grandchildren will laugh at those who predicted global warming. We'll be cooler by then, if the Lord hasn't returned... The fact is that there is no global warming." He went on to call global warming "a myth," bragged about driving a GM Suburban, and concluded by recklessly urging "everyone to go out and buy an SUV today!" Unfortunately, in just a few short years, things have taken such a dramatic turn for the worse that even many fundamentalists are taking notice. The Evangelical Environmental Network,[1] for instance, publisher of *Creation Care Magazine*, has written an "Evangelical Declaration on the Care of Creation," which suggests those who worship and honor the Creator must cherish and care for creation; that environmental pollution and destruction is sin; that Christ's healing and compassion should be extended to the suffering Earth and its creatures; and that creation must be restored to wholeness if it is to continue sustaining us and our children. The Declaration summarizes sin against creation as land degradation, deforestation, species extinction, water and air pollution, and calls human poverty both a "cause and consequence" of environmental degradation. It goes on to state, "The cosmos, in all its beauty, wildness, and life-giving bounty, is the work of our personal and loving creator," and concludes by promising, "We make this declaration knowing that until Christ returns to reconcile all things, we are called to be faithful stewards of God's good garden, our earthly home."

---

[1] www.creationcare.org.

Believe it or not, the EEN really is a conservative organization that bases its concern for the environment on the Bible. And it's not alone! In a 2005 article, *The Greening of Evangelicals*, Blaine Harden of the *Washington Post* wrote, "There is growing evidence—in polling and in public statements of church leaders—that evangelicals are beginning to go for the green. Despite wariness toward mainstream environmental groups, a growing number of evangelicals view stewardship of the environment as a responsibility mandated by God in the Bible."[2] Instead of calling it *environmentalism*, however, they're speaking in terms of "creation care." This is so, according to Harden, because "it does not annoy conservative Christians for whom the word 'environmentalism' connotes liberals, secularists, and Democrats."[3]

The article also quotes Ted Haggard, then president of the 30-million member National Association of Evangelicals, who said point-blankly, "There are significant and compelling reasons why [the environment] should be a banner issue for the Christian right." In its Evangelical Call to Civic Action, that same year, the organization affirmed, for the first time, the Christian responsibility to care for creation. "We affirm that God-given dominion is a sacred responsibility to steward the earth and not a license to abuse the creation of which we are a part."[4] This statement, which also noted that the "government has an obligation to protect its citizens from the effects of environmental degradation,"[5] has been signed by conservative evangelicals as noteworthy as James Dobson and Chuck Colson.

Also in 2005, *Christianity Today*, a popular evangelical magazine, took up the issue for the first time by declaring, "Christians should make it clear to governments and businesses that we are willing to adapt our lifestyles and support steps

---

[2] **The Greening of Evangelicals: Christian Right Turns, Sometimes Warily, to Environmentalism,** by Blaine Harden, *Washington Post* Staff Writer, Sunday, February 6, 2005, Page A01.

[3] Ibid.

[4] Ibid.

[5] Ibid.

towards changes that protect our environment."[6] Perhaps most remarkably, in August 2005, Pat Robertson, who had debunked global warming in the past, called himself "a convert" during his *700 Club*. "...It is getting hotter," he admitted, "and the ice caps are melting and there is a build up of carbon dioxide in the air, and I think we really need to address the burning of fossil fuels. If we are contributing to the destruction of this planet, we really need to do something about it."[7]

This sudden about-face by so many members on the Christian right is as alarming as it is welcome. For we all know conservatives don't change easily—that's why they're called "conservatives." Thus, their sudden shift in consciousness may be a harbinger of just how serious our environmental crisis has become. "There is no such thing as an atheist in a foxhole," as the saying goes, and now, at what may be the eleventh hour for life on Earth, even the believers have become believers! At the same time, it is a relief to have conservatives actually standing for conservation, rather than merely the puritanical preservation of traditional values and ideas. It further indicates that care for creation may have become a universal value that not only crosses religious barriers, but can also cross partisan, social, and economic divisions as well. Thus, it may be our universal concern for the health of our planet that unites us all, regardless of our beliefs and backgrounds. For none of us can afford to go on viewing our planet as an endless frontier waiting to be conquered. As we are discovering, it does have its limitations!

William Blake suggested we can "see a world in a grain of sand." Perhaps that's all our world really is, just a small blue grain of sand afloat in the Milky Way, with limited resources and limited energy. This is not unlike Julian of Norwich, the 14th Century Christian mystic, who had a vision in which God put something into her hand the size of a hazel nut. "I looked at it with the eye of my soul and thought, 'What is this?' And this is the answer that came to me; *It is all that is made.* I was astonished that it managed to survive: it was so small that I thought that it might disintegrate. And in my mind I heard this answer: 'It lives

---

[6] Ibid.
[7] *700 Club*, August 2, 2005.

on and will live on forever because God loves it.' So every single thing owes its existence to the love of God."[8]

In comparison to the celestial ocean in which it swims, the Earth may be far less than either a hazelnut or a grain of sand. Still, there is enough within their tradition to inspire all Christians, along with the rest of us, to fully embrace this blue spec of cosmic dust. Even though Christianity, as we have seen, is largely a product of the dominator culture, and has historically ignored the actual teachings of Jesus in favor of the dominator Myth of Redemptive Violence, it does seem that a better understanding of his attitude toward the environment should be the starting point for a Christian doctrine of Creation Care.

The problem, of course, is that to speak of Jesus' attitude about anything is presumptuous at best! As has been previously noted, there is precious little written, particularly in the Christian scriptures, that tells us anything about the historical Jesus. Among the letters of Paul, whom scholars widely agree is the "true founder of Christianity,"[9] we find nothing of Jesus' teachings. As Geza Vermes, translator of the Dead Sea Scrolls, writes, "After a meticulous combing of the whole corpus of his writings, the information relating to the prophet of Nazareth would add up to precious little."[10] Scholars also agree that the fourth Gospel, pseudonymously attributed to John, gives us nothing on the historical Jesus; not only because it was written in the second century, between 70 and 100 years after Jesus lived, but because its author was clearly a Hellenistic mystic whose only purpose was to fabricate a story about Jesus that would support and promote his own esoteric beliefs. With the exception of a few other epistles, this pretty much leaves us with the synoptic gospels—*Mathew*, *Mark*, and *Luke*—all of which, as we have seen, are uniquely different and contradicting, yet contain enough similarities that it is clear they all shared a common source. It is the remnants of this common source, which may be a lost writing or based purely on

---

[8] Armstrong, Karen, *Visions of God*, Bantam Books, New York, NY, 1994, p. 184.
[9] Vermes, Geza, *The Changing Faces of Jesus*, Penguin Compass, New York, NY, 2000, p. 64.
[10] Ibid. p. 74.

oral tradition, that can inform us most about the historical Jesus and what he may have really said and done.

What little this original tradition does tell us is that he was born in Nazareth, not Bethlehem, during the reign of Herod the Great; to parents who were likely named Mary and Joseph; that he was an itinerant teacher who engaged with social outcasts; and that the Romans executed him as a public nuisance. Although he was also a healer, stories about his immaculate conception, virgin birth, performance of miracles, and resurrection, are all later fabrications, as is most of what he is reported to have said. In addition, the synoptic gospels may provide us with some of Jesus' authentic sayings and parables, but always in an altered context. Again, as Vermes explains, "The Sermon on the Mount is an assemblage of unconnected sayings loosely stitched together by Matthew, a good many of which... may ultimately go back to Jesus."[11] In other words, Jesus never came off a mountain to deliver his teachings in a single sermon. The author used this as a literary device for the convenience of stringing together many of Jesus' well known teachings all at once, and to compare him to Moses in the minds of his Jewish audience, who also came off a mountain carrying the Ten Commandments. In short, we can assume many of the proverbs and parables attributed to Jesus in the synoptic gospels were handed down through oral tradition, even if we can't be certain of their original set and setting.

Thankfully, the fact that he did speak in proverbs and parables happens to tell us a great deal about Jesus and his connection to nature. In Hebrew, the word for "proverb" is *mashal*, which is literally translated, "a comparison." The root of the word means, "rule," and might be used like "pattern," or "paradigm." So Jewish proverbs, in particular, are meant as rules to live by; like, "There is gold and abundance of costly stones; but the lips informed by knowledge are a precious jewel,"[12] and, "Can fire be carried in the bosom without burning one's clothes?"[13] When expanded into lengthier stories, these comparisons become parables, which are also metaphors of some deeper truth. In

---

[11] Ibid., p. 26.
[12] Proverbs 20:13.
[13] Proverbs 27:7.

Jewish tradition proverbs and parables became part of Hebrew Wisdom literature, which include the *Book of Proverbs*, the *Book of Job*, *Ecclesiastes*, *Ecclesiasticus* (*Sirach*), *Wisdom of Solomon*, some of the *Psalms*, and, perhaps, portions of the *Song of Songs*. Those Jewish philosophers who spoke in proverbs and parables were, therefore, considered Wisdom teachers.

The Hebrew word for "wisdom" is *Hokma*, translated into Greek as *Sophia*, from which we get *philosophy*, the "love of wisdom." But Hebrew philosophy is unique in that it came to personify Wisdom as the feminine expression of God manifested through Creation. As Proverbs 8:1 asks, **"Does not wisdom call, and does not understanding raise her voice?"** Speaking on her own behalf, Wisdom goes on to say:

> **The Lord created me at the beginning of his work, the first of his acts of long ago.**
> **Ages ago I was set up, at the first, before the beginning of the earth...**
> **When he established the heavens, I was there, when he drew a circle on the face of the deep, when he made firm the skies above, when he established the fountains of the deep, when he assigned to the sea its limit, so that the waters might not transgress his command, when he marked out the foundations of the earth, then I was beside him like a master worker; and I was daily his delight, rejoicing before him always, rejoicing in his inhabited world and delighting in the human race.**[14]

So, in ancient Hebrew thought, Wisdom is more than clever sayings and stories, it is the presence of God wherever it is manifested, not only in wise teachings and sacred texts, but, even more overtly, in God's Creation, that is, in nature. This Wisdom

---

[14] Proverbs 8:22-31.

tradition, then, represents Jewish animism, the idea that God is in all things. The Kabbalah says, for example, "Divinity flows and inheres in each thing that exists. This is the secret meaning of the verse; 'God's presence fills the entire world.' Contemplating this, you are humbled, your thoughts purified."[15] Wisdom, then, as "purified thoughts," comes through this recognition of God in all things, that is, through awareness of God's presence in the natural world. "Sparks of holiness intermingle with everything in the world, even inanimate objects," the Kabbalah continues, "Even by eating, you bring forth sparks that cleave to your soul."[16] Yes, according to this Wisdom tradition, the food we eat doesn't merely come from God; it is God! "'What is this enjoyment and pleasure? What is it that I am tasting?' Answer yourself, 'This is nothing but the holy sparks from the sublime, holy worlds that are within the food and drink.'"[17] Mechtild of Magdeburg, a 13th century Christian mystic, once explained how she came upon such Wisdom; "The day of my spiritual awakening was the day I saw, and knew I saw, all things in God and God in all things."[18] And Meister Eckhart, another Christian mystic, puts it most succinctly in his claim that, "Every creature is a word of God, and a book about God."[19]

That we can comprehend God best through nature is also, rather humorously, illustrated in the Biblical story of Moses' encounter with Yahweh. "**Show me your glory**," Moses prayed. God responds by promising to "**make all my goodness pass before you**," but cautions, "**you cannot see my face; for no one shall see me and live**."[20] This story clearly suggests that while it's possible to see, taste, and breath in God's "goodness" through God's handiwork, Creation, it is not possible for any of us, given

---

[15] Matt, Daniel C., *The Essential Kabbalah*, Quality Paper Back Book Club, New York, NY, 1995, p. 28.

[16] Fox, Matthew, *One River, Many Wells*, Jeremy P. Tarcher/Putnam, New York, NY, 2000, p. 64.

[17] Ibid.

[18] Fox, Matthew, *Wrestling with the Prophets*, Jeremy P. Tarcher/Putnam, New York, NY, 1995, p. 40.

[19] Fox, Matthew, *Original Blessing*, ibid.. p. 35.

[20] Exodus 33:20.

the limitations of our senses and our knowledge, to fully comprehend the Divine. This is why the Jews don't dare speak or write the "name" of God; For, as the Kabbalah, says, "All the divine names, whether in Hebrew or any other language, provide merely a tiny, dim spark of the hidden light for which the soul yearns when it says, 'God.' Every definition of God leads to heresy; definition is spiritual idolatry."[21]

So, to satisfy Moses' request, as much as is humanly possible, Yahweh continues, **"See, there is a place by me where you shall stand on the rock; and while my glory passes by I will put you in a cleft of the rock, and I will cover you with my hand until I have passed by; then I will take away my hand, and you shall see my back; but my face shall not be seen."**[22] Although the English translators clean the story up a little, the implication here, quite literally, is that God mooned Moses! The amusing point of the story, then, is to suggest that the only way to see God is to see what God leaves *behind*—Creation, Nature.

> **O Lord, how manifold are your**
> **Works!**
> **In wisdom you have made**
> **them all;**
> **the earth is full of your**
> **creatures,**
> **Yonder is the sea, great and wide,**
> **creeping things innumerable**
> **are there,**
> **living things both small and**
> **great.**
> **Where ships sail,**
> **and whales play.**
> **These all look to you**
> **To give them their food in due**
> **Season;**
> **when you give to them, they**
> **gather it up;**

---

[21] Matt, ibid., p. 32.
[22] Exodus 33:21-23.

> **when you open your hand, they**
> **are filled with good things.**
> **When you hide your face, they**
> **are dismayed;**
> **when you take away their**
> **breath, they die**
> **and return to their dust.**
> **When you send forth your**
> **Spirit, they are created;**
> **And you renew the face of the**
> **ground.**[23]

Because Jews understood Wisdom in this way, as the phenomenological expression of God, Jesus would not have been considered a Wisdom teacher simply because he taught in proverbs and parables, but because he was inspired by nature—seeing God in all things. His spirituality was a form of what Matthew Fox calls *Creation Spirituality*, expressed and experienced in four ways—the *positive* path, the *negative* path, the *creative* path, and the *transformative* path. He describes the first of these paths by explaining, "The creation spirituality journey begins with awe, wonder, and falling in love. The first commandment, the *Via Positiva*, is that of praise that flows from beholding the awe of our being here."[24] Clearly Jesus experienced life as positive, as abundance, in which even the sparrows and lilies are fed and clothed without effort. He was a positive person who encouraged us not to worry about life, about what we'll eat or drink, or where we'll live and what we'll wear; "Do not worry about tomorrow," he said, "for tomorrow will worry about itself."[25] And so his teachings are based on love, abundance, and blessing:

> *Blessed* are the poor in spirit, for theirs is the kingdom of
> heaven.

---

[23] Psalms 104:24-30.

[24] Fox, Matthew, *Creation Spirituality*, Harper San Francisco, Harper Collins Publishers, New York, NY, 1991, p. 19.

[25] Matthew 6:34.

Blessed are those who mourn, for they will be comforted.
Blessed are the meek, for they will inherit the earth.
Blessed are those who hunger and thirst for righteousness, for
they will be filled.
Blessed are the merciful, for they will be shown mercy.
Blessed are the pure in heart, for they will see God.
Blessed are the peacemakers, for they will be called sons of
God.
Blessed are those who are persecuted because of righteousness,
for theirs is the kingdom of heaven.[26]

"Creation is original blessing," Fox tells us, "and all the subsequent blessings—those we give our loved ones and those we struggle to bring about by healing, celebration, and justice making—are prefigured in the original blessing that creation is, a blessing so thoroughly unconditional, so fully graced, that we go through life hardly noticing it at all."[27] But Jesus did notice this unconditional blessing, and, because of it, he taught us to love our friends and enemies alike, for God "makes the sun rise on the evil and on the good, and sends rain on the righteous and on the unrighteous."[28] Jesus learned about God's unconditional love, not from Scripture, but from sun and rain—from his experience of the Living Word!

But Jesus was also a man of great depth, and to have depth, one must travel into the deep, into the abyss. This is the *via negativa*, the negative path, that teaches us, often through hard knocks, the value of letting go and letting be. Fox says it "can be a bottoming out experience of profound spiritual depth and a source for new birth."[29] We cannot be certain of the nature of Jesus' own "bottoming out experience,"—whether it involved being born a *mamzer* (bastard) in an intolerant world, or among a people horribly oppressed by Roman tyrants who thought nothing of executing hundreds of them at a time—but we can be confident that when he said, "You must be born again," he was speaking

---

[26] Matthew 5:3-10.
[27] Fox, ibid., p. 11.
[28] Matthew 5:45.
[29] Fox, Matthew, *Wrestling with the Prophets*, ibid., p. 21.

from personal experience. Somewhere along the way, Jesus' own suffering birthed his compassion for others, and it was out of such compassion that his ministry was based. As Julian of Norwich said, "Compassion is a kind and gentle property that belongs to a Motherhood in tender love. Compassion protects, increases our sensitivity, gives life, and heals."[30] Jesus was a kind and gentle healer, and a lover of life, because, somewhere along the line, he fully entered his own pain, his own *dark night of the soul*. And though, as we have seen, his message remained positive and life affirming, Jesus, like anyone who truly steps upon the negative path, could never fully escape its impact or influence. Like the mythical nymph Persephone, who must spend three months a year in Hades because she once ate of its fruit, none who have dwelled for a time in darkness can live purely in the light. But such darkness, if we enter it courageously and willingly, eventually becomes a friend, a source of life, a womb of birth and rebirth. "You darkness that I come from," the poet Rilke sang:

> *I love you more than all the fires*
> *that fence in the world,*
> *for the fire makes*
> *a circle of light for everyone,*
> *and then no one outside learns of you.*
>
> *But the darkness pulls in everything:*
> *shapes and fires, animals and myself,*
> *how easily it gathers them! —*
> *powers and people —*
>
> *and it is possible a great energy*
> *is moving near me.*
>
> *I have faith in nights.*[31]

---

[30] Ibid., p. 95.
[31] Bly, Robert, trans. & ed., *Selected Poems of Rainer Maria Rilke*, HarperCollins Publishers, New York, NY, 1981, p. 21.

Rilke's love of darkness is reminiscent of San Juan de la Cruz who said of his own time in the abyss, "In deep loneliness, I saw with wisdom... I was so far beyond—so lost and absorbed—I lost all my senses... and my spirit was filled, with knowledge not knowing... for this is the dark cloud that brings light to the night."[32] And so the negative path, this Dark Night, can be enlightening and beautiful—the place of calm, quiet, and stillness that enabled Jesus to say, "Have no worries," and to live without possessions. "A return to the dark is also a return to our origins," Fox writes, "we were all conceived in the dark, lived our first nine months in the dark, and were from all eternity in the dark heart of the God-head that preceded the creation of fire and light."[33] So Jesus, having traversed upon this negative path, found his way back to this origin of all things, to the first moments of creation, to that dark and mysterious womb through which each of us is born again.

As a creation spiritualist, he would also have traversed upon the creative path, the path upon which, as Fox explains, "we judge and make a choice of what images to trust."[34] In other words the *via creativa* represents the visionary path. It is that place from which we dream dreams and visions of a better world. The following adaptation of Martin Luther King's famous "I Have a Dream" speech, for example, expresses my own personal vision of the world I want to help create, demonstrates the kind of creativity that keeps our hopes from becoming sedentary, and enables us to move our collective dreams forward;

> I have a dream that one day this nation will rise up and live out the true meaning of its creed: "We hold these truths to be self-evident: that all men [and, might I add, women, and children] are created equal."
> I have a dream that one day in the red states of America's political map, the children of religious extremists and the children of gay parents will be

---

[32] de Nicolas, Antonio T., *St. John of the Cross: Alchemist of the Soul*, Paragon House, New York, NY, 1989, p. 135f.
[33] Fox, *Creation Spirituality*, ibid., p. 20.
[34] Ibid., p. 75.

able to sit down together at a table and welcome each other as children of God.

I have a dream that one day even the bigoted state of mind, an intolerant and hateful state, sweltering with the heat of fear, injustice and oppression, will be transformed into an oasis of freedom and justice, of love and kindness.

I have a dream that my own two children, as well as your children, will one day live in a nation, indeed, in a World, where they will not be judged by the color of their skin, or the creed of their religion, or the nation of their origin, or the size of their parents' bank account, or who they choose to love, but by the their open-minded and open-hearted character.

I have a dream today.

I have a dream that one day the state of Kentucky, whose governor's lips are presently dripping with the words of intolerance and discrimination,[35] will be transformed into a situation where gay boys and gay girls of all ages will be able to join hands with straight boys and straight girls and walk together as sisters and brothers.

I have a dream today.

I have a dream that one day every one who has ever felt the poverty of oppression shall be lifted up; and everyone who has unjustly taken more for themselves than they need at the expense of others, will be brought down to Earth; that every one who experiences rough patches will find their burdens eased; and white collar crooks will enter again into right relation with those unfortunates they exploit; and the glory of God's Creation will be honored by all of us together.

This is our hope. This is the faith we must return to our country and to our planet. With this faith we will be able to hew out of the mountain of despair a stone of hope! With this faith we will be able to transform the jangling discords of our bipartisan nation into a beautiful symphony of unity and harmony! With this faith we will be able

---

[35] This statement refers to Governor Ernie Fletcher's (R-KY 2003-2007) April 11, 2006 executive order repealing antidiscrimination protections for gay, lesbian, bisexual, and transgender state employees—the very same day he had proclaimed "Diversity Day."

> to work together, to pray together, to struggle
> together, to, when necessary, go to jail together,
> and get fired from our jobs together, to stand up for
> freedom together, to march in parades together, to
> grieve together and celebrate together, knowing
> that we will all be free together one day!

Jesus had such a dream, a vision of "the Kingdom of God among us," of people living together as brothers and sisters, forgiving each other, sharing our belongings, loving one another, caring for those who have been marginalized, accepting those who have been ostracized, in a world without violence or enemies. Out of our woundedness comes compassion, and out of our compassion, a new vision is born, a dream of how things ought to be. Jesus dreamt big; he dreamt of Heaven on Earth!

Re-visioning the world in this way, however, is meaningless unless we are willing to make our dreams come true. The transformative path is the path of justice making. It is part of Creation Spirituality because all of Creation is just—all things working together in harmony. The Greek goddess, Justice, holds a pair of scales in her hands to depict this cosmic balance through which all things function together as part of the intricate fabric of Creation. If one thread is removed, the air, the water, the honeybees, the polar ice sheets, even microbes in the soil, the whole thing starts to unravel. The *via transformativa*, therefore, is the path of faith in action; the path upon which our *dogma* becomes *pragma*; upon which Jesus' teachings must be lived out. If we are not living out our spirituality to make justice, to make the world a better place—a more balanced and harmonious place— then our spirituality is a meaningless lie, a mere opiate that keeps us numb to our own suffering and to the suffering around us. **"Take away from me the noise of your songs; I will not listen to the melody of your harps. But let justice roll down like waters, and let righteousness like an ever-flowing stream."**[36]

Like Amos, who spoke these words, Jesus was a prophet who stood against those forces and institutions responsible for exploiting others. "The prophet interferes with injustice," Fox tells us, "the unnecessary pain, that rains on the earth and its creatures

---

[36] Amos 5:22-24.

when humans neglect justice and compassion."[37] Jesus, like all true prophets, lived out his passion for life by putting his radical faith into radical action. He put his reputation on the line by associating with outcasts, he completely refused to participate in unjust economics, he violated unjust laws, and, ultimately, he laid his own life on the line.

He clearly demonstrated the four paths of Creation Spirituality during his brief life. The author of *Matthew* even has his ministry begin with a retreat into the wilderness, like a wanderer on a vision quest. Yet, he did not take this journey to remove himself from the world, but to rejuvenate himself by communing with nature. Fox says, "The basic spiritual discipline in the creation tradition is decidedly not asceticism, but the development of the aesthetic."[38] As a Wisdom teacher, Jesus needed his time alone in nature, not to escape, but to recreate. As Master Ueshiba, the founder of Aikido, the Way of Harmony, advises, "On occasion it is necessary to seclude yourself among deep mountains and hidden valley's to restore your link to the source of life."[39] Some might argue, however, that, as one who gave up all possessions, Jesus was decidedly ascetic, meaning he lived a life of austerity and self-denial. Although it cannot be denied that he was austere, having not a penny to his name, or a "place to lay his head," he functioned primarily, as has already been noted, from a perspective of abundance, not self-denial. He did not own things because he did not need things. It was no burden or struggle for him to give things up. His closeness to nature, to the origin of all things, taught him that all his needs had already been met. As the Don Williams' song goes, "I've got silver in the stars... gold in the morning sun." Jesus knew he was wealthy beyond measure because he understood that nature, Lady Wisdom, provided all his needs without any effort or concern on his part.

As a creation spiritualist, he may have interfered with injustice, but he was wise enough not to interfere with Mother Nature. To do so, to worry about tomorrow, to store more than we

---

[37] Fox, ibid., p. 23.
[38] Fox, ibid., p. 21.
[39] Ueshiba, Morihei, ibid., p. 21.

need in banks and barns, instead of trusting the Earth to give us our "daily bread," as it has for millions of years, is itself a form of injustice that is now threatening our entire planet. As Masanobu Fukuoka, author of *The Natural Way of Farming*, has expressed, "My greatest fear today is that of nature being made the play thing of the human intellect."[40] Like Jesus, Fukuoka, came to realize that our interference with nature makes things worse, not better. "The seeds sown by nature are not so weak as to grow only in plowed fields," he writes, "Plants have always grown by direct seeding, without tillage. The soil in the fields is worked by small animals and roots, and enriched by green manure plants."[41] By interfering with these natural processes, however, through overuse of chemicals and tillage, we have destroyed much of the microbial ecosystem that makes the soil itself alive. The dead ground beneath us then becomes dependent on unnatural and unhealthy agriculture practices that require far too much time, expense, and resources. Yet, in restoring the soil on his farm to a more natural state, Fukuoka has proven able to produce as much rice per acre as anyone else, with little effort or expense. "After thirty years at it, I have managed to reduce my labor to essentially just sowing seeds and spreading straw. Human effort is unnecessary because nature, not man, grows the rice and wheat."[42] That's trust in God's Creation. That's Wisdom. Nothing may be perfect by itself, but all things are made to work perfectly together, and Jesus knew it. He saw the harmony, the balance, the justice, that is nature, and felt no need to worry about tomorrow.

Yet Christians have long mistaken Jesus' aestheticism (sensuality) as its opposite, asceticism (self denial), and, as a result, have too often engaged in life threatening, rather than life sustaining, practices. Early Christians, as noted earlier, became so used to being persecuted that they came to take a certain pride in being martyred, even to the point of advocating martyrdom among themselves. In 107 CE, for instance, when it was still a crime to be a Christian, Ignatius, the Bishop of Antioch, was arrested and

---

[40] Fukuoka, Masanobu, *The Natural Way of Farming*, Japan Publications, Inc., 1985, p. 7.
[41] Ibid., p. 5.
[42] Ibid., p. 16.

sentenced to death. On his way to Rome to be killed by wild animals, he wrote a letter begging his followers not to interfere with his execution. "Allow me to follow the example of my suffering God,"[43] he said. This propensity toward death became so widespread that some Christian leaders, like Clement of Alexandria, complained that those "who have rushed to death" were, in his words, "an accomplice in the crime of the persecutor."[44] For the most part, however, those Christians who caved to the fear of martyrdom, and those who simply did not believe such was necessary to prove their faith, were treated, at best, as marginal Christians, and, at worst, as "heretics."

It wasn't until Ireland was Christianized in the early 5ᵗʰ century that this penchant toward martyrdom took a unique turn. Thomas Cahill, author of *How the Irish Saved Civilization*, suggests this may have occurred because Ireland is, "the only land into which Christianity was introduced without bloodshed."[45] Like all Christians, the Irish admired the stories they heard of Christians willing to give up everything they had, even their own lives, for their faith. "If all Ireland had received Christianity without a fight," Cahill continues, "the Irish would just have to think up some new form of martyrdom—something even more interesting than the wonderfully grisly stories they had begun to learn in the simple continental collections, called 'martyrologies.'"[46] The result is what has come to be called, *green martyrdom*. Instead of sacrificing their lives, as "red" (blood, death) witnesses, they simply retreated into nature, becoming "green" (nature, life) witnesses. "The Green Martyrs were those who, leaving behind the comforts and pleasures of ordinary human society, retreated to the woods, or to a mountaintop, or to a lonely island—to one of the green no-man's-lands outside tribal jurisdictions—there to study the scriptures and commune with God."[47] But many came to

---

[43] Chidester, ibid., p. 77.

[44] Ibid., p. 84.

[45] Cahill, Thomas, *How the Irish Saved Civilization*, Random House, Inc., New York, NY, 1995, First Anchor Books Trade Paperback Edition, March 1996, p. 151.

[46] Ibid.

[47] Ibid.

admire those who spent their lives communing with God through nature, and followed these green martyrs into the wild where they constructed huts to live in, establishing the rudimentary beginnings of what became monasteries and the monastic way of life—Christianity's first contemplatives.

Jesus also retreated into nature to commune with God. Though he was crucified, he did not die to prove his faith in anything. On the contrary, he died because he lived out his faith—a faith inspired by the beauty he saw in nature, encouraged by his dream of a better world, and lived out through his relationships with others. He was not a red martyr, but the original green martyr, hoping to help fashion a society that might reflect the same beauty and balance he found in nature. He was not an ascetic who denied life, but an aesthetic who embraced life. Indeed, it was only through his deep connection to nature that he was able to step outside the corrupt economy of his day, refusing to use money or own anything, because he trusted God, through nature, to meet every need. "Look at the birds of the air,"[48] and, "consider the lilies of the field."[49] The birds do not sow, harvest, or store away, yet they are fed. The flowers do not toil are spin, yet they are clothed. "Foxes have holes, and birds of the air have nests; but the Son of Man has nowhere to lay his head."[50] Though he was homeless and penniless, with nothing more than the clothes on his back, Jesus operated from a mindset of abundance, not poverty. He considered himself rich, and looked at those who store treasure in barns and banks as impoverished in both body and soul.

Yet he did not want anyone to live in poverty, nor to work endlessly just to make ends meet. Why is it so easy for the birds and the flowers, yet so difficult for us? The Earth managed to produce and sustain life for nearly 3.5 billion years before humans arrived on the scene. Now, through our tinkering with Wisdom's natural rhythms and systems, through technology and agriculture, we've brought ourselves to the edge of doom. Jesus experienced the Earth as a potential paradise, a Garden of Eden, in which we can all be free to romp about enjoying the abundance all around

---

[48] Matthew 6:26.
[49] Matthew 6:28-29.
[50] Matthew 8:20.

us, sharing what we have, and working very little to meet our basic needs.

Jesus' wisdom, his parables and proverbs, are filled with creation metaphors. How are we to recognize genuine teachers? "You will know them by their fruits." he said, "Are grapes gathered from thorns, or figs from thistles? In the same way, every good tree bears good fruit, but every bad tree bears bad fruit."[51] His *Parable of the Sower* tells of a man who scatters seed, some of which falls on the path and is eaten by birds; some of which fall on rocky ground where there isn't much soil and grows quickly, but is easily scorched by the sun; some of which fall among thorns and are choked out; and some that fall upon good soil and bring forth lots of grain. Whatever else this might mean, it is clear that Jesus saw healthy soil, the Earth, as good and necessary for growing and sustaining life.

Another of his parables tells of a farmer who plants his wheat in a good field, but an enemy scatters weeds in it while he sleeps. Instead of trying to eradicate the weeds, however, the man decides to let them grow together so as not to accidentally uproot the wheat. Perhaps this is a parable that modern agribusinesses — currently doing what nature never intended, by genetically modifying crops to withstand heavy dousing of herbicides, while killing everything else in the soil, including the microorganisms necessary to help plants eat and breath — ought to pay attention to. All things are made to work perfectly together, weeds and wheat, sinners and saints, heaven and earth. To eradicate one, is to eradicate everything. Jesus understood this deep connection between all things, and often used earthly metaphors to describe Heaven. Like William Blake, he understood that a single mustard seed is as precious as the whole world. "The kingdom of heaven," he said, "is like a merchant looking for fine pearls. When he found one of great value, he went away and sold everything he had and bought it."[52] Jesus, it appears, truly did give up everything for the pearl of Wisdom he had found in Creation, the rare blue pearl we call Earth. Yet he did not try to hoard it for himself, but instinctively understood that to cling to

---

[51] Matthew 7:16-17
[52] Matthew 13:45-46.

the world is the surest way to lose it. Instead, he tried to share its splendor and its riches with everyone, reminding us that it's possible for everyone to have abundance, if only we can learn to let Wisdom do what she does best, create and sustain life.

For far too long the Christian world has forgotten this most important lesson from Jesus, and has, instead, promoted the deadly idea that the Earth is a vile place full of sin and ungodliness, a place God disdains so much that it will eventually be destroyed in a fit of divine wrath. Fortunately, this is one area in which the Christian world is starting to come around, realizing, like many of us, that Wisdom requires us to care for Creation. For, as the apocryphal *Book of Wisdom* explains, **"She is the breath and power of God, and a pure emanation of the glory of the Almighty; therefore nothing defiled gains entrance into her. For she is a reflection of eternal light, a spotless mirror of the working of God, and an image of his goodness."**[53] Or, perhaps it is enough for us to simply reflect upon the first law of Creation told of in *Genesis*, **"God saw everything that had been made, and indeed, it was very good."**[54]

---

[53] Book of Wisdom 7:25-26.
[54] Genesis 1:31.

CHAPTER XII

Jesus Was a Person for the Ethical Treatment of Animals

*"Blessed are those who hunger and thirst for righteousness,
for they will be filled."*

The only food items Jesus is reported to have eaten in the Gospels include, bread, heads of grain, figs, and wine. *The Gospel of John* tells us (probably fictitiously) that during the Temple ruckus, "**Making a whip of cords, he drove all of them out of the temple, both the sheep and the cattle**,"[1] effectively saving the lives of these sacrificial animals during his fatal act of civil disobedience. Obviously it would be quite a stretch to make the claim he was a vegetarian and animal rights activist based on such slim evidence. Like everyone else in his culture, it seems likely that Jesus would have eaten meat, especially fish, on those occasions it became available. Yet, based solely on those stories of his feeding the multitudes with a few fish, his occasional mention of fish to illustrate a point, or the fact that he lived in a fishing community, it would also be a stretch to suggest he was a ravenous carnivore who completely objectified his fellow creatures; or, more importantly, that someone as compassionate as Jesus could support the heinous brutality against animals that has become indicative of modern agribusiness. On the contrary, as a Wisdom teacher, Jesus would have shared the proverbial sentiment that, "**The righteous know the needs of their animals, but the mercy of the wicked is cruel**,"[2] which is why he himself once asked, "Which one of you, having a hundred sheep and losing one of them, does not leave the ninety-nine in the wilderness and go after the one that is lost until you find it?[3]

This is so, from a practical standpoint, because, as John Robbins explains in *The Food Revolution*:

---

[1] John 2:15.
[2] Proverbs 12:10.
[3] Luke 15:4.

Since ancient times, the industries of people who raise animals for meat, milk, and eggs were obligated to make sure that the basic needs of the animals in their care were met. If many animals fell sick or suffered from lack of food, water, or protection, the productivity of the operation suffered, as well as the animals. Livestock operators had a vested interest in the wellbeing of the animals they raised. They did well only if the animals did well.[4]

More important than the practicality of caring for the creatures that make our lives and livelihoods possible, however, is the spiritual need to manifest compassion for all beings; to those we like, and those we dislike; to those we *are* like, and those we *are* dislike. For when it comes to compassion, Jesus expects us to, "Be perfect, therefore, even as your heavenly Father is perfect."[5] Meister Eckhart, who said, "Compassion is the outburst of everything God does,"[6] also said, "Every creature is a word of God, and a book about God."[7] Eckhart, following in the footsteps of Jesus, was, like all genuine mystics, a creation spiritualist. He recognized some aspect of God in every creature. This doesn't mean he made an idol out of Creation, or that he didn't understand God is more than Creation. Like Moses came to discover, Eckhart realized the only way our limited senses can perceive the Divine is by observing what it leaves *behind*. To comprehend the nature of God, we must look to Nature itself. This is not to say, therefore, that a squirrel is God, but that a squirrel, like all creatures, reflects some aspect of God. We don't have to worship squirrels, but we should care for them as part of God's good Creation, just as we should care for all creatures.

Indigenous peoples throughout world history have largely been *panentheistic* and *animistic*, meaning, respectively, they see God in all things, and all things have souls. The very word, *anima*, the Greek word for "soul," is the root of the word

---

[4] Robbins, John, *The Food Revolution*, Conari Press, Boston, MA, 2001, p. 168.
[5] Matthew 5:48.
[6] Fox, Matthew, *Creation Spirituality*, ibid., p. 35.
[7] Fox, Matthew, *Original Blessing*, ibid., p. 35.

"animal." *Animal* literally means "soul." The squirrel is a soul, the bird is a soul, the cat is a soul, the whale is a soul, even the amoeba and the bacterium are a soul. Hildegard of Bingen, who said, "It is God whom human beings know in every creature,"[8] also understood that, "no creature, whether visible or invisible, lacks a spiritual life."[9] Injustice against animals is, therefore, a sin against the Holy Spirit, against souls. As a man of justice, a man of compassion, and a Wisdom teacher, Jesus would not have been able to stomach cruelty to animals, or the cold, callous objectification of God's magnificent Creation in any of its multifarious forms.

One of the difficulties in studying the Earth-centered beliefs of most indigenous peoples, however, is that they don't tend to write about them. There is no Aboriginal Bible, or Native American Vedas, or Pagan Koran to reflect upon. This is so because Earth-centered cultures experience's God's word as a Living Word ("Every creature is a word of God, and a book about God"). Why read about God when you can experience God for yourself? It is those societies that have become separated from the world of nature that seem to rely more upon scripture. As Erich Fromm once explained, "The social history of man started with his emergence from a state of oneness with the natural world to an awareness of himself as an entity separate from surrounding nature and men."[10] As a result of this separation, "civilized" humans need an authoritative source to explain the workings of the world, usually in the form of texts held to be sacred. "In the west especially," Creation mystic, Father Thomas Berry, says, "the mystical bonding of the human with the natural world was progressively weakened;"

> Humans, in differing degrees, lost their capacity to hear
> the voices of the natural world. They no longer heard
> the voices of the mountains or the valleys, the rivers or
> the sea, the sun, moon, or stars; they no longer had a

---

[8] Fox, Matthew, ed., *Hildegard of Bingen's Book of Divine Works*, Bear & Company, Santa Fe, NM, 1987, p. 36
[9] Ibid., p. 281.
[10] Fromm, Erich, *Escape from Freedom*, ibid., p. 39.

sense of the experience communicated by the various animals, an experience that was emotional and esthetic, but even more than that. These languages of the dawn and sunset are transformations of the soul at its deepest level.[11]

Perhaps writing, in light of this, is, at it's core, both our attempt to explain a world that once needed no explanation for us, and to reconnect, through communication, with other people, with those we've stopped seeing, like Jesus understood, as our "brother and sister and mother." Reading, however, is an intellectual activity that may open the mind to new possibilities, but it is only by closing our books and entering fully into the world that we can explore these possibilities by truly communing with others and nature. To seek God purely in books may be theologically stimulating, and may even give us some dim insights about God, but it cannot allow us to experience God. To do so, we must turn to others; nay, we must reconnect with others, including other creatures. "Men love jargon," Martin Buber explained, "It is so palpable, tangible, visible, audible; it makes so obvious what one has learned; it satisfies the craving for results. It is impressive for the uninitiated. It makes one feel that one belongs."[12] But, in the end, he added, "Jargon divides men into Us and Them," into human and nature, friend and enemy, soldiers and terrorists, male and female, people and animals. Could this be the reason fundamentalists are so typically bibliolatrous, because, in their separation from God and the world, they are desperate to find belonging somewhere, somehow? Indigenous animists, on the other hand, do not need written scriptures to *tell* them what is holy because they experience it for themselves in the natural world around them, through their connection and communion with all creatures. Books are important, Scripture can hold deep meaning, but how could the Divine possibly be confined to mere pages?

---

[11] Berry, Thomas, & Swimme, Brian, *The Universe Story*, Harper Collins, New York, NY, 1992, p. 199.

[12] Buber, Martin, *I and Thou*, Charles Scribner & Sons, New York, NY, 1970, p. 15.

Contemplate the workings of this world,
Listen to the words of the wise,
And take all that is good as your own.
With this as your base,
Open your own door to truth.
Do not overlook the truth that right before you,
Study how water flows in a valley stream —
Freely and smoothly between the rocks.
Also learn from holy books and wise people.
Everything, even mountains, rivers plants, and trees
Should be your teacher.
—Morihei Ueshiba[13]

During a recent meeting of our Sunday evening Spirituality Group at church, I asked participants to forgo our usual "check-in" in anticipation of a "check-out" before its close. After speaking a few minutes about animism and panentheism — about the Divine in all things — I asked them to begin by each taking a few minutes of solitude walking the surrounding neighborhood in search of something that might inspire or connect them to Spirit. After about twenty minutes we reassembled. Some told of stones, plants, trees, and broken shards of glass that had spoken to them as profoundly as any text could have. What I had not expected, however, is what happened a little later when I invited each participant to check-out by talking about how they were feeling. To my delight — unlike our usual check-ins, which are often self-centered, shallow, and depressing — each participant, having connected but a few moments with the Divine in all things, spoke of their concerns for others and nature. One woman, for instance, talked of her concern for two perfect strangers she had quietly passed during her walk, wondering about their lives, their struggles, their personal histories. Each also expressed feeling more at peace with themselves because they had gotten away from their own navels, their own problems, long enough to see a bigger picture. To my astonishment, this twenty-minute exercise in "practical animism" had enabled everyone who participated to become less self-absorbed by reconnecting with the larger world around them. Again, as Ueshiba said, "There is evil and disorder

---

[13] Ueshiba, Morihei, ibid., p. 26.

in the world because people have forgotten that all things emanate from one source. Return to that source and leave behind all self-centered thoughts, petty desires, and anger. Those who are possessed by nothing, possess everything."[14]

Jesus, as we have seen, possessed nothing, and, because of this, possessed everything. "Ask and it will be given to you; seek and you will find; knock and the door will be opened to you. For everyone who asks receives; one who seeks finds; and to one who knocks, the door will be opened."[15] As an itinerant teacher, he went on lots of long walks and must have had plenty of time to commune with nature, which may be why he appreciated Scripture, but wasn't adverse to going beyond it, "You have heard that it was said to those of ancient times... but I say to you..." Jesus saw God in all things and was inspired by all creatures—birds of the air, lilies of the field, foxes, trees, stones, sun, and rain. And though it might be logical to presume, as a person of nonviolence and compassion, he may have personally chosen not to eat meat; it seems more likely, to me, that he would have eaten meat when it was available. Eating meat and having compassion are not mutually exclusive, at least not in Jesus' day when people understood the importance of treating animals mercifully, and eating all things with humility and gratitude toward the Creator. But if he were alive today, his nonviolent and compassionate values would leave him little choice but to exclude meat and most animal products from his diet.

This is so because eating meat in today's world is harmful and unjust on many levels. Firstly, as a healer, concerned with the spiritual and physical wellbeing of others, Jesus would have to advise against eating meat and dairy. "Even the American Meat Institute and National Dairy Council acknowledge that the primary suppliers of saturated fat in the American diet are animal products—beef, cheese, butter, chicken, milk, pork, eggs, and ice cream."[16] Saturated fat, as most of us know, can lead to higher cholesterol levels, which, in turn, is the number one cause of heart disease. Yet studies indicate the blood cholesterol levels of those

---

[14] Ibid., p. 16.
[15] Matthew 7:7-8.
[16] Robbins, John, ibid., p. 18.

who *don't* eat animal products (vegans) may be as much as 35 percent lower than those who do.[17] Cancer is also much less prevalent among those who don't eat animal products than others. According to a 1997 report by the American Institute for Cancer Research and the World Cancer Research Fund, it would help prevent 60 to 70 percent of cancers if people "Choose predominately plant-based diets rich in a variety of vegetables and fruits, legumes, and minimally processed starchy staple foods."[18] We also know that obesity is rising at epidemic proportions in the U.S., a direct result of eating too much fat and too many calories. This is not so, however, among vegans, who have a mere 2 percent obesity rate, as compared to the more than 20 percent obesity rate among Americans in general. None of this even touches upon growing concerns over the potential effects to humans caused by treating livestock with heavy doses of antibiotics and growth hormones, or the risk of getting food-borne diseases from animals crammed into unsanitary conditions on factory farms and corporate feedlots.

Heart disease, stroke, cancer, obesity, and now *E. coli, Bovine Spongiform Encephalopathy* (Mad Cow Disease), *Swine Flu* and *Avian Influenza* (Bird Flu) are diseases of affluence, and were not around in Jesus' day. Yet, as one who worked to restore the health and wholeness of others, he would, no doubt, be greatly disturbed by today's unhealthy eating habits. Although he resisted puritanical dietary restrictions, stating, "it is not what goes into the mouth that defiles a person, but it is what comes out of the mouth that defiles,"[19] he also understood the link between our bodies and what we eat. "**While they were eating, Jesus took a loaf of bread, and after blessing it he broke it, gave it to his disciples and said, '**Take, eat; this is my body.**' Then he took a cup, and after giving thanks gave it to them, saying, '**Drink from it, all of you, for this is my blood...**"** [20] Whatever else we may make of the "last supper," it is clear that Jesus understood, on

---

[17] Ibid., p. 19.
[18] Ibid., p. 38.
[19] Matthew 15:11.
[20] Matthew 26: 26-28.

some level, we are what we eat. Unhealthy food leads to unhealthy bodies!

More significantly, as a Wisdom teacher who saw Creation as the manifestation of God, Jesus would be appalled by what our modern eating habits have done and continue to do to the environment. It is one thing for a family to raise enough livestock for themselves, and, perhaps, to sell to members of their nearby community, but it is quite another to allow corporate farms and big agribusiness to deplete the Earth's resources at an unsustainable and suicidal rate in the name of profit. For example, according to Soil and Water Specialists with the University of California Agricultural Extension Department, it takes more than 5200 gallons of water to produce one pound of California beef.[21] The same specialists also estimate it takes more than 1600 gallons to produce a pound of pork, and over 800 gallons to produce a pound of chicken, as compared to only 49 gallons of water to produce a pound of apples, and 23 gallons for a pound of lettuce or tomatoes. In fact, according to *Audubon* Magazine, "Nearly half the water consumed in this country is used for livestock, mostly cattle."[22] This is a real concern when we consider that the Ogallala, one of the largest bodies of fresh water on Earth, stretching from South Dakota to Texas, which had remained virtually unaffected by human usage until the recent advent of factory farming and feedlot beef, is today being depleted to the tune of 13 trillion gallons of water annually, the majority of which is being used to grow grain for beef production—more than is used to grow all the fruits and vegetables in the entire country.[23] To help comprehend the enormity of the situation, keep in mind that a trillion seconds ago was 31 thousand years ago! Because the Ogallala is an underground fossil aquifer from a melted Ice Age glacier, rains or streams don't replenish it. Once it's used up, it's gone forever. Nevertheless, as John Robbins explains, "the Ogallala's water tables are dropping precipitously, and some wells are going dry. In northwest Texas, by the early 1990's, one-quarter of the Texas share of the aquifer had been depleted. By then more than a third

---

[21] Schulbach, Herb, et al., in *Soil and Water* 38 (Fall 1978).

[22] *Audubon*, December, 1999.

[23] Robbins, John,, ibid. p. 238.

of the land in Texas that had been irrigated in the 1970's had lost its water, and had become parched and unable to grow food. Without water, these once fertile farmlands will be deserts forever."[24]

Tragically, the same scenario is being played out with other precious water resources around the globe. Mechanized agriculture (not to mention the growing bottled water industry) is rapidly sucking one of our most precious and vital natural resources dry in the name of meat production. Although 71 percent of the Earth's surface is water, 97 percent of it is salty, making it toxic to terrestrial beings. And because most of the fresh water on Earth is locked away in glaciers and ice sheets too deep to reach, only 0.0001 percent of fresh water is readily accessible.[25] Despite water's scarcity, however, world meat production, with the expansion of mechanized animal farming, has quadrupled in the last 50 years,[26] and, according to "The Browning of America," a 1981 *Newsweek* article, "The amount of water that goes into a 1,000 pound steer would float a (Naval) destroyer."[27]

Sadly, and, perhaps, tragically, water usage isn't our only worry regarding modern meat production. There are currently 20 billion livestock animals living on Earth—more than triple the number of human beings. In the U.S. alone, there are more turkeys processed each year than there are people—300 million turkeys vs. 280 million Americans,[28] and there are more chickens processed annually than there are people in the entire world—7.6 billion chickens vs. 6.9 billion people.[29] According to a 1999 *Time Magazine* article, "In the United States, livestock now produces 130 times as much waste as people do."[30] Because the amount of

---

[24] Ibid., p. 238f.

[25] Suzuki, David, *The Sacred Balance: Rediscovering Our Place in Nature*, Vancouver, BC, Greystone Books, 1997, p. 66.

[26] Durning, Alan, and Brough, Holly, "Taking Stock: Animal Farming and the Environment," Worldwatch Paper 103, July 1991, p. 11.

[27] "The Browning of America," *Newsweek*, February 22, 1981, p. 26.

[28] Ibid.

[29] Lang, John, "Environmentalists Rap Factory Farms for Manure Productions," Scripps Howard News Service, June 9, 1998.

[30] Ayers, "Will We Still Eat Meat?" (*Time*, 1999).

corporate feedlot waste is too much to feasibly return to nourish the soil, as in years past, much of it ends up polluting our already scarce water supply instead. Former hog producer, Don Webb, laments, "North Carolina has been known for its natural beauty, mountains, and beaches. The hog industry is turning it into America's toilet bowl."[31] When large amounts of animal waste pollute waterways, it depletes them of oxygen, suffocating the life therein. Members of the Natural Resources Defense Council in Washington, D.C., have noted, "As a result of animal waste pollution, there is now, in the Gulf of Mexico south of Louisiana, a 'dead zone' of nearly 7,000 square miles that can no longer support most aquatic life."[32]

On top of this, farmers, instead of using animal waste, must now depend on chemicals to fertilize soil, a practice that, according to Robbins, is destroying precious topsoil. "The amount of topsoil we are losing from Iowa alone would fill 165,000 Mississippi River barges a year."[33] According to environmentalists, John Ryan and Alan Durning, "The production of every quarter-pound hamburger in the United States causes the loss of five times the burger's weight in topsoil."[34] In addition to this, beef production, in particular, requires a huge amount of land because cattle, unlike pigs and chickens, which are housed in confined feeding operations, do spend most of their lives grazing outdoors. Livestock grazes on about 525 million acres in the U.S., "nearly 2 acres for every person in the country," according to Robbins, who also points out that, "Seventy percent of the land area of the American West is currently used for grazing livestock. More than two-thirds of the entire land area of Montana, Nevada, Utah, and Idaho is used for rangeland."[35]

As a prophetic activist, Jesus would also loathe the modern meat industry because of the many social injustices it causes to people, especially given that it's propped up by the same

---

[31] Robbins, ibid., p. 243.
[32] Ibid.
[33] Ibid., p. 241.
[34] Ryan, John, and Durning, Alan, *Stuff: The Secret Lives of Everyday Things*, Seattle, Northwest Environment Watch, 1997, p. 55.
[35] Robbins, ibid., p. 248.

169

dominator system that in his own day allowed one or two percent of the population to control all the available resources. Most our nation's grazing lands, for example, are publicly owned, which means corporate ranchers are able to externalize their production costs by shifting them onto the backs of tax payers. Again, according to Robbins' research, "Currently, 70 percent of the land in western National Forests and 90 percent of Bureau of Land Management land are grazed by livestock for private profit."[36] In 1994 taxpayers paid $105 million to manage publicly owned lands used by ranchers for grazing, yet received only $29 million in return.[37] In New Mexico, where 99 percent of trust land is open to grazing, Governor Bruce King, in 1994, was allowed to graze his cattle on 17,372 trust acres for only 65 cents an acre, and the candidate for Land Commissioner, Sterling Spencer paid only 59 cents per acre to graze his cattle on 20,000 acres.[38] Yet there are only three states in the U.S. with higher taxes on the poor, and none with a greater percentage of women living in poverty.[39] And speaking of poverty, "nearly 40 percent of the world's grain is fed to livestock... in the United States, livestock now eat twice as much grain as is consumed by the country's entire human population."[40] The result is that far more of the Earth's resources are going toward meat production to feed one-fourth of the world's human population than are going to provide for the "least among us." According to World Bank estimates, "The world's 630 million poorest people lack the resources to provide themselves with sufficient calories for a healthy diet."[41] It has been made abundantly clear that Jesus, who said, "I have compassion for the crowd... because they have nothing to eat,"[42] would not stomach such injustice, especially given that such poverty directly results from those who take more than they need. As Alan Durning points out, "Indirectly, the meat-eating quarter of

---

[36] Ibid., p. 249.
[37] Ibid.
[38] Ibid.
[39] Ibid.
[40] Ibid., p. 285.
[41] Schut, ibid., p. 93f.
[42] Mark 8:2.

humanity consumes almost half the world's grain—grain that fattens the livestock they eat."[43] It's estimated, furthermore, that much of the water used for meat production leaves nearly two-thirds of humanity with "no option but to drink water that is often contaminated with human, animal, and chemical wastes."[44]

Today, especially, in an age of oil wars due to the peak oil consumption, global water shortage is also becoming a major cause of conflict. During a 1994 lecture presented at the Geneva Conference on the Environment and Quality of Life, British journalist, Adel Darwish warned, "Water is taking over from oil as the likeliest cause of conflict in the Middle East." According to Vandana Shiva's *Water Wars*, "The water crisis is the most pervasive, most severe, and most invisible dimension of the ecological devastation on earth."[45] In her country of India, named after the great Indus River, the average water availability dropped from 3,450 cubic meters to 1,250 cubic meters between the 1950's and the 1990's, and is expected to drop to 760 meters by the year 2050.[46] This dramatic reduction in water is due largely to deforestation for India's paper industry, but the same thing is happening in others parts of the world, including the Amazonian rainforests, the lungs of the Earth, to provide more grazing land for livestock. Forest systems naturally store water, and when they're gone we end up with deserts. Even so, the U.S. imports hundreds of millions of pounds of beef each year from Central American countries where two-thirds of the rainforests have been cleared to raise meat for U.S. consumers, equal to approximately 55-square-feet per hamburger.

Socrates, according to Plato, linked war to meat consumption, which he considered an unnecessary luxury. A country of meat consumers, he said, "which [had] enough to support the original inhabitants will be too small now, and not enough."[47] So, in the end, in order to maintain its luxuriant

---

[43] Schut, ibid., p. 94.

[44] Ibid., p. 95.

[45] Shiva, Vandana, *Water Wars*, Pluto Press, London, 2002, p. 1.

[46] Ibid., p. 2.

[47] Plato, *The Five Great Dialogues*, Walter J. Black – Roslyn, New York, NY, 1942, p. 273.

lifestyle, "a slice of our neighbor's land will be wanted by us for pasture and tillage, and they will want a slice of ours, if, like ourselves, they exceed the limit of necessity, and give themselves up to the unlimited accumulation of wealth... and so we shall go to war."[48] Meat eating, especially in today's age, is an act of aggression and war against the Earth, other creatures, and other people. Jesus, who prayed, "Give us this day our daily bread," and said, "Do not store up for yourselves treasures on earth," would not have stood for it.

Nor would he have stood by and watched corporations lure children into their diners of iniquity with promises of clowns, playgrounds, and toy surprises—especially in light of the current health crisis regarding childhood obesity. If Jesus walked into a McDonalds today, he'd probably turn over more than a few tables, happy meals and all, if they weren't bolted to the floor! Jesus, who said, "suffer the children not," warned those who abuse children that "If any of you put a stumbling block before one of these little ones who believe in me, it would be better for you if a great millstone were fastened around your neck and you were drowned in the depth of the sea."[49] Jesus understood, probably from personal experience, that "Occasions for stumbling blocks are bound to come," and no matter how much we try to protect our children they will end up facing their own struggles, "but woe to the one by whom the stumbling block comes!"[50] Children must overcome far too many obstacles in this complex life as it is, without having to deal with the health issues and social stigma that come with obesity. Yet, according to the Mayo Clinic, "The [childhood] obesity epidemic is especially evident in industrialized nations where many people live sedentary lives and eat more convenience foods, which are typically high in calories and low in nutritional value."[51] It goes on to say that, "In just two decades, the prevalence of overweight doubled for U.S. children ages 6 to 11—and tripled for American teenagers,"[52]

---

[48] Ibid.
[49] Matthew 18:6.
[50] Matthew 18:7.
[51] www.mayoclinic.com/health/childhood-obesity/DS00698, 2007
[52] Ibid.

adding up to nearly one-third of our nation's children. If evoking the name of Jesus really does have the power to cast out demons, then I implore those corporations profiting from injustice against children to stop, in the name of Jesus, stop! It is immoral, you know it, and you must stop!

Finally, Jesus would not tolerate today's meat production practices for the sole reason that they are horrendously and unnecessarily cruel to animals. In addition to destroying the natural habitat of other creatures for cattle grazing, contributing to the extinction of nearly 130 species each day, this industry is diabolically cruel to most the 20 billion livestock animals it feeds upon. "Blessed are the merciful," he said, "for they will receive mercy."[53] Tragically, the meat industry is far from merciful. It does not, as the proverb suggests, recognize the "**needs of its animals**." Its "**mercy is cruel**." Such cruelty is no longer reserved for those unfortunate calves we've all heard about that are kept isolated and immobile in dark crates to produce veil. Today many factory farms cram cows, chickens, and pigs, and turkeys into spaces that are severely uncomfortable, breeding grounds for disease, filthy, and frightening. Pigs are sometimes stacked into cages, barely larger than their own bodies, on top of each other, forcing them to defecate and urinate on each other, or confined together into spaces so tightly that these unusually social and active creatures turn on each other. Although it's against Federal standards, it is often the case that cows butchered for meat aren't fully stunned before they are skinned alive and dismembered. Dairy cows don't have it any easier. In the U.S. their natural lifespan of twenty to twenty-five years is reduced to only four. Chickens, crammed so tightly into cages that they can't spread their wings, often have their beaks clipped off to prevent them from pecking each other to death in their desperation for space. Cock fighting is more humane! In addition, the distressingly cramped quarters all of these animals are kept in incubate diseases, which means they must have a steady regiment of antibiotics to keep them fit for human consumption, a practice leading to the evolution of super-diseases immune to antibiotics. Many of these unfortunate creatures are also given steroid treatments to make

---

[53] Matthew 5:7.

them grow at abnormal rates, preparing them for an early trip to the market, often so fast that they are crippled by bodies that grow larger and faster than their legs can support. Sadly, these conditions only touch upon the cruelty being done to these Living Words of God. Surely these horrific circumstances are completely contrary to what Jesus meant when he said, "God's kingdom is among you." Whether or not you believe eating meat is natural for humans, and is part of the circle of life, there is nothing natural about modern meat production, nor does it operate within Creation's sustainable lifecycle. On the contrary, it is part of the circle of death that is currently killing us, killing our children, and killing our planet. It must stop! In Jesus name, it must stop!

CHAPTER XIII

Jesus Was a Feminist

"Mary has chosen the better part, which will not be taken away from her."

The 2006 film, *Water*, directed by Deepa Mehta, tells the story of a group of widows in 1938 India. It begins with the father of a little girl named Chuyia, asking the eight-year-old child if she remembers having been married a few years earlier, in an effort to explain why she must now be sent away to live the rest of her life in a widow's colony. Needless to say, the little girl doesn't remember her marriage, nor understand why she must be separated from her family. But, according to Hindu tradition, a woman is half of her husband, and once he dies she becomes half a person. A widow, therefore, has no choice but to burn on the funeral pyre with her husband's corpse, marry his younger brother if possible, or live the rest of her life in self denial, as if she were half dead, by joining a widow's colony, shaving her head, dressing in plain white clothes, begging for food, and sleeping on a cold hard floor, in order to atone for the sins that must have caused her husband's untimely demise, while the rest of society considers her untouchable.

In 1938, Gandhi was actually trying to change this attitude toward widows, as well as all untouchables, but enough of it still lingers today that when *Water* was being filmed in India, Hindu fundamentalists made death threats to its producers, and staged violent protests, burning down the sets, eventually forcing them to finish the film in Sri Lanka. What is worse, this idea, that women are less than men, and only have meaning in relation to their husbands, typifies the attitude that still dominates too much of the Middle Eastern world. In many Muslim countries, women must keep themselves covered and veiled while in public, and might be accused of prostitution if accompanied by any man other than their husbands or fathers. No matter how they try to spin these archaic attitudes, they are rooted in oppression, inequality, and patriarchy. Hiding our faces from others is a universal expression of shame, which is why the word "shame" contains *sham* as is root. We cover ourselves, or hide ourselves, when we are ashamed, and the expectation that women should cover themselves, suggests they ought to be ashamed.

Here in the "civilized" West, we like to think that we're above this sort of thing, that women and men are treated as equals, but we all know this isn't exactly true. It wasn't until 1920 that women in America, considered inferior to men, were granted the Constitutional right to vote. Since then, they have continued to struggle for equality. It wasn't until 1963 that congress passed the *Equal Pay Act*, making it illegal to pay women less than men. A year later the *Civil Rights Act* made it illegal for employers to discriminate against people based on race or gender. Another year later the Supreme Court struck down the last remaining state law prohibiting the use of contraceptives. Eight years later, in 1973, the Supreme Court gave women the right to make their own reproductive choices in the controversial Roe v. Wade decision. Three years later, the first law making it illegal for husbands to rape their wives was passed in Nebraska. And it wasn't until 1978 that legislation was passed to prevent pregnant women from employment discrimination.

The point is, here in the West, *land of the free*, these basic rights have been denied women until relatively recently. And, in many cases, women are still treated like second-class citizens, as if they are less than men. We may not ask them to cover their faces with a sham, but, keep in mind, it is the women in our society whom makeup companies market to. It is also true that men are allowed to expose much more of their bodies in public than are women. Just remember what happened in 2004 after Janet Jackson exposed her breast for a split second during the Super Bowl's halftime show. Almost immediately afterward laws were changed and fines were levied (though nothing is being done to shield our children from televised male violence). The public exposure of that part of a woman's body that is so distinctly feminine is still considered lewd and lascivious by mainstream society. There remain many places in our country today where it is not legally safe for women to breast feed in public, which is not only demeaning and difficult for mothers, but denies infants the very right to eat when and where they are hungry! Nor should I neglect to mention former U.S. Attorney General John Ashcroft, who ordered curtains to cover the statue of Lady Justice at the Justice Department in 2002, after her cast aluminum breast appeared above his head in a television interview during which, ironically, he was discussing a report on pornography.

Asking where this discrimination comes from is like asking, *which came first, the chicken or the egg?* Does it stem from the Biblical tradition at the core of many of our Western values, or was the Bible written to reflect those biased attitudes already prevalent in patriarchal dominator cultures? In either case, we know the bias against women, both at home and abroad, in the past and the present, is rooted in some of the world's most ancient beliefs, and it is not until we are able to alter them within ourselves that we can truly proceed to transform our culture into the egalitarian society toward which Jesus aspired.

As recently as 1998, for example, the Southern Baptist Convention, representing 16 million Americans, adopted a resolution requiring women to "graciously submit" to their husbands, and, a year later, affirmed their policy prohibiting women from becoming ministers. This attitude, that women are less than men, stems, in part, from the *Genesis* story in which Eve is blamed for introducing sin into the world, much like the Greek myth of Pandora who opened a box to release sorrow, sickness, and death. Afterward, Yahweh says to Eve, "**I will greatly multiply your pain in childbirth, in pain you will bring forth children. Yet your desire will be for your husband and he will rule over you.**"[1] This dominator perspective of women is carried over into the Christian scriptures in words attributed to the apostle Paul, "**Wives should be subject to their husbands as to the Lord, since as Christ is head of the Church and saves the whole body, so is a husband the head of his wife; and as the Church is subject to Christ, so should wives be to their husbands, in everything.**"[2] This, more than anything else, seems to be the basis of the Southern Baptist resolution, which states similarly, "A wife is to submit graciously to the servant leadership of her husband even as the church willingly submits to the

---

[1] Genesis 3:16.
[2] Ephesians 5:22-23.

headship of Christ. She, being 'in the image of God' as is her husband and thus equal to him, has the God-given responsibility to respect her husband and to serve as his 'helper' in managing their household and nurturing the next generation."

In truth, it is widely held that the words attributed to Paul in *Ephesians* were written by somebody else, and directly contradict his notion that, "**There is neither Jew nor Greek, slave nor free,** *male nor female*, **for you are all one in Christ Jesus**."[3] It is clear that Jesus himself accepted women into his circle of companions and treated them as equals. Yet, as time proceeded, the role of women in his life became more and more obscured by Christian writers reinserting the patriarchal dominator viewpoint, until, as in the case of *Ephesians*, an entire work is written and attributed to Paul to contradict his more authentic and egalitarian writings.

It seems the best place to begin, then, is with Jesus himself. In rediscovering his openness and inclusion of women, perhaps we can begin to alter the age-old paradigm that continues to justify the subjugation of women today. Unfortunately, this is not an easy task, given that the Gospels, which are, for the most part, the only record we have of the historical Jesus, were themselves written by authors with their own political agendas and macho biases. Like all else, then, it is necessary to dig beneath their surfaces to find remnants of the historical Jesus' legitimate teachings.

With the exception of the *Gospel of John*, written in the second century, long after Jesus' death, which seems to contain little to nothing new that can be taken as historically true, the gospels don't portray women as playing any significant role. All of them write primarily of the relationship Jesus has with his twelve male disciples. But this number is probably only a literary convention meant to evoke an association with the fictional twelve tribes of Israel. In realty, Jesus had many disciples, some of which, at least, we're women. "**The twelve were with him, as well as some women who had been cured of evil spirits and infirmities: Mary, called Magdalene, from whom seven demons had gone out, and Joanna, the wife of Herod's steward**

---

[3] Galatians 3:28

178

Chuza, and Susanna, and many others, who provided for them out of their resources."[4] In fact, his inclusion of women into his circle was revolutionary. For, at the time, as theologian Andrew Harvey points out:

> Women had few rights: they could not be witnesses in a court of law; they could not initiate divorce proceedings; they could not be taught the Torah. Both childbirth and menstruation were considered ritually impure. In public life, moreover, women were separated from men as they still are in parts of the Arab world. Middle- and upper-class women did not go out of the house unescorted by a family member; adult women had to be veiled at all times when they were out in public. Meals outside the family were male-only occasions; if women were present, they were thought of as harlots and courtesans. A woman's identity in the world derived totally from her husband or father.[5]

So, by including women, as well as other social outcasts, Jesus opened himself up to lots of criticism. Indeed, it is likely that onlookers would have considered many of the women in Jesus' company prostitutes since they accompanied men who were not necessarily their husbands or fathers.[6] Just as Gandhi later took the untouchables of his culture by their hands and led them into Hindu temples, Jesus, by associating with those considered unclean and unworthy, championed the least in his society. "I tell you the truth," he said to his critics, "the tax collectors and the prostitutes are entering the kingdom of God ahead of you."[7] Jesus seems to have understood that women, like other outcasts, were victims of injustice, not its cause. Women, in particular,

---

[4] Luke 8:1-3

[5] Harvey, Andrew, *Son of Man*, Jeremy P. Tarcher/Putnam, New York, NY, 1998, p. 32.

[6] Some scholars suggest, however, that it may have been appropriate for women to accompany prophets as celibate "companions" or "spiritual wives," reflecting the spiritual marriage between Heaven and Earth, God and "man," and, eventually, Christ and Church.

[7] Matthew 21:31.

were often considered "spoiled goods" after being taken advantage of by men. If a woman was raped or had sex with a man who wasn't willing to marry her, she was considered a prostitute, whether she sold her favors for sex or not. Sadly, many women, after being so victimized, would have had to engage in prostitution just to survive, since, afterward, no man would ever consider marrying her. Yet, by associating publicly with such women, Jesus modeled the truth of his own axiom, "Whoever is least among you all is the greatest."[8]

The *Gospel of Matthew*, in particular, is interesting because it seems to get at the significance of women in Jesus' life rather subversively, perhaps in an attempt to make the work more overtly acceptable to its patriarchal audience. The author begins the work, for instance with Jesus' genealogy. Normally, since individuals were identified paternally, such a genealogy would connect Jesus solely to his father, Joseph, but, in this case, it ends by saying, **"Joseph, the husband of Mary, of whom was born Jesus, who is called Christ,"**[9] emphasizing that Jesus came from Mary. Even more unusual, this genealogy also mentions the names of four other women, *Tamar*, who, in Hebrew scripture, poses as a prostitute in order to be impregnated by her father-in-law; *Rahab*, who harbors spies in her home to assure her family's safety; *Ruth* who pursued Boaz to keep from suffering the difficult life of a widow and a foreigner; and the adulteress *Bathsheba*. These were all desperate women who did whatever it took, no matter how unsavory, to survive in their patriarchal society. *Matthew*'s association of these women, and no others, with the birth of Jesus seems to be a symbolic and subversive attempt to portray Jesus in light of his historical relation to such women, including his own mother's proverbial "shot-gun wedding," before a patriarchal culture that could not have accepted such a notion had it been spelled outright.

It should also be noted that in his, so called, "Sermon on the Mount," Jesus specified that "anyone who looks at a woman lustfully has already committed adultery in his heart,"[10]

---

[8] Luke 9:48.
[9] Matthew 1:16.
[10] Matthew 5:28.

suggesting that women are not to be treated like sexual objects, and that it is men, not women, who are guilty of this transgression. Singling out the men in a culture that victimizes women, then blames them for their own ills, appropriately shifts the blame back on those men who were incapable of taking responsibility for their own abusive behavior. He goes on to say, "I tell you that anyone who divorces his wife, except for marital unfaithfulness, causes her to become an adulteress,"[11] which, again, puts the blame on the man, rather than the woman. In such a deeply patriarchal society, marriage was a woman's only form of social security and welfare. Should a man divorce her, or not fulfill his obligation as a husband after sexual consummation, the woman, again, would have been outcast as a sinner, harlot, or adulteress. Jesus let the men around him know, "It's your fault, not theirs. Act responsibly."

Thus, in shear defiance of cultural expectations, Jesus not only associates with the victims of patriarchal oppression, he champions them at every turn by placing the shame, the *sham*, where it belongs, on those who exploit the weaknesses of others. *Matthew* even tells the story of a woman who had been bleeding for twelve years who approaches Jesus and touches his cloak in order to be healed. Jewish law, you will recall, has many prohibitions against men coming into contact with women who are menstruating, including their own wives. So, for a woman and stranger who has been bleeding a dozen years (there's that symbolic number 12 again) to dare touch a holy man would offend the moral sensitivities of any self respecting Jew. Yet Jesus simply and lovingly responds by saying, "Take heart daughter, your faith has healed you."[12]

At this point, it might be thought odd that I haven't referred to the *Gospel of John* in this discussion of Jesus' attitude toward women, especially since it, more than the other three Gospels combined, portrays Jesus as having significant interactions and relationships with women. Some of these stories, like that of his encounter with the Samaritan woman at the well, and the woman caught in adultery, mentioned in my introduction,

[11] Matthew 5:32.
[12] Matthew 9:22.

are quite meaningful accounts, and do seem, in some ways, to be in keeping with the spirit of what Jesus stood for. Throughout this work, however, it has been my intent to uncover, as best I can, the genuine attitudes of the historical Jesus in consideration of how they might pertain to certain contemporary issues. As has already been noted, there is little to nothing original to *John* that can be counted as historical. It is simply too unreliable a reference upon which to base a discussion of the historical Jesus.

It is my personal belief, however, that Jesus is resurrected whenever and wherever we practice his teachings among us, "For where two or three are gathered in my name, I am there among them." It would be possible, therefore, to consider *John* in terms of the risen Spirit of Jesus; that is, it's possible to ask ourselves, *what of* John *reflects the spirit of Jesus' life and teachings*? Certainly, it's possible to read Jesus' inclusive and loving nature into some of his Johannine interactions, as in those examples previously mentioned. For the most part, however, *John*'s portrayal of women is decidedly patriarchal, and cannot, therefore, be considered in keeping with Jesus' feminist attitude. In her work, *The Women in the Life of the Bridegroom*, Johannine scholar, Adeline Fehribach, concludes, "Like their female counterparts in the Hebrew Bible, the primary function of women in the Fourth Gospel is to put emphasis on the male hero, further the career of the hero, and/or support androcentric or patriarchal principles."[13]

Fehribach's well argued work suggests *John*'s entire account was written to portray Jesus as a "messianic bridegroom who has come to give those who believe in him the power to become children of God and therefore have eternal life."[14] To accomplish this, its author uses conventional type-scenes involving female characters whose roles would have been easily recognized by its original audience. The story of the Samaritan woman, for instance, who meets Jesus at a well, gives him a drink of water, then rushes home to tell her friends and family about him, is reminiscent of typical betrothal stories in the Hebrew

---

[13] Fehribach, Adeline, *The Women in the Life of the Bridegroom*, The Liturgical Press, Collegeville, Minnesota, 1998, p. 175.

[14] Ibid., p. 169.

Scriptures. In *Genesis* Abraham sends one of his servants to the foreign city of Nahor to find a bride for his son Isaac. Once there he sees several women of the town coming out to draw water from a well. He then prays, **"Let the girl to whom I shall say, 'Please offer your jar that I may drink,' and who shall say, 'Drink, and I will water your camels'—let her be the one whom you have appointed for your servant Isaac."**[15] Immediately afterward the servant encounters Rebekah who responds precisely as he had prayed. After the stranger had given her gold jewelry, she **"ran and told her mother's household about these things."**[16] Later on in *Genesis* we find the story of Jacob's entrance into **"the land of the people of the east,"**[17] where he soon sees Rachel arriving to water her sheep at a nearby well. **"Now when Jacob saw Rachel... Jacob went up and rolled the stone from the well's mouth, and watered the flock... Then Jacob kissed Rachel, and wept aloud... and she ran and told her father."**[18] Reflecting upon the similarity of these stories, Robert Alter explains, "The betrothal type-scene, then, must take place with the future bridegroom, or his surrogate, having, journeyed to a foreign land. There he encounters a girl... or girls at a well. Someone, either the man or the girl, then draws water from the well; afterward, the girl or girls rush to bring home news of the stranger's arrival..."[19]

We can see from just this one example that *John's* fictional stories of Jesus' encounters with women were used as literary devices to portray him as a typical hero figure, supported by women functioning in traditional patriarchal roles. But, as we have already seen, there was nothing traditional about Jesus' encounters with women, especially in light of those critics who complained, **"If this man were a prophet, he would have known who and what kind of woman this is who is touching him—**

---

[15] Genesis 24:14.

[16] Genesis 24:28.

[17] Genesis 29: 1.

[18] Genesis 29:10-12.

[19] Alter, Robert, *The Art of Biblical Narrative*, Basic Books, Perseus Books Group, U.S., 1981, p. 52.

that she is a sinner."[20] The relevance of *John* to our discussion, then, is to point out that its use of female stereotypes runs contrary to Jesus' atypical treatment of women. He did not treat them in the typical fashion; like sex objects subservient to men. *Luke*, for example, which, unfortunately, may be only slightly more reliable than *John*, offers an original account of Jesus' visit to the home of Mary and her sister Martha. While there, Martha complains that Mary has been sitting, like a disciple, at Jesus' feet, while she's left to wait on their guests. **"Lord, do you not care that my sister has left me to do all the work by myself? Tell her then to help me.**"[21] Jesus responds, "Martha, Martha, you are worried and distracted by many things; there is need of only one thing. Mary has chosen the better part, which will not be taken away from her."[22] Luke is known for his embellishments, to say the least, but if there is any truth to this story, which certainly rings true to the risen Spirit of Jesus, it proves that Jesus, breaking with tradition, refused to validate the paradigm that women should serve men, that they should not receive educations, that men should order them around, or that he, or anyone else, has the right to keep knowledge, freedom, or equality away from anyone, including women!

Luke also gives us the clever story of a woman who **"had been crippled by a spirit for eighteen years,"** and was **"bent over and unable to stand up straight."**[23] She came to Jesus while he was **"teaching in one of the synagogues on the Sabbath."**[24] Despite her forbidden intrusion upon an all male meeting, Jesus takes her compassionately by the hand and exclaims, "Woman, you are set free from your ailment."[25] Although it is extremely unlikely there is any historic truth to this story, it can be taken as a metaphor of Jesus' well-known concern for the plight of women. As such, we can take this woman's "crippling spirit" as an indicator her condition was spiritual, not physical. She was, for all

---

[20] Luke 7:39.
[21] Luke 10:40.
[22] Luke 10:41-42.
[23] Luke 13:12.
[24] Luke 13:10.
[25] Luke 13:12.

practical purposes, as a woman, unable to stand up against the oppressive patriarchal forces of her dominator culture. Thus, Jesus correctly relates her "ailment" to the loss of liberty she's suffered nearly her entire life. "Woman you are set *free* from your ailment." Yet, his response merely acknowledges the restoration of her true stature brought about by her own liberating action. She finally got so "bent out of shape," as Walter Wink puts it, that she found the fortitude to at last "stand erect in a male religious space."[26] Despite those who criticized him for violating Sabbath law, Jesus goes on to coin a new phrase, calling this brave woman a, "daughter of Abraham," a term that would have stood out in sharp contrast to the conventional, male only, phrase, "son of Abraham." Stand up women! You are children of God too, and, as such, you are equal to any man!

Unlike *Luke* and the other Gospels, however, *John*, written at the start of the 2nd century CE, long after Jesus' death, has the highest Christology among the Gospels, claiming, in its preamble, that Jesus, as *Logos* (the Word), has been around since the beginning of time. **"In the beginning was the Word, and the Word was with God, and the Word was God. He was in the beginning with God. All things came into being through him, and without him not one thing came into being."**[27] These words seem intentionally reminiscent of Wisdom's first person claim of herself in *Proverbs*, **"The Lord created me at the beginning of his work, the first of his acts of long ago. Ages ago I was set up, at the first, before the beginning of the earth."**[28] The not so subtle difference here emphasizes the entire problem with *John*'s view of women in Jesus' life. *John* begins his story by replacing "Wisdom," *Hokmah*, with *Logos*, "the Word." Wisdom, as you will recall, is decidedly feminine—the feminine expression of God manifested through Creation, to be exact. *Logos*, by contrast, is Logic, a function of the masculine left side of the brain. If *John* were truly in keeping with the Jewish tradition, he would have substituted the Greek feminine word, *Sophia*, for *Hokmah*, not the Greek masculine word, *Logos*. In doing so, the Fourth Gospel

---

[26] Wink, ibid., p. 71.
[27] John 1:1-3.
[28] Proverbs 8:22-23.

shifts from the Jewish idea of the *manifestation* of God as Lady Wisdom (Mother Nature), to the Hellenistic *incarnation* of Father Reason (Athena born from Zeus' head); from feminine right-brain creativity, to male left-brain thinking; from experiencing God, to merely having ideas about God; from behavior to belief; from *pragma* to *dogma*.

Jesus believed that, in the end, men and women will be equals, "like the angels in heaven," he said, "they will neither marry nor be given in marriage."[29] And when his family came looking for him, he did not give them special privilege, but pointed to his disciples, saying, "Here are my mother and my brothers. For whoever does the will of my Father in heaven is my brother and sister and mother."[30] It is clear from this that Jesus not only had female disciples, brothers and sisters and mothers, but that he considered them all to be equals, which explains how, in at least one of his parables, he likens God to a woman, "The kingdom of heaven is like yeast that a woman took and mixed into a large amount of flour until it worked all through the dough."[31] I wonder what the world might be like if more of us imagined God as a woman making bread? No matter what our ideas of God, or what beliefs we have about women, Jesus' inclusive and compassionate attitude toward the plight of women has proven strong enough to survive its patriarchal cover up, and calls upon all of us to treat the other half, perhaps our better half, our mothers and daughters and sisters, as if they too are born in the image and likeness of God.

---

[29] Matthew 10:30.
[30] Matthew 12:49-50.
[31] Matthew 13:33.

CHAPTER XIV

Jesus was a Gay Rights Advocate

"Love one another, as I have love you."

During the 2004 national elections, voters in Kentucky passed a constitutional amendment banning marriage for gays and lesbians—one of 11 similar bills passed around the country at the same time. At the time I was working as a full-time corporate video producer in Louisville, in addition to my role as minister at Clifton Unitarian Church. I was so disturbed and offended that the government had begun officially telling me who I can and cannot offer my ministerial services to that the following Sunday I informed my congregation I can no longer in good conscience marry anyone until I'm free to marry everyone. They gave me a standing ovation and a few weeks later our church board passed a policy prohibiting wedding ceremonies in our building until we're free to open our doors equally to all, including gays and lesbians. Because my stance was so extreme, "Minister Says No More 'I Do's,'" the local media ran with the story. Less than a week later my secular employers called me into a meeting and essentially reprimanded me, demoted me, and asked for my resignation. After I realized what had happened, I hired an attorney to work out a severance agreement. Less than two months later they fired me outright without even giving me the two-weeks severance the law requires, or the vacation pay they owed me, citing several trumped up charges, including that I had not received advanced permission from my supervisor to be off work sick. Company officials claimed the fact that its policy manual, the basis of its lobbying efforts, included the statement, "The institution of marriage should only be recognized as the legal union of a man and a woman," had nothing to do with my termination.

During the Fall of that same year, prior to the election, the largest church in the Commonwealth, Southeast Christian Church, with more than 18,000 members, one the largest mega-churches in the U.S., weighed in on the matter by launching an expensive advertising campaign promoting the slogan, "One Man, One

Woman: God's Plan for Marriage;" which was attributed with helping to pass the "Marriage Amendment Act" in Kentucky. Three years later, in 2007, when the University of Louisville and the University of Kentucky both decided to offer domestic partner benefits to gay and lesbian employees, bills were immediately proposed in the Kentucky House and Senate to prevent them from doing so. State Rep. Stan Lee (R-Lexington, KY), the sponsor of one of the bills, complained, "I think it undermines families. It's a public university... that is using taxpayer dollars to support and promote a lifestyle that the overwhelming *majority of people* in this state don't agree with."[1] Fortunately, these bills were defeated before ever coming up for a vote, but the alarming thing here is that a State legislator, sworn to uphold the Constitution, isn't shy about indicating he determines morality based on majority opinion rather than the law. What ought to be truly frightening for all of us, however, is that this "might makes right morality" seems to be the basis of what many politicians today view as *representative Government*. Far too many of them stick their fingers in the air to see which way the political wind is blowing before making their decisions. Always listening to one's constituents, in this way, may be a pretty effective strategy for reelection, but it doesn't reflect the kind of government our nation's founders truly aspired toward. Ours is not merely a representative government, not merely a democracy in which the majority rules, it is a *constitutional democracy* with laws, including a Bill of Rights, designed especially to protect minorities from mob justice. I personally feel so strongly about this matter that in September of 2005 I wrote the following letter to the editor of our local paper:

> I, for one, am tired of all your front-page stories about polls telling us what most people think!
>
> In a democracy, which includes everyone, under a Constitution that protects minorities and in a country that's supposed to practice the rule of law, mob mentality ought to be rendered meaningless.

---

[1] *Lexington Herald-Leader*, July, 2006, by Brandon Ortiz.

It should not matter, therefore, that
(according to your recent article) a majority of
Americans favor teaching "creationism" in school.
Our great Constitution protects us from such
religious tyranny—no matter how many people vote
for it!

Perhaps the majority would favor writing a
new Constitution, like the one in Iraq that won't
allow any laws that conflict with the Quran.

So much for Democracy. Score another
point for the Christian Taliban!

Regardless of our Constitution, there is tremendous
pressure placed upon individuals in all groups to conform to the
will of the majority. In our society such pressure is administered,
not only by our own families and peers, but also, as we have seen,
by our government, the corporate sector, and, especially, by our
religious institutions. It is this truly immoral marriage between
church and state that seems to have riled Jesus the most. Herzog
explains that during Jesus' time, "As the priestly elites curried
favor with Rome in order to cement their own standing, they
increasingly shifted the interests of the temple from serving the
people of the land to exploiting them for the resources they needed
to consolidate and maintain their positions."[2] Again, as numerous
scholars have pointed out, it was likely Jesus' response to this
unholy union that got him killed. Geza Vermes says point blank,
"Had he not been responsible for a fracas in the Temple of
Jerusalem... very likely Jesus would have escaped with his life."[3]

Today the same unholy union between Temple and
Empire exists between Church and State. The Republican Party,
in particular, has been able to win elections and remain in power
by appealing to conservative religious values, especially regarding
abortion, and, more recently, gay rights. Conservative churches
have likewise been able to advance much of their social and
political agenda by using their influence to help elect sympathetic
politicians. What may not be so obvious, however, is that
discriminating against women (denying reproductive rights) and
homosexuals (denying equality) props up the dominator system

[2] Herzog, *Jesus, Justice and the Reign of God*, ibid., p. 193.
[3] Vermes, Geza, ibid., p. 280.

through which the patriarchy governs (capitally) from the top down. In other words, the dominator system, propagandized by the Myth of Redemptive Violence, which, as you will recall, is, "the real myth of the modern world," benefits successful men (top guys) more than anyone else. And because the dominator culture views power as violence, those competitive men capable of beating others—physically, politically, or economically—are revered more than most. The problem with this, as historian Riane Eisler points out, "lies in a social system in which the power of the Blade is idealized—in which men and women are taught to equate true masculinity with violence and dominance and to see men who do not conform to this ideal as 'too soft' or 'effeminate.'"[4] The real reason, then, that both Church and State are threatened by homosexuals, especially gay men (because they don't fit the macho stereotype), is that the dominator system is sustained by men who compete with each other, not by men who love each other. Men who love each other, as Jesus instructed them to do, threaten to bring the entire dominator system crashing down!

I am intentionally singling out gay men from gay women here because, in a dominator society, which is decidedly patriarchal, men who love each other are more of a threat than women who love each other. Men, after all, are expected to be on top, women are not. Many men, in fact, are actually turned on by the thought of lesbian sex. In patriarchal Muslim countries, for instance, women caught in Lesbian relationships are usually lashed, whereas gay men are immediately executed. Similarly, in Nazi Germany, lesbians were often considered sick or mentally ill and were sent for "treatment," while gay men were automatically sent to concentration camps to be killed. But this is not to suggest in any way that the injustices committed against lesbians are any less horrific than those committed against gay men. One of my dearest mentors in life is a lesbian woman, a fellow minister, who, after being caught with another woman in her youth, was sent to a psychiatrist to get "fixed." This psychiatrist was himself a narcissistic dominator who once accused her of wearing pants simply to undermine his male authority. Sadly, this dear woman

---

[4] Eisler, Riane, *The Chalice and the Blade*, HarperCollins, New York, NY, 1987, 1995, p. xviii.

and dear friend, became convinced there was something wrong with her and ended up marrying a man she could never wholly love. Many years passed, having raised their children, before she found the courage to divorce and live the life she was truly meant to live, with a woman she's now been with more than two decades. No, the psychological, emotional, and physical abuse of "homosexuals," male or female, is inexcusable! My intention here is to simply point out that dominators, by their very nature, are more greatly threatened by men who love each other than by women who love each other, because men are expected to uphold the dominator system of violence and oppression. If men start loving each other, look out!

I wish I could say my own experience is unique, that it's rare to suffer economic and social consequences for supporting gay rights; and unusual for States to pass laws singling out gays and lesbians for discrimination; and for churches, professing to represent Jesus, to campaign against equality. But the truth is these things are happening everywhere in our country because men who love each other are a threat to our national way of life—the domination of others from the top down. This is why, prior to his reelection in 2004, President Bush called for a ban on all same sex marriages, explaining, "Marriage cannot be severed from its cultural, religious and natural roots without weakening the good influence of society." That same year he also asked Congress to draft a Constitutional amendment "defining and protecting marriage as a union of a man and a woman as a husband and wife." Notice that he unabashedly cites "religion" as a major reason for his position, despite the First Amendment, which states emphatically, "Congress shall make no law respecting an establishment of religion." In other words, the President, our nation's "top man," has blatantly asked lawmakers to violate the most important law in our land. Like Rep. Stan Lee, Bush knows the Constitution doesn't really matter so long as he has the mob on his side. If people want to discriminate against others, then, by God, let's change the Constitution so they can, or, as is more often the case, simply ignore it!

Thus, when people like Bush speak of gay marriage "weakening the good of society," they're really speaking of it weakening our patriarchal system of domination over others. As linguistics professor, George Lakoff explains in his book, *Moral Politics*, "Gay and lesbian couples simply do not fit the Strict Father model of the family. Homosexuality challenges the monolithic authority of the Father."[5] Church and State attacks against gay marriage aren't really protecting the "sanctity of marriage," they're protecting male dominance by defending an archaic "Father Knows Best" model of family in which the man is the "head of the household;" correctly intuiting that the demise of dominator relations among families and individuals will inevitably lead to the demise of the entire dominator system itself.

Indeed, the dominator system, framed as "strict father morality" by Lakoff, is the basis of Christian theology. It begins, of course, with God as a "Father" above all others. Then, by elevating human Jesus to divine Christ, the Father's Son becomes the "cap," or "head," of the church. In Catholicism, in particular, Christ's avatar on Earth is the *Pope*, a title derived from the Greek word meaning "Father," or "Poppa." Beneath him are his *bishops*, another Greek term once reserved for government officials that means "overseer." Beneath these overseers are individual parish priests who are also called "Father" by those parishioners they preside over. These parishioners are further expected to emulate this top down patriarchal system by making the father the head of their household, above the mother, who is above the children, who must eventually grow up to dominate those "beneath" them, and to willfully submit to those authorities above themselves.

Strict Father Theology

Heavenly Father
↓
Christ
↓
Pope
↓
Bishop
↓

---

[5] Lakoff, George, *Moral Politics*, 2nd ed., The University of Chicago Press, Chicago, IL, 1996, 2002, p. 225.

Priest
↓
Father
↓
Mother
↓
Children
↓
Subordinates
↓
etc.

It shouldn't take a Freudian, therefore, to detect what is most obvious; Christianity represents the collective wish of hundreds of millions of narcissistically wounded souls to finally gain the love and approval of their own emotionally distant and unforgiving fathers who often punished them psychologically, emotionally, and/or physically, which is also why the primary object of their worship remains the figure of a punished child, the crucified Christ. This is true, not only of Christianity, but of every religious group that depends upon the approval of the wider culture—group think—for its sense of belonging. As Erich Fromm once noted, even "the animal god of totemism is the elevated father."[6] In such a society, in which everyone is expected to act and believe alike. "God is always on the side of the rulers," who are, psychologically speaking, hierophants—God's patriarchal representatives on Earth. "In this psychological situation of infantile bondage," Fromm continues, "resides one of the principle guarantees of social stability. Many find themselves in the same situation they experienced as children, standing helplessly before their father; the same mechanisms operate now as then."[7] Thus, he concludes, religion "offers the masses a certain measure of satisfaction that makes life sufficiently tolerable for them to prevent them from attempting to change their position from that of obedient son to that of rebellious son."[8] In other

---

[6] Fromm, *The Dogma of Christ*, ibid., p. 27.
[7] Ibid., p. 26.
[8] Ibid.

words, as Matthew Fox more succinctly says, "All fundamentalists have father wounds."[9]

Yet Jesus, as we have seen, was not the obedient crucified son promoted by Paul who wrote, "**And being found in appearance as a man, he humbled himself and became obedient to death—even death on a cross! Therefore God exalted him to the highest place and gave him the name that is above every name, that at the name of Jesus every knee should bow, in heaven and on earth and under the earth, and every tongue confess that Jesus Christ is Lord, to the glory of God the Father.**"[10] Rather, Jesus was himself a rebellious son who opened the eyes and ears of those who had grown accustomed to turning a blind eye and deaf ear toward the oppressed, and the mouths of those such oppression had silenced.

Hence, without its humanity, that is, without Jesus' humanitarian teachings, the Church is little more than a religion of primitive ancestor worshippers trying futilely to get Father's love and approval—futile because he's so strict no one can possibly live up to his high standards, for "**all have sinned and fall short of the glory of God.**"[1] Focusing on such "unworthiness" is especially prevalent among Protestants who often exclude the centrality of women from their theology altogether, making it entirely patriarchal. This position, as we have seen, is often manifested in the exclusion of women from ministry and other important leadership positions. The problem with excluding women, and, more significantly, the maternal nature of the Divine, is that we negate the experience of unconditional love, depriving ourselves of the psychological necessity of being loved *for who we are*. Paternal love, on the other hand, is conditional, and loves us only *for what we do*. Both are necessary. Motherly love validates our true self. Fatherly love asks us to consider our roles and responsibilities among others. Without it we would be lost in the world. Unconditional love alone leaves us extremely narcissistic—living as if "it's all about me." But conditional love by itself leaves us feeling empty inside because we've completely abandoned our own inner truth, our most sacred calling, and have,

---

[9] Fox, Matthew, *A New Reformation*, ibid., p.18.
[10] Philippians 2:8:12.

instead, become mindless automatons—cogs in the social machine! "In the nature of father love," writes Fromm, "lies the fact that obedience becomes the main virtue, that disobedience is the main sin—and its punishment the withdrawal of fatherly love."[11]

We can see from this why a religion based solely on Father worship becomes domineering, dispassionate, strict, and punitive, and why, based on our most sacred values, it ends up permeating all sectors of our lives. "The strict father is moral authority and master of the household," writes Lakoff, "dominating the mother and children and imposing needed discipline. Contemporary conservative politics turns these family values into political values: hierarchical authority, individual discipline, military might."[12] This further explains why, under the dominator model, marriage must exist, as father-worshippers define it, as *the union of a man and a woman.* "Marriage in the strict father family must be heterosexual marriage," Lakoff continues, "The father is manly, strong, decisive, dominating—a role model for sons, and for daughters a model of a man to look up to."[13] Perhaps theologian Matthew Fox—excommunicated by the Pope for publishing his book, *Original Blessing*, which suggests, maternally, that Creation is good and none of us are born "short of God's glory,"—explains strict father morality best; "One worships a punitive Father and seeks obedience at all costs. It is patriarchal and demonizing of women, the earth, other species, science and gays and lesbians. It builds on fear and it supports empire builders. Its theology includes a Punitive Father in the Sky and a teaching of original sin."[14] Or, as Riane Eisler more succinctly says, "In the name of religion, there is a push to again deny women reproductive choice, to maintain rigid male control over women's sexuality, and to demonize homosexuality."[15]

---

[11] Fromm, Erich, *The Art of Loving*, ibid., p. 36.
[12] Lakoff, George, *Don't Think of an Elephant*, Chelsea Green Publishing, White River Junction, VT, 2004, p. 47f.
[13] Ibid., p. 48.
[14] Fox, Mathew, *A New Reformation*, ibid., p. 11.
[15] Eisler, Riane, *The Power of Partnership*, New World Library, Novato, CA, 2002, p. 52.

This explains why, even though the Bible says little to nothing about homosexuality, so many in our culture treat gays and lesbians with particular contempt, yet ignore many other more prominent prohibitions. To avoid going into great detail about some of these, perhaps another of my whimsical editorials will suffice in getting the point across. I wrote the following in April of 2005, in response to, then, Senate Majority Leader Bill Frist's appearance at a Louisville Baptist church to promote "Justice Sunday," in his attempt to thwart the efforts of, so called, "activist judges" who were upholding the Constitution by ruling in favor of gay marriage:

> I for one am really looking forward to the day the likes of George Bush, Bill Frist and other leaders of the Christian Taliban succeed in replacing our Democracy with a Theocracy, our Constitution with the Bible, and our Federal Judges with conservative Bible-thumpers.
>
> There'll be no more noisy neighborhood dogs or pesky house cats around because the Bible says, "all that walk on their paws among the animals... are unclean for you."
>
> All of us married guys will have to stay away from our "unclean" wives a whole week after menstruation, which should greatly reduce the divorce rate.
>
> We can also forgo the tedium of shaving everyday since it's a sin to "mar the edges" of our beards.
>
> The Bible also instructs us to practically take the entire month of July off work, or else be ostracized by our friends and families.
>
> That will give us plenty more quality time to spend with our children and spouses (unless our wives are menstruating).
>
> Nobody will work Saturdays, unless they want to get stoned, and I'm not talking recreationally!
>
> I'm also looking forward to Jubilee every seventh year when my bank and creditors must forgive my debts.
>
> This is especially needed now that the Republicans have made it more difficult for the poor to file bankruptcy.

> Although the economy may suffer under
> these Biblical policies, we can always reinstitute
> slavery and sell our daughters in a pinch.

How is it that so many Christians are easily willing to overlook numerous other Biblical requirements and restrictions, yet obsess about homosexuality? The answer, it seems, is that people who genuinely love each other, as equals, represent a grave threat to the strict father morality through which a few men control everyone else, obtaining untold riches for themselves in the process. This is so, as we have seen throughout, even though Jesus himself stood against the dominator system and asked us to base our relationships on love instead of violence. **"'You shall love the Lord your God with all your heart, and with all your soul, and with all your mind.' This is the greatest and first commandment. And a second is like it: 'You shall love your neighbor as yourself.' On these two commandments hang all the law and the prophets."**[16] But our domineering society greatly fears this commandment to love one another, and demonizes those who do, because love makes us all equals, it makes us partners, and the last thing we want in a dominator culture are loving partnerships! This is the fundamental reason the powers-that-be, in both Church and State, deny gay partners the right to marry, and are against institutions providing domestic partner benefits — because their values are based on domination rather than love, on capital (being on top) rather justice.

It ought to be clear by now that Jesus was not patriarchic, and that, in fact, he not only resisted the dominator system of his own day, but lost his life in doing so. True, he often referred to God as "*abba*," a word usually translated as "Father," but is really a colloquialism that is more accurately translated "daddy." Since he clearly could not have gotten by in his culture with calling God "mother," he did the next best thing by making the Jewish idea of a strict father god more loving and accepting by using baby-talk. Jesus tried to bring theology back down to Earth by presenting God horizontally, as *Immanuel*, "God with us." As in his parable of the prodigal son, Jesus' God was not a punitive father, but a

---

[16] Matthew 22:37-40.

loving and forgiving father who rushes out to meet us unconditionally no matter *who we are* or *what we've done.* "But while he was still far off, his father saw him and was filled with compassion; he ran and put his arms around him and kissed him."[17] This is the kind of "daddy" who openly kisses his son and is so happy to have him home that he doesn't hear his unnecessary plea for forgiveness because he's too busy planning a welcome home party.

It's especially noteworthy that when Jesus was informed about the presence of his awaiting mother and brothers, he's reported to have asked rhetorically, "'Who are my mother and my brothers?' **And looking at those who sat around him, he said, 'Here are my mother and my brothers! Whoever does the will of God is my brother and sister and mother."**[18] Notice he omitted "and my father" from this list. Having resoundingly promoted himself as both a "son of God" and, therefore, a part of the human race, a "son of Man," worthy of respect and dignity, Jesus refused to endow any human being with patriarchal authority over him. "**Call no one your father on earth, for you have one Father—the one in heaven.**"[19] He knew all too well what happens under the dominator system when patriarchs assume divine authority, and he refused to have any part of it. For him, God is not a strict father who judges and condemns us, but understands and embraces us, unconditionally, more like a mother, even if he couldn't come right out and call her "mama."

In Lakoff's frame, we might say Jesus' idea of God comes from "nurturing parent morality," which he describes as, "protective and caring, builds trust and connection, promotes family happiness and fulfillment, fairness, freedom, openness, cooperation, community development."[20] Although the stereotype may be heterosexual, Lakoff adds, "there is nothing in the nurturing family model to rule out same-sex marriage."[21] As one of my college Bible professors used to say, "You'll always treat

---

[17] Luke 15:20.
[18] Mark 3:32-35.
[19] Matthew 23:9.
[20] Lakoff, ibid., p. 48.
[21] Ibid.

others the way you think God treats you!" If we think God loves us, then we treat others with love. If we think God is strict, then we tend to be judgmental. If we think God is going to burn us in Hell, we treat others like hell! It's clear that Jesus' nurturing parent theology led him to treat others in a nourishing way. We all know that he was often criticized for associating with those his society considered outcasts, and if he were living today, no doubt, he would be criticized for having similar associations with the modern equivalent of the social pariah—homosexuals.

Although Jesus never actually spoke on the issue, and the word "homosexual" doesn't exist anywhere in the Bible, we can be sure Jesus encountered the ancient equivalent of those we now call "gays and lesbians," given that 8 to 10 percent of the human population is and always has been sexually attracted to members of their own gender. We can take his silence on the matter as an indication he really didn't care who we love, so long as we "love one another."[22] In other words, Jesus didn't talk about "homosexuality" because it wasn't an issue for him. He simply had bigger fish to fry!

His primary mission, as we have seen, was about bringing an end to the dominator system that allowed a few sadists to exploit and oppress everyone else. Men who love each other, and women who love each other, were the least of his concerns, and, in fact, were part of his prescribed solution. Though he may not have ever spoken in depth about sexual relationships of any kind, and is presented by the gospel writers as rather asexual and androgynous himself, the one thing we can be most certain of is that Jesus would have been as much against sexual exploitation as he was all forms of exploitation. This is an important point because dominator societies aren't as much against man-on-man sex as they are, again, against men who truly love each other. In fact, it has been common throughout history for dominators to sexually abuse those they are subjugating in an attempt to humiliate and bring them under submission. Dominator societies have traditionally shut a blind eye to such abuses, sexual or otherwise, so long as those carrying out these atrocities are "on top of things." Women, children, and men, continue to be raped and

---

[22] John 5:12.

sodomized to this day by government soldiers around the globe. The chilling stories coming out of Northern Africa today, involving bands of soldiers murdering the parents of children they then gang-bang to death, are too nightmarish to recount! The rape of men and women, boy and girls, has long remained a weapon of war and domination. Sadly, as we must all now admit, even American soldiers have recently committed such crimes. The torture and sexual humiliation of detainees at the Abu Ghraib prison are only one example we know of. The 14-year-old Iraqi girl, Abeer Hamza, forced to watch three U.S. soldiers murder her family before raping her and putting a bullet through her head is another.

What is most unthinkable, though not usual, however, is that the perpetrators of these crimes blame their helpless victims for such abuses, not themselves. In their minds, poisoned by the dominator Myth of Redemptive Violence, those they abuse deserve exactly what they get, if for no other reason, because they are weak and helpless, not strong and victorious. As one U.S. tank driver lamented in a recent magazine article, "Sure, some Iraqi kids had been killed. It's like seeing a dead dog on the side of the road. We hated them and were happy to have killed one. That's how those kids on the news were able to rape the 14-year-old girl, shoot her in the face, and kill her whole family. They just didn't care, they still don't care, they couldn't make themselves care if they tried."[23] Dominators are stuck at the lowest level of theological development, viewing God, as Fromm puts it, "as a despotic, jealous God, who considers [people] whom he created, as his property, and is entitled to do with [them] whatever he pleases."[24] Because we "treat others the way we think God treats us," those with this perspective feel justified in abusing others (just as the ancient Aryans thought they were emulating Indra when conducting raiding parties). Riane Eisler explains, "what happens is that when people relate to each other as 'superiors' and

---

[23] "Why Iraq Veterans Can't Stay Silent," by Sarah Olson, *Yes! Magazine*, Summer, 2007, p. 13f.

[24] Fromm, *The Art of Loving*, ibid., p. 57.

'inferiors,' they develop beliefs justifying these kinds of relations."[25]

Nowadays gays and lesbians are treated as 'inferiors,' which justifies much of the discrimination and violence committed against them by those who feel they are morally 'superior.' This position of dominance is justified by the belief that God's disdain for homosexuals is made abundantly clear throughout the Bible, and since God can do whatever "he" wants to "his" subjects, it's okay for us to emulate God by exploiting, oppressing, torturing, discriminating against, abusing, and, even murdering, those he despises. After all, *they do have it coming*! Just look at what happened to the inhabitants of Sodom and Gomorrah who wanted to have sex with those guys visiting Lot's house, "**the Lord rained on Sodom and Gomorrah sulfur and fire from the Lord of heaven**."[26] The real point of this story, however, is not that the men of these cities were asking these strangers out on a date in the hope they might end up making love together—they wanted to rape them! Again, this kind of sexual abuse is a common dominator method used for humiliating and subjugating others. Isn't it more reasonable, therefore, to assume the men in this story were destroyed, not because they wanted to love these strangers, but because they wanted to harm them? It's obvious! Of course this was the case! Especially in light of the many Biblical prohibitions against the mistreatment of strangers, "**You shall not oppress a stranger. You know the heart of a stranger, for you were strangers in the land of Egypt**,"[27] something Jesus reiterated when he said, "I was a stranger and you welcomed me."[28]

How so many can misinterpret this story as justification for mistreating homosexuals seems incomprehensible! The only explanation for this, again, is that those under the spell of the dominator myth cannot see that there is anything wrong with abusing their "inferiors"—those strangers among us with all their strange ideas, strange ways, and strange lifestyles. The prophet

[25] Eisler, Riane, *The Power of Partnership*, ibid., p. xvii.
[26] Genesis 19:24.
[27] Exodus 23:9.
[28] Matthew 25:43.

Ezekiel, who criticized Israel, in part, because, "**the stranger has been oppressed in your midst**,"[29] clearly understood the story of Sodom in its proper context. "**Now this is the sin of your sister Sodom**," he explained, "**She and her daughters were arrogant, overfed and unconcerned; they did not help the poor and needy**."[30] Notice the prophet goes out of his way to identify the city as feminine, as if to completely stay away from the misnomer the city was destroyed because of man-on-man sex. On the contrary, it was destroyed because it was unjust and oppressive. Yet, because dominators simply cannot grasp that there's something terribly wrong with oppressing and abusing others, the "least" among us, the point remains lost on them, and we've ended up making the word "sodomy" a synonym for gay sex rather than sexual abuse.

In 2005, for example, when Representative Mark Foley (R-FL) was accused of sending sexually suggestive emails to a 16-year-old male congressional page, former House Speaker Newt Gingrich (R-GA) excused his party's decision to leave Foley as Chair of the House Caucus on Missing and Exploited Children, of all things, by saying, "Had they overly aggressively reacted to the initial round, they would have also been accused of gay bashing." Clearly Gingrich doesn't understand what was wrong with Foley's actions—that it was not his desire to have sex with another male, but the use of his position of power to potentially exploit someone less powerful. We've seen the same thing happen in recent years in regard to the child sexual abuse scandal that has plagued the Catholic Church in the U.S. In September of 2005 the Vatican announced that in response to the scandal it would begin investigating all of its 229 American seminaries for "evidence of homosexuality." As in the case with Foley, those in power, who contributed to these injustices through gross negligence, cannot seem to differentiate between consensual sexual relationship among mature adults, and the sexual abuse of children.

Still, there are many fundamentalists who would argue such animosity toward homosexuals is warranted in light of Biblical verses like *Leviticus* 18:22, which states emphatically,

---

[29] Ezekiel 22:7.
[30] Ezekiel 16:49.

"Do not lie with a man as one lies with a woman; that is detestable;" *Leviticus* 20:13, which states, similarly, **"If a man lies with a man as one lies with a woman, both of them have done what is detestable. They must be put to death; their blood will be on their own heads;"** and *Deuteronomy* 23:17-18, **"There shall be no whore of the daughters of Israel, nor a sodomite of the sons of Israel. Thou shall not bring the hire of a whore, or the price of a dog, into the house of the Lord thy God for any vow: for even both these are abominations unto the Lord thy God."** These three verses, which, incidentally, are the only verses in the Hebrew Scriptures that concern same-sex encounters, may seem pretty clear-cut at the outset, but putting them in their proper context makes it obvious they concern sexual exploitation, not homosexuality. Firstly, it's important to remember these verses were written as part of the Jewish *holiness code* for Temple priests and those participating in Temple worship—a code that could be summed up in the familiar cliché, "Cleanliness is next to Godliness." Thus, the word that is usually translated into English as "detestable" or "abomination" might be better translated as, "ritually unclean," as it is elsewhere in the Hebrew Scriptures. Because the Jewish idea of sin is separation, anything that isn't completely whole (holy, pure) would be improper to use in a ritual setting. Spotted animals, for instance, could not be sacrificed upon the altar, nor could fabric woven from differing materials be worn.[31]

Nowadays it goes without saying that people, gay or straight, shouldn't have sex during a church service. But in ancient times many people included sexual rituals in their religious practices, often in the hope of assuring an abundant harvest. It was common for Temple priests and Temple prostitutes to help men ejaculate in order that their semen might fecundate the Earth. Because women were excluded from many of these ritual settings, it was up to men to assist other men in this way. This would have been particularly true of the Jewish Temple, which contained certain areas women were not allowed to enter. This explains why the ancient Hebrews, who struggled to keep their cultic practices

---

[31] Although I don't consider myself puritanical, I do agree, in looking back at the 70's, polyester ought to be considered a sin!

separated from those of neighboring peoples, would be concerned with bringing **"the hire of a whore, or the price of a dog into the house of the Lord**," to begin with. Thus, a more accurate interpretation of verses like these might be, "Temple sex is ritually unclean," or, more simply, "It's inappropriate to have sex during a church service."

Yet we must not ever lose sight of the fact that Judaism's unique gift to World Religion is that it comes from the perspective of an oppressed people, and, therefore, can speak to and for oppressed people everywhere in all ages. Spotted goats, for instance, were not considered "ritually unclean" simply because they somehow smell worse than unmarked goats. Rather, the separation delineated in their markings is a symbolic reminder of what it means to be separated in a society that singles you out as inferior, considers you unworthy of equal rights and protections, and thinks you deserve to be discriminated against and exploited. Thus, the first of their Ten Commandments states, **"I am the Lord your God, who brought you out of the land of Egypt, out of the house of slavery. You shall have no gods before me."**[32] The litmus test for worship, for what we hold *worthy*, is always liberation! If it doesn't free us, it's not worthy of our devotion and does not come from God. It's from this perspective we come to ask ourselves, then, what is the injustice caused by a **"man lying with a man the way one lies with a woman?"** Or the injustice of paying prostitutes for their services?

In answering this question, it's important to note that the restriction here is very specific, prohibiting men from lying with men **"the way one lies with a woman."** It says nothing about sexual engagement between women, or of men engaged in mutual sex with each other. Rather, this prohibition is specifically singling out "top guys." This was necessary because, as we have seen, men who are on top tend to project their own guilt onto those they exploit. Although the authors of the holiness code obviously believed it was improper for prostitutes to solicit business on holy ground, which most Jews would have already known, they found it necessary to let those exploiting them know that they too were in the wrong. Again, the dominator mindset doesn't recognize that

---

[32] Exodus 20:2-3.

it's unjust to take advantage of people in lesser circumstances because, in their minds, they deserve it. Therefore, those men using Temple prostitutes would have placed the blame for such indiscretion entirely upon the prostitutes themselves, unable to recognize that they had any role in it. This is particularly disturbing when we recall that these prostitutes were at the absolute bottom tier of their agrarian society. They were from the *expendable* class, considered "ritually unclean" because their desperation and destitution forced them to engage in despicable trades. They included women who had been raped or taken advantage of by men who refused to marry them, thus leaving them "spoiled goods" with no choice but to engage in "activities considered offensive or unclean to the population."[33] Many of them, in addition, were children whose parents could no longer afford to care for them, and, as Herzog explains, "were people with nothing left to sell but the energies of their bodies or their animal energies."[34] Since, again, women were forbidden entrance to certain parts of the Temple, it would have been left up to these orphaned boys to meet the needs of those men wishing to engage in ritual sex—which, in retrospect, ought rightly be called *detestable*!

Outside of these three verses, along with the story of Sodom and Gomorrah, the Hebrew Scriptures say nothing about anything that might be construed or misconstrued as "gay sex." The Christian Scriptures contain only two such references. The first of these is found in Paul's letter to the Romans, "**For this reason God gave them up to degrading passions. Their women exchanged natural intercourse for unnatural, and in the same way also the men, giving up natural intercourse with women, were consumed with passion for one another.**"[35] Taken out of context, this passage also seems rather black and white. It is clear, however, that these sentences are merely a part of a larger conversation Paul is having about the old holiness code that was so strict it was impossible to adhere to, which, for him, was its entire point. Although Paul, admittedly, did not concern himself

---

[33] Ibid.

[34] Herzog, *Parables as Subversive Speech*, ibid., p. 65.

[35] Romans 1:26-27.

with the teachings of Jesus, he was not of a dominator mindset (even if the religion he invented has ended up that way). On the contrary, Paul tried to loosen many of the impractical restrictions placed on people by the "strict father" religion they had been accustomed to. Rules, for him, which are paramount under the strict father model, are, quite literally, made to be broken. **"If it had not been for the law, I would not have known sin."**[36] Paul brings these taboos up in *Romans*, along with many others, merely to point out just how impossibly strict they are. In promoting a more egalitarian society, in which there was **"no longer Jew or Greek, slave or free, male or female,"** he found it necessary to encourage understanding and acceptance. Thus, immediately after presenting a long list of ritual taboos, including those against **"unnatural intercourse,"** he states emphatically, **"Therefore you have no excuse, whoever you are, when you judge others; for in passing judgment on another you condemn yourself."**[37] Perhaps Paul's entire argument, then, is summed up in *Romans* 8:1, **"There is therefore now no condemnation for those who are in Christ Jesus."** The translators of the King James Version of the Bible found Paul's openness here so disturbing, particularly in light of their strict-father culture, that they added the line, **"...for those who walk not after the flesh, but after the spirit,"** a line that has been correctly omitted from modern translations.

The other verse, found in *I Corinthians*, says, **"Know ye not that the unrighteous shall not inherit the kingdom of God? Be not deceived: neither fornicators, nor idolaters, nor adulterers, nor effeminate, nor** *abusers of themselves with mankind*, **nor thieves, nor covetous, nor drunkards, nor revilers, nor extortioners, shall inherit the kingdom of God."**[38] In this case, I cite the King James translation because it does appear to be more accurate than those modern translations that wrongly translate the Greek word, *arsenokoitai*, as "homosexual." The precise meaning of this unusual word is rather vague, but it most definitely has to do with sexual abuse, not homosexuality. What *King James* calls **"abusers of themselves with mankind,"**

---

[36] Romans 7:7.
[37] Romans 2:1.
[38] I Corinthians 6:9.

might better be translated simply as, "abusive men," or, perhaps, as "child abusers." The word preceding it, *malakoi*, is translated as "effeminate," or "soft," or "male prostitute." Like the author of *Leviticus*, Paul is making it a point to let the "top guys" know that they too are to blame for taking advantage of male prostitutes, those, who, again, were most likely children.

Although this might seem rather obvious, it must be continually spelled out for dominators because, as I cannot overstate, they don't comprehend that it's possible for them to abuse those they dominate. This is why we must have a Bill of Rights in a country that's supposed to be free to begin with! Because dominators just don't seem to get it! They always end up blaming those they oppress — women, minorities, the poor, homosexuals — for the injustices they themselves perpetrate. In Paul's day this was the case involving men who "mentored" boys in exchange for sexual favors. This common practice, known as *pederasty*, meaning "boy-love," became quite controversial in ancient Greek society, so much so, in fact, that the philosopher Plato became well known for his stance against it. This is the reason why, to this very day, we refer to non-sexual relationships as "platonic." Paul, in adding "abusive men" to his list of indiscretions, was taking a clear position on this very controversial subject. Thus, as with all the other scriptures we have dealt with, the real issue here is about injustice, not puritanical notions about whom we can and cannot love!

But even if these half dozen references did condemn such behavior, it still would not justify the blatant discrimination against gays and lesbians that's happening in our country today — at least not anymore than the Biblical sanction of slavery and genocide justifies these unholy practices. Even though this odd collection of works, written by numerous authors over a period of more than a thousand years, holds many contradictions, the Bible, as a whole, is remarkably cohesive in its universal devotion to justice. This is so from the Torah (Law) that correctly places blame upon those who exploit the weaknesses and difficult circumstances of others; to prophets like Ezekiel who tell us "it's not about sex, it's about oppression;" to Paul who asks, "**Why do**

you pass judgment on your brother or sister?"[39]; to Jesus himself who encouraged us to, "Love one another, even as I have loved you."[40]

Earlier in this work Oliver North was quoted as saying, "After the Christian majority takes control, pluralism will be seen as immoral and evil and the state will not permit anybody the right to practice evil." This statement reflects the typical dominator mindset of "might makes right," and proves its desperation to make everyone act and think just alike. It's desperate because, despite North's prediction, the strict father model is losing its grip on our society and the religious right is panicking. According to the 2000 census, less than 55 million of the approximately 105 million U.S. households belong to married couples. It also shows the number of unmarried-partner households is on the rise, up from 3.2 million in 1990 to 5.5 million in 2000. 1 in 9 of these belong to same sex partners, representing more than half a million American households. Are we to believe that Jesus, who himself rejected the strict father family model, really wants us to exclude and persecute so many people whose only real fault is that they *love one another*? Partnerships are rising like a phoenix from the ashes of the failing dominator system, and this, for no other reason, is why our gay neighbors are being persecuted by both the Church and State—two entities joined together in the only unholy matrimony any of us should be concerned with.

---

[39] Romans 14:10.
[40] John 15:12.

INTRODUCTION TO

The Gospel According to Todd

"What have you to do with me, Jesus, Son of the Most High God?"

As previously mentioned, I have strived throughout this work to confine my remarks concerning the meaning of Jesus' life and teachings to what I consider is a reasonable interpretation of who he really was based on the evidence of scholarship. *The Gospel According to Todd*, however, is entirely impressionistic on my part, and represents no attempt to accurately translate the scriptural material. What I think it does represent is an example of the process the original Gospel writers may have gone through when writing there own biased versions of Jesus' story. Like them, I've simply taken the material available to me (in this case, the three synoptic gospels, as well as *John*'s, so called, "Gnostic" gospel) and recompiled a gospel story reflecting more directly my own theological bias. Admittedly then, you cannot take my gospel as gospel, anymore than you can take any of my sources as historically true.

It is my hope that students of religion in particular may find this useful in studying how the authors of the four gospels overlaid their own agendas on the material they had available to them. In my case, I used *Mark* as both my template and primary source. It should be easy to ascertain, however, that *Matthew* is also an important source for many of the parables and teachings I've included in my version. Nor will it take an astute student to also find some scarce material borrowed from *Luke* and *John*. I particularly enjoyed replacing *John*'s interpolative story about "the woman caught in adultery," with my own completely fictional interpolation of a man caught in a sexual act with another man [12:67-78]. There are also many inconveniences I intentionally omitted, including many of the preposterous healing and miracle stories that would otherwise diminish my entirely human presentation of Jesus. I have personally found this experience so rewarding and enlightening that I would encourage theology professors to require their students to attempt such an undertaking themselves, and invite anyone interested in the historical Jesus to undergo this enriching process.

Finally, it should be understood, despite the acknowledgment that my gospel cannot be taken seriously as an accurate translation, I do consider it to be true! It may not be an accurate representation of the historical literature, or of history, for that matter, but it does reflect my impression of who Jesus really was based on my humble understanding of the scholarship I've researched. My narrative, like those of my canonized predecessors, is merely a literary method of stringing together material that may or may not be rightly attributed to the historical Jesus; but I am by no means reluctant to admit that I believe my version to be a more probable, realistic, meaningful, and profound version of the gospel than has ever been told. This is necessary, I believe, because, after centuries of separation from the unique cultural, social, and economic circumstances prevalent when the original Gospels were written, a literal translation makes it difficult, if not impossible, for a modern reader to understand how they must have impacted the thoughts and feelings of their original audience. Indeed, it is likely our own modern *sitz im leben* may sometimes cause us to react to ancient scripture in a way completely opposite of what its authors originally intended.

This is precisely what Clarence Jordan, a celebrated New Testament Greek professor at Southern Baptist Theological Seminary and civil rights activist in the 1960's, succeeded in accomplishing with his series of "Cotton Patch" versions of various New Testament works. These translations represent his attempt to impress upon his own racist southern culture the true spirit of Jesus' egalitarian teachings by presenting the material in the vernacular of the very culture he was trying to influence. The following example is Jordan's version of the *Parable of the Good Samaritan*:

> One day a teacher of an adult Bible class got up and tested him with this questions: "Doctor, what does one do to be saved?"
> Jesus replied, "What does the Bible say? How do you interpret it?"

The teacher answered, "Love the Lord your God with all your heart and with all your soul and with all your physical strength and with all your mind; and love your neighbor as yourself."

"That is correct," answered Jesus. "Make a habit of this and you'll be saved."

But the Sunday school teacher, trying to save face, asked, "But... er... but... just who *is* my neighbor?"

Then Jesus laid into him and said, "A man was going from Atlanta to Albany and some gangsters held him up. When they had robbed him of his wallet and brand-new suit, they beat him up and drove off in his car, leaving him unconscious on the shoulder of the highway.

"Now it just so happened that a white preacher was going down that same highway. When he saw the fellow, he stepped on the gas and went scooting by.

"Shortly afterwards a white Gospel song leader came down the road, and when he saw what had happened, he too stepped on the gas.

"Then a black man traveling that way came upon the fellow, and what he saw moved him to tears. He stopped and bound up his wounds as best he could, drew some water from his water-jug to wipe away the blood and then laid him on the back seat. He drove to Albany and took him to the hospital and said to the nurse, 'You all take good care of this white man I found on the highway. Here's the only two dollars I got, but you all keep account of what he owes, and if he can't pay it, I'll settle up with you when I make pay-day.'

"Now if you had been the man held up by the gangsters, which of these three—the white preacher, the white song leader, or the black man—would you consider to have been your neighbor?

The teacher of the adult Bible class said, "Why, of course, the nig—I mean, er... well, er... the one who treated me kindly."

211

Jesus said, "Well, then, *you* get going and start living like that!"[1]

The Decalogue, from the Hebrew Scriptures, may serve as another good example. From our contemporary perspective, it can only be interpreted as a rigid and puritanical set of laws that must be obeyed in all circumstances, even if doing so should prove harmful to others. Ask a modern Biblicist, for example, to name the first commandment and, inevitably, the response is, "have no other gods before me." This, however, is but the tail end of the entire commandment as it is recorded in both Exodus and Deuteronomy:

Exodus 20:2-3 & Deuteronomy 5:6-7
I am the Lord your God, who brought you out of the land of Egypt, out of the house of slavery; you shall have no other gods before me.

To detach the simple commandment from its context also detaches its meaning from the cultural situation in which it was written. The narrow command, "**you shall have no other gods before me**," says nothing about the quality of the god we *are* to put before us, and leaves us open to any interpretation from any charismatic religious leader or threatening mob that should impose its particular theology upon us. The context for this commandment and the others, however, is stated explicitly at the beginning and should not be ignored; "**I am the Lord your God, who brought you out of the land of Egypt, out of the house of slavery.**" Thus the Ten Commandments are not a set of puritanical bonds, but are quite the opposite; they are a set of principles based on a kind of liberation theology that could only have emerged from a culture that had been historically oppressed and enslaved.

As modernists it is difficult for us to grasp this liberation perspective from the text itself given the chasm of differences

---

[1] Jordan, Clarence, *The Cotton Patch Version of Luke and Acts*, A Koinonia Publication, Association Press, New York, NY, 1969, 1970, p. 46f.

between then and now. It is necessary, therefore, to examine and understand the historical, social, political, and cultural circumstances during which the text was written in order to more accurately understand the intentions of its author/s and what it may have meant to its original audience. It is equally important, as I am attempting to do in the forthcoming pages, to offer today's readers an impressionistic translation of scripture that may not be an accurate grammatical translation of the text, but may leave us with a more reliable impression of how the material impacted its original audience. The following, side-by-side, comparison of the Decalogue translated verbatim into English in the NRSV with my own impressionistic translation illustrates the point.

Deuteronomy 5:6-21	Impressionistic Translation
I I am the Lord your God, who brought you out of the land of Egypt, out of the house of slavery; you shall have no other gods before me.	I I'm the kind of God that sets people free. Don't put anything before your liberty.
II You shall not make for yourself an idol, whether in the form of anything that is in heaven above, or that is on the earth beneath, or that is in the water under the earth. You shall not bow down to them or worship them; for I the Lord your God am a jealous God, punishing children for the iniquity of parents, to the third and fourth generation of those who reject me, but showing steadfast love to the thousandth generation of those who love me and keep my commandments.	II Don't become so materialistic that you forget what's really important in life. Materialism will cause your children and grandchildren to suffer for years to come. Justice cannot coexist with the elitism you pass down from one generation to the next. Love is all you need. It will sustain the whole world for thousands of years.
III You shall not make wrongful use of the name of the Lord your God, for the Lord will not acquit anyone	III Don't arrogantly assume you can know the unknowable mind of God by attributing your behavior

who misuses his name.	to God's will.
IV Observe the Sabbath day and keep it holy, as the Lord your God commanded you. For six days you shall labor and do all your work. But the seventh day is a Sabbath to the Lord your God; you shall not do any work—you, or your son or your daughter, or your male or female slave, or your ox or your donkey, or any of your livestock, or the resident alien in your towns, so that your male and female slave may rest as well as you. Remember that you were a slave in the land of Egypt, and the Lord your God brought you out from there with a mighty hand and an outstretched arm; therefore the Lord your God commanded you to keep the Sabbath day.	**IV** Take a break at least once a week, and make sure everyone, including your livestock and farm animals, has the same opportunity. The Earth is a masterpiece! Respect and enjoy it! Do not discriminate between men and women, rich and poor, animals and humans, citizens and foreigners—nobody deserves to be oppressed. Remember the times in life you've been oppressed, and how good it felt when you were liberated from such oppression. That's why you should give everyone, every creature, and everything a break. Rest and recreation are sacred; keep it that way.
V Honor your father and your mother, as the Lord your God commanded you, so that your days may be long and that it may go well with you in the land that the Lord your God is giving you.	**V** Have a system in place to provide for your elders so that when you become elderly you too will be provided for.
VI You shall not murder.	**VI** Don't kill—period!
VII Neither shall you commit adultery.	**VII** Don't ever make sex one-sided.
VIII Neither shall you steal.	**VIII** Don't take more than you need at someone else's expense.

| IX
Neither shall you bear false witness against your neighbor. | IX
Don't lie about others to benefit yourself. |
| X
Neither shall you covet your neighbor's wife. Neither shall you desire your neighbor's house, or field, or male or female slave, or ox, or donkey, or anything that belongs to your neighbor. | X
Don't let your greed cause you to obsess about taking good things away from other people. |

Unfortunately, an impressionistic response can seldom, if ever, be derived by a literal translation of the material, which is why preachers and theologians exist to begin with—so they can give us their impressions about its actual meaning. Scripture requires interpretation, and that interpretation, right or wrong, comes from the interpreter's own hermeneutic (method of interpretation). Just as a literal translation cannot by itself get at the original meaning of a text, neither can a literal interpretation. It is necessary to delve into the historical, social, economic, political, literary, and cultural circumstances from which scripture springs. Although these circumstances cannot be factored into a literal translation, they can be expressed in a more impressionistic interpretation, which is something Jesus himself attempted when, after generations of oppressive literalism, he chose to summarize the Decalogue in his own impressionistic way, "'You shall love the Lord your God with all your heart, and with all your soul, and with all your mind.' This is the greatest and first commandment. And a second is like it: 'You shall love your neighbor as yourself.' On these two commandments hang all the law and the prophets."

THE GOSPEL ACCORDING TO

Todd

Belonging for the First Time

1 This is the story of Jesus, later called "Christ," and later still, "the Son of God." ²He began his life without a father, and was known only as the illegitimate son of a young maiden named Mary. ³After he was grown, he became a disciple of a popular, though peculiar, wilderness prophet named John, who emphasized the forgiveness of sins through repentance and baptism. ⁴Growing up fatherless in his society often made Jesus feel dirty and ashamed because he'd been taught that he was born in sin and was forever unclean in the eyes of God. ⁵He was often ridiculed, ostracized, and discriminated against because of it. ⁶But at the moment of his own baptism in the sacred Jordan River, Jesus felt he'd been washed completely clean. ⁷Even while still emerging from the cold water he suddenly understood that he too was worthy of God's love, and for the first time in his life he knew what it was like to belong. ⁸"Your are my child," God's All-Inclusive Spirit seemed to say, "I love you and am very pleased with you."

Inspired by Nature

9 Afterward, he disappeared into the wilderness for a long time to reflect upon what had happened and to consider what it might mean for his life. ¹⁰This allowed him to clear his mind, because there, among the wild animals, he felt God's presence most clearly.

Beginning his Ministry

11 This experience of worth and dignity gave Jesus the fortitude to leave John the Baptist and to begin proclaiming his own message of hope and healing to others who had been outcast and oppressed. ¹²He called it his "good news," saying, "God's love and goodness is available right here, right now. You can count on it!"

Finding Followers

13 The kindness and inclusion with which Jesus greeted others, especially those

who had been marginalized by society, inspired many to follow him, including a few poor fishermen he met on the shores of Galilee. ¹⁴"Come on," he said, "Let's go catch some people." ¹⁵Among them were some of his more well known followers, like Peter and Andrew, along with Zebedee's sons, James, and John. ¹⁶In a sense, these two brothers left their earthly father in order to know their Spiritual Father who never leaves anyone out.

A Cleansing in the Synagogue

17 One Sabbath, while in Capernaum, Jesus entered the synagogue and began teaching his astounding message about God's universal love. ¹⁸He seemed to teach with confidence, from his heart, instead of merely quoting the scriptures like the literalists do. ¹⁹Just then, a man the authorities had demonized burst in and started yelling, "What good is your good news to people like me Nazarene? ²⁰Aren't you just another holy man who wants us destroyed because you find us repulsive?" ²¹But Jesus countered, "Stop talking like that! You're a child of God.

There's nothing repulsive about you, so cut it out!" ²²The man was so moved that he began shaking and cried out in a loud voice. ²³Those who saw it were amazed and began asking, "What is this? ²⁴This teaching of universal love is like nothing we've ever heard before, yet he teaches it with such confidence! ²⁵He even welcomes those the authorities say are mad!" ²⁶Incidents like this caused Jesus' fame to spread throughout the region.

Jesus Becomes Known as a Healer

27 Another time, they happened to visit the home of Peter and Andrew at the same time Peter's mother-in-law had come down with a high fever. ²⁸Even though the sickness made her unclean and it was considered inappropriate for a man who wasn't her husband to touch her, Jesus tried to comfort her by holding her hand, and soon she began feeling better. ²⁹Before long she was on her feet again, and started serving her guest.

30 By nightfall everyone who was sick or demonized ended up at the door. ³¹It seemed the entire town had surrounded the house. ³²Jesus

comforted as many of the sick as he could, and welcomed those who had been demonized.

Jesus Seeks time Alone

33 Having worked all night, Jesus was worn out, and found it necessary to find a quiet place where he could pray while it was still dark. ³⁴When they discovered him missing, his followers began searching for him. ³⁵When they found him they said, "Everyone is looking for you." ³⁶But Jesus said, "It's time to leave and head to some other places. ³⁷I have to stay focused on my message of universal love. ³⁸That's what I'm really all about." ³⁹And so he went throughout Galilee proclaiming his good news in their synagogues, and embracing those who had been marginalized.

Jesus Cleanses a Leper

40 One time a man who had been excluded from the synagogue because he once had a skin condition and was considered ritually unclean came to Jesus kneeling and begging for help. ⁴¹"If you want to," he pleaded, "you can declare me clean." ⁴²Jesus was moved with compassion and responded, "Of course I want to. You are clean." ⁴³The man then stood up straight and proud, and Jesus instructed him to go immediately to the synagogue and let the priests know he would go through their cleansing rituals, but that he had every right to enter. ⁴⁴But he no longer seemed to care about entering the synagogue, and instead began telling everyone that Jesus had bypassed the Law of Moses, and declared him clean without it. ⁴⁵This got Jesus into a bit of trouble with the authorities, and forced him to stay out of the towns for a while, so that the people had to come out to him in the country.

Jesus Empowers a Helpless Man

2 When he finally felt it was safe enough to return to Capernaum, it didn't take long before word got out that he was home. ²Soon the house he was in filled up with people. ³There wasn't even enough standing room for everyone who wanted to hear him speak about his good news. ⁴Four men brought their paralyzed friend to see Jesus, but, because of the crowd, they

couldn't get near him. ⁵So they climbed onto the roof, dug through it, and lowered the man on his mat. ⁶When Jesus saw how determined they were, he said to the paralyzed man, "Your condition is no fault of your own. God is forgiving and does not curse us with such ailments." ⁷But some of the religious authorities, who had come to see what all the commotion was about, found Jesus' words extremely offensive. ⁸"How dare he! Who does he think he is? It's blasphemy! Only God can forgive sins." ⁹Jesus knew what they were thinking and said, "What's wrong with your hearts? ¹⁰It's no more difficult to say 'God loves you,' than to simply say, 'Get up, take up your mat, and walk.' ¹¹But just so you might understand that anyone on earth has the power to forgive," he turned to the powerless man and said, "Stand up, take your mat and go home." ¹²And the man stood up—proud and tall—then took his mat and walked out in front of everyone. ¹³So they were all astounded and praised God, saying, "This way of looking at things is completely new to us!"

Jesus Includes Outcasts

14 Another time, after Jesus had been teaching a crowd by the sea, he met a tax collector named Levi. ¹⁵Because he made his living exploiting his own people on behalf of Rome, other Jews treated him disdainfully. ¹⁶Even so, Jesus said, "I'll include you. Come with me." ¹⁷So Levi became a student.

18 Soon afterward, Jesus and his many followers enjoyed a good meal in Levi's home, while sitting and communing with several others who were considered social outcasts. ¹⁹When the religious authorities caught wind of it they complained to his students, "Why does he eat with people so unworthy of God's love?" ²⁰But when Jesus found out what they were saying he responded, "Just as doctors care for the sick, not the healthy, I'm here to share God's love with those who need it most."

A Question about Fasting

21 Once, during a time of fasting, when both John's students and the Pharisees were not eating, many curious people asked, "Why don't your disciples follow the examples

of John and the Pharisees?" [22]Jesus responded, "Why should we snub our noses at the gifts God has given us? [23]It's like a wedding banquet around here! We should enjoy and celebrate God's gifts while we have them. [24]We'll fast when the party is over, and not before.

25 "If you sew a new patch on an old coat, it will shrink and pull away, making the tear worse than ever. [26]And if you put new wine into old wine skins, the wine will burst and spill all over the place. [27]New wine needs new wine skins, and new teachings need new ways."

Eating When You're Hungry

28 One Sabbath when they were making their way through some grain fields, Jesus and his students began plucking a few heads of grain. [29]The religious authorities said, "Hey, you're breaking the law!" [30]Jesus responded, "Haven't you ever read about what David did when he and his companions were hungry? [31]He entered into the Temple, right in front of the High Priest, and ate bread dedicated to God, which isn't lawful for anyone but priests to eat, then he shared some with his companions." [32]Then he concluded, "The Sabbath was made to benefit people, not the other way around. [33]Us humans are superior to the Sabbath."

Doing the Right Thing

3 Another time he entered the synagogue and met a man who felt cursed because he had severe arthritis in his hands. [2]The authorities kept an eye on Jesus to see what he would do, hoping they might find cause to accuse him of wrongdoing. [3]"Come here," he said to the arthritic man. [4]Then he turned to the religious experts and asked, "Is it best to do good or to do harm on the Sabbath, to save a life or to kill?" [5]They all kept quiet. [6]It made him mad, and he grieved that their hearts had grown so hard, and he said to the man, "If you'll stretch yourself a little, you'll come to understand that you're condition is not a curse; that you're a child of God worthy of love and respect." [7]The man did stretch himself and went away feeling good. [8]Some of the religious authorities felt threatened by Jesus because of this and began conspiring against him.

Jesus' Popularity Grows

9 Jesus and his students went to the seaside and were soon followed by a huge crowd from Galilee. ¹⁰When others heard about all he was doing and saying, they also came in larger numbers from Judea, Jerusalem, Idumea, beyond the Jordan, and the region around Tyre and Sidon. ¹¹He asked his students to find a boat he could use to keep from being crushed by the multitudes; for he had made so many feel better, that those hoping for the same began pressing in around him. ¹²When those who had been demonized bowed before him and acknowledge that he was indeed, "a child of God," he asked them to get up and quit making such a big deal.

Jesus Shares his Authority

13 Jesus had many followers and he told all of them that they too had the power to validate those who had been marginalized and demonized by society. ¹⁴Among them were numerous men and women whose names have become lost to us.

Jesus is Demonized

15 While visiting his hometown the crowds became large again; so large they began overwhelming the local food supply. ¹⁶When his family heard about all the chaos he was causing, they decided they would try to get a handle on him, saying, "He's out of his mind!" ¹⁷And the religious rulers from Jerusalem, in an effort to discredit him said, "He has Beelzebub in him, the ruler of demons, which is why those with unclean spirits listen to him." ¹⁸So Jesus responded by comparing them to thieves, ¹⁹"How can an unclean spirit cast out an unclean spirit? ²⁰A community divided against itself cannot endure. ²¹And a home divided against itself cannot thrive. ²²And one who is inwardly split apart is doomed." ²³Jesus Laughed. ²⁴"What's really happening here is that you know you cannot get control of a strong man, or take charge of his belongings unless you can first restrain him; ²⁵then you can plunder his home and take what doesn't belong to you.

26 This you can be sure of; everything you consider blasphemy is no big deal, ²⁷but whoever works against

universal love, God's Holy Spirit, is the true blasphemer and will forever be in the wrong." [28]This he said because they had called his inclusive spirit, "divided" and "unclean."

Brothers and Sisters

29 Then his mother and brothers finally showed up outside and asked to see him. [30]Some in the crowd informed him, "Your mother and your brothers are outside asking for you." [31]And he replied, "Who are my mother and my brothers?" [32]Then, looking around at those with him, he said, "Here are my mother and my brothers! [33]Whoever extends my Spiritual Father's universal love to others is my mother and my brother and my sister." [34]He also used to say, "Don't subjugate yourself to any human patriarch, for your Spiritual Father is all you need."

Parable of Seeds

4 Jesus often spoke in parables. One of his favorites went something like this: [2]"Listen up! A man was scattering seed. [3]Some fell straightaway on the path and were eaten up by birds. [4]Those that fell on rocky ground sprouted quickly as a result, but soon burned up in the sun because they didn't have time to establish deep roots. [5]Others fell among weeds and were choked out before they got a good start. [6]But some fell upon good soil and ended up yielding fruit and multiplying themselves greatly. [7]You really should listen to what Mother Nature is saying here!"

A Hidden Lamp

8 Another of his parables goes like this: [9]"Is a lamp supposed to be placed under a basket, or under the bed, rather than on a lampstand? [10]Sooner or later everything comes to light. Pay attention to this." [11]He also used to say, "Pay attention to how things work; you get as much as you give, and sometimes even more. [12]But those who routinely take more than they need, eventually end up losing everything."

Parable of Growing

13 Sometimes he told this one: "A Godly community works like someone who simply throws seed on the ground, then goes about life,

rising and sleeping, trusting them to sprout and grow on their own. [14]For the earth produces this miracle all by itself, first the stalk, then the head, then the head full of grain. [15]Then, at the proper time, all one has to do is go out and harvest it."

Parable of Small Things

16 Here's another: "What can I say a Godly community is like? How about this? [17]It's like the tiniest of seeds, perhaps a mustard seed, that is sown in the ground and grows up to become so large that many different kind of birds come to make their homes in its shade."

Weeds among the Wheat

18 He also liked to tell this one: "A rich landowner once had perfectly good seed sown upon his field. [19]But when no one was watching, weeds also managed their way into the field, carried in by the wind and wild animals. [20]So when the good seeds began to sprout, there were many unwanted plants among them. [21]When the slaves working the field informed their master, he became paranoid and said, 'An enemy has done this!' [22]The

slaves asked, 'Should we remove them?' But he replied, 'No, I'm worried you might pull up some of my valuable wheat in the process. [23]Let them grow together until harvest, then we'll collect all the weeds first and have them destroyed, and can store the wheat safely in my barn so I don't suffer a loss.'"

Parable of a Woman Making Bread

24 Here's another good one; "A Godly community is like a woman kneading leavened bread, mixing various ingredients together until the whole thing rises as one."

The Use of Parables

5 Jesus seldom explained his parables to anyone, including his students, because they were simple enough for anyone to understand, [2]yet remained aloof enough to keep him out of trouble with the authorities.

Parable of the Absentee Landlord

3 Here's a good example: "A rich landlord planted a vineyard, put a fence around it, dug a pit for his wine press, and built a watchtower to keep

223

an eye on his investment. [4]But when he grew bored with it, he leased it out to tenants and moved far away to another country. [5]When it was time to harvest he sent his slaves to extort more than he deserved from his tenants. [6]But this made them so angry they beat one up, killed another, and stoned a third, then sent them away empty-handed. [7]The landlord was so out-of-touch that he sent even more slaves, who were treated no better than the first. [8]But the landlord was so far removed that he still couldn't understand the magnitude of the situation and decided to send his own son to collect his payment. [9]'Surely they'll respect my son,' he thought. [10]But when the angry tenants realized who it was, they said to themselves, 'This is the old bastard's boy who will one day come and claim this land for himself. [11]Let's kill him and keep what it rightfully ours!" [12]So, in a fit of rage, they captured and killed him."

13 When the authorities realized what he meant by all of this, that it was really about them, they wanted to arrest him, but were afraid of his popularity among the crowds.

[14]So they usually left him alone.

Parable of the Sadist

15 Here's another they didn't much care for either: [16]"A rich landowner goes out one morning to hire day laborers to work in his vineyard. [17]After agreeing on an amount to pay them for the day, he put them to work. [18]Then, about mid-morning, he saw other workers in the marketplace and sent them into his vineyard too. [19]'I promise to pay you whatever is right,' he said. [20]He ends up doing the same thing again at noon, at three o'clock, and at five. [21]'Why are you just standing around?' he mocked them. 'Because nobody has hired us,' they responded. [22]So he put them all to work in his vineyard. [23]But when evening came he instructed his manager to assemble all of them together, then intentionally instructed him to begin paying those who had worked the least, first. [24]When those who had been working all day saw what those who had worked but a few hours received, they, naturally, expected a little more. [25]But when it came their turn, they

were paid exactly the same as everyone else. [26]They began complaining among themselves, 'This isn't right! We worked all day in the scorching heat and have been paid the same as those who worked only an hour!' [27]But the landowner responded, "Friend, I'm not doing you any harm. [28]I paid you exactly what you agreed to this morning, so take it and get lost. [29]I can pay whatever I want to whomever I want. [30]Can't I do what I want with my own money? [31]Quit giving me dirty looks. [32]Are you jealous because I'm so generous?' [33]Someday the high and mighty will be last, and the last will become important."

Jesus Explains about the Wheat and Weeds

34 Some of his students once asked him to explain the meaning of his story about the wheat and weeds: [35]"The master of the field represents those who wrongfully claim what God has given to everyone for themselves alone. [36]He exploits those who work the field and deserve to benefit from it most by making them his slaves. [37]This goes against the natural order of things, just as it's unnatural to expect a field not to have weeds. [38]But he considers nature, the Wisdom of God, his enemy. [39]This is so because of his greed, which is why he is compelled to destroy everything in nature he feels he doesn't need, and keep everything else locked up securely in his private storehouse. [40]This separation is the real sin. [41]It's the sin against oneness, against the All-Inclusive Spirit who causes all things to grow together."

Parable of the Lenient Accountant

42 Sometimes he told this story: "A rich man once threatened to fire an accountant that he suspected was squandering his property. [43]The accountant was incapable of doing any other job and worried about how he would survive. [44]Then he devised a plan that would make others welcome him into their homes after his dismissal. [45]He called his master's debtors one by one, asking the first, 'How much do you owe my master?' [46]He answered, 'A hundred jugs of olive oil.' [47]The accountant responded, 'Let's make it fifty.' [48]Then he asked another who replied, "A

hundred containers of wheat.' ⁴⁹Again he replied, 'Make it eighty.' ⁵⁰And so, even this shrewd accountant understood the power of compassion. ⁵¹How much more compassionate are the children of light who make themselves eternally welcome wherever they go?"

A Chasm between the Rich and Poor

52 "Once there was a very wealthy rich man who dressed in the finest clothes and feasted on delicacies everyday. ⁵³At the same time a very poor man named Lazarus, who was starving and covered with sores, sat at the man's gate, hoping for a few scraps from his table, and for his dogs to come lick his wounds. ⁵⁴Eventually the poor man died and was carried into the arms of father Abraham. ⁵⁵The rich man also died and was buried. ⁵⁶In Hades, where he was in torment, he saw Lazarus at Abraham's side and called out for mercy, ⁵⁷'Please father Abraham, send Lazarus to give me but a taste of water, for I am miserable in these terrible flames.' ⁵⁸But Abraham responded, 'Child, don't you remember in life all the good things you received, yet did nothing to help poor Lazarus who was suffering each day right in front of you? ⁵⁹Besides, you have helped create an insurmountable chasm between the rich and poor so that nobody can cross over it.' ⁶⁰The rich man pleaded, 'Will you at least send a messenger to my family to warn them so that they won't end up like me?' ⁶¹But Abraham responded, 'I'm sorry, but they have already received everything they need to know about justice from the Law and the Prophets. ⁶²It's now up to them.'"

Some other Parables

63 He also used to say: "A Godly community is like a treasure buried in a field, which someone discovers and is willing to give everything for."

64 "It's like a merchant who discovers fine pearls and sells everything to obtain them."

65 "It's like a net thrown into the sea that catches fish of every kind."

The Lost Lamb

66 When he was criticized for associating with those

considered outcasts and sinners, he often used to say; [67]"God's love is like someone who loses one sheep out of a hundred, and leaves the ninety-nine alone in the wilderness to look for it. [68]When he finds it, he lays it gently across his shoulders and rejoices all the way home. [69]And when he returns home he expects his friends to rejoice with him because he has found his little lamb. [70]In the same way, God loves everyone, even those who aren't in the fold, and expects you to do the same."

The Lost Coin

[71]"In the same way, if a woman with ten silver coins loses but one, she lights a lamp, sweeps the floor, and searches the entire house until she finds it. [72]And when she does, she gathers her friends so they can celebrate together, saying, 'Rejoice with me for I have found the coin I lost.' [73]God's love doesn't leave anyone out, whether they're part of the group or not, and we ought to rejoice with those who embrace them, not question their integrity."

The Prodigal Son and His Self Righteous Brother

[74] To further illustrate this point he sometimes used tell this story: [75]"There was once a man with two sons. One day the youngest asked him for his share of his inheritance. [76]So he divided it between his two sons. [77]The younger son then gathered his belongings and set off to explore the world, squandering everything he had in the process, so that he ended up living in destitution. [78]A sever famine throughout the region made it impossible for him to find food. [79]In desperation, he hired himself out to a pig farmer. [80]He would have been satisfied just to eat some of the husks the pigs ate, but nobody gave him anything. [81]Finally he came to his senses and thought, "My father's hired hands have more than enough to eat, and here I am starving to death! [82]I'll go home and apologize to him and ask if he'll hire me as a servant, even if I'm no longer worthy to be considered his son.' [83]So he set off for home. [84]But while he was still a distance from the house, his father spotted him and rushed out to greet him on the road. [85]He ran up and threw his arms around him and began kissing him. [86]Then his son started his speech, 'Father, I have sinned

against you…' but his father was so excited he didn't hear anything he had to say. [87]Instead he ordered his servants to bring out clean clothes for him, including a robe, a fine ring, and sandals for his tired feet. [88]Then he had them prepare the best calf to celebrate his son's return, saying, 'I thought my son was lost, maybe even dead, but here he is, alive! He was lost and is found!' [89]And they began to celebrate.

90 "Now the elder son, who, according to the custom, deserved, not half his father's estate, but everything, returned from the field after a hard day's work and wondered what all the music and dancing was about. [91]'Your brother has come home,' a servant explained, 'and your father has slaughtered his best calf to celebrate his safe return.' [92]This made him angry and he refused to join the celebration. [93]So his father came out and asked him what was wrong. [94]'Listen!' he replied, 'I've worked my ass off for you my entire life and have never disobeyed you, yet you've never given me so much as an old goat to share with my friends! [95]And now this degenerate son of yours, who

has squandered your property on whores, returns home and you give him your best calf!' [96]Then his father said, 'My boy, don't you know that everything I have is already yours? [97]You don't have to ask for it, or wait for me to give it to you. [98]But we have to celebrate and rejoice because your brother whom we thought was dead is alive, he was lost and has been found.'"

The Secret to Happiness

6 Sometimes Jesus spoke more directly to those who came out to hear him, like when he taught them about happiness:

2 "To be happy you should stop clinging to possessions, for those who let go, possess everything.

3 "To be happy you should first learn to grieve, for those who do will eventually find peace.

4 "To be happy you should walk gently, for those who leave few footprints will preserve the earth.

5 "To be happy you should crave the just distribution of wealth, for those who do know that this is more than enough.

6 "To be happy you should forgive others, for those who do will be forgiven by others.

7 "To be happy you should keep things simple, for those who are simple comprehend much.

8 "To be happy you should be a peacemaker, for those who practice nonviolence act just like God.

9 "To be happy you should risk taking a stand when necessary, for those who do help create Heaven on Earth.

10 "To be happy you should expect lots of trouble from those who represent the status quo. [11]This is a good sign; it means your making a difference, and can consider yourself in good company.

Saying about Salt and Light

12 "You're the saltshakers of the earth; so why not shake things up? [13]An empty saltshaker is useless.

14 "You can light up the world if you're not afraid to shine. [15]A light on a hill really stands out, but a light tucked away is pointless. [16]Shine forth!

Do More than is Expected

17 "Don't confuse me for an anarchist. I'm just trying to get at the heart of the Law and the Prophets. [18]On the contrary, I don't want to get rid of them, I want to surpass their expectations. [19]I don't think much of those who break these laws, or teach others to do the same. [20]I think we should teach and follow them, just not in a rigid legalistic way that is without compassion.

Be More than Law Abiding

21 "The law says, "Do not kill,' and 'whoever kills will be prosecuted.' [22]What I'm saying is that if you hold hatred in your heart for your brothers and sisters you're in the wrong, and if you but curse at them you're violating God's law of universal love. [23]So don't talk about how much you love God if you're creating conflict among others. [24]Living in harmony with others is the only way to consecrate your faith. [25]Work things out with others and don't hold grudges. [26]If not, if you harbor ill will toward others, things may eventually get way out of hand and you might do something stupid and end up getting yourself in trouble. [27]Hatred has too high a price to pay!

28 "The law says, 'Don't commit adultery.' But the

point I'm trying to make is that your heart is in the wrong if you objectify anyone. [29]If looking at others you find yourself wanting to use them for your own selfish purposes, cut it out! [30]If your interactions with others aren't mutual and evenhanded, keep your hands to yourself! [31]Giving yourself over to such abuses is a hell of a thing!

32 "The law says, 'Divorce is permissible," but I'm telling you that you must continue treating your partner lovingly, even when you do separate; [33]and that means making sure your resources are divided equitably so that neither of you is left without.

34 "The law says, 'Don't perjure yourself, and keep your contracts,' but I'm suggesting you should strive to be the kind of person who is trustworthy without needing to swear or make formal agreements. [35]It's far too easy to make promises that can't be kept. Just say 'yes' or 'no' and mean it, so that you can be taken at your word.

36 "The law says, 'let the punishment fit the crime,' but I say do not return injustice for injustice. [37]But if someone strikes you on one side of the face, turn the other cheek.

[38]And if anyone lays claim to what's rightfully yours, be as generous as possible; give them the shirt of your back! [39]If someone pressures you to go farther than they should, go twice as far. [40]Be generous to those who ask for help, and kind to those who need a handout.

41 "The law says, 'Be just to your neighbor, but unjust to your enemy.' [42]But I'm saying you have to love your enemies too, and want good things for those who treat you wrongly. [43]That's how others will know that you are children of God, whose love is universal and showers blessing upon the best and worst among us. [44]Love that loves only those who love you in return is not God's universal love. [45]Even crooks do that. [46]Of course you're supposed to love the people in your immediate family, but even those who don't understand this divine love can go that far. [47]Your love must be universal, like the universal love of your Spiritual Father."

Practicing your Religion

7   "Don't be a show off! Keep your good deeds to yourself and let your reward come from within.

2 "And don't make a lot of noise blowing your own horn like a lot of narcissists do at every opportunity. [3]Rather, the practice of your faith should come so naturally and be so effortless that even you aren't aware you're doing it. [4]This is a much more rewarding way to live than being the center of attention all the time.

5 "And try not to pray a lot in front of others like those seeking publicity for themselves. [6]It's really not worth much. [7]Prayer should be a contemplative experience; peaceful, quiet, and alone.

8 "And when you do pray, keep it simple, like this:
Oh Great Spirit
Father,
Whose name
cannot be named,
[9]Dwell among us,
Move within us,
To create heaven
here on earth.
[10]Give us just enough
for today,
[11]And go easy on us,
And help us go easy
on others.
[12]Keep us out of harm's
way,
And away from
bad company.
13 "For why should you receive forgiveness if you're not willing to forgive others? [14]If you don't forgive others, you won't know forgiveness yourself.

15 "And keep in mind your spiritual practice should not make you look miserable like so many pious frauds who are really starving for something better. [16]Practice your religion privately, for your own edification, and don't brag about how hard you have it. [17]Inner satisfaction is reward enough."

Higher Mind

18 "Don't make your life about acquiring wealth. [19]Money comes and goes, things break, get lost, or are stolen, and in the end you can't take any of it with you. [20]There are things a lot more rewarding than wealth that don't break, and can't get lost or stolen. [21]Strive for these things.

22 "Looking at things in a just way sheds light on everything you do. [23]But injustice is darkness, and if that's how you see things, you're very dark indeed!

24 "You can't have it both ways; you will either love justice, or strive to amass great amounts of money. [25]There's absolutely no way to do what

231

is right and take more than your fair share.

26 "So don't obsess so much about the future, about how you'll get your food, drink, health, or clothing. ²⁷Life is so much more than these things. ²⁸Look to the birds; they don't plant seeds, or harvest, or store food in barns, yet God has provided plenty for them to eat. ²⁹Are you any less important than they are? ³⁰Besides, the future is out of your control, so there's no use stressing too much over it. ³¹And why make such a fuss about fashion? Look to the flowers in the field. ³²They grow without effort and are clothed more magnificently than the wealthiest of kings. ³³If God has provided a way to adorn field grass, which so quickly comes and goes, don't you think there's also enough for you? ³⁴So stop stressing about, 'What will we eat?' or 'What will we wear?' ³⁵God's creation provides these things and more with no effort on your part. ³⁶So focus your efforts on justice making and these other things will automatically come your way too.

37 "Don't obsess about a future that doesn't exist yet while ignoring current issues. ³⁸Now is enough for now.

Mercy and Kindness toward Others

8 "When you judge others you're really judging yourself, so the degree to which you condemn others is the degree to which you condemn yourself.

2 "How is it you can so easily project minor faults onto others, but do not recognize the overwhelming faults in yourself? ³Or how can you say to your neighbor, let me solve your problem, when you can't even solve your own? ⁴Worry about your own issues before you worry about what's wrong with everyone else!

5 "Don't waste your time and resources on things that aren't worth it, or on those who don't appreciate your efforts. ⁶Dogs should not be fed caviar, and pigs will quickly trample on your treasures then turn on you!

7 "Why ask when it is already yours? Why search when it is already found? Why knock when the door is already opened for you? ⁸Who would feed their children stones instead of bread, or poisonous snakes instead of fish? ⁹How much more then has your Spiritual Father, whose love is universal, provided everything you need and then some!

10 "Everything in the Law and the Prophets can be summed up in one sentence, 'Always do for others what you would have them do for you!'

Practice My Teachings

11 "These teachings are not easy to follow. There are simpler paths that many choose to follow toward their own destruction. [12]But the gateway to life is narrow and difficult, and, for this reason, few look for it.

13 "Lookout for misguided teachers who look harmless enough, but are really pursuing their own selfish desires. [14]You'll know who they are by looking at the results they produce. [15]Grapes don't come from thorn bushes and rotten trees don't bear tasty fruit. [16]Good trees, on the other hand, only produce good fruit. [17]Those that don't aren't good for anything but firewood. [18]That's how you'll know them, by their fruits.

19 "Not everyone who uses religious jargon is on the path that leads to our Spiritual Father. [20]In the end, many will say the right words, 'Lord this, and Lord that,' and will accomplish many things they claim are for the glory of God; [21]but God won't know what the hell they're talking about!

22 "It's not enough to just listen to these teachings, you have to act on them, in the same way a smart person builds a house on a solid foundation so it can withstand hurricanes. [23]On the other hand, those who listen to such teachings but are too dumb to do anything with them are just wasting time. [24]All their efforts will be as futile as building a house on shifting sands.

25 The crowds always responded well to these teachings, because they seemed fresh and new, unlike the same old stuff they often heard repeated by the literalists.

Jesus Validates a Demonized Man

9 Once, while on the other side of the Sea of Galilee, in the country of Jerash, Jesus and his companions were confronted by a man living in the tombs who had been demonized by the local authorities. [2]They had often tried to restrain him by binding him with chains and shackles; but his anger made him so strong that nothing could hold him for very long. ³He raged like a madman all day and night, and often hurt himself among the rocks. ⁴He seemed very deranged and dangerous, but when he saw Jesus coming he ran up and knelt before him, shouting at the top of his lungs, "What are you doing here holy man? Are you here to treat me as vile as everyone else?" ⁵But Jesus responded, "There's nothing about you I find vile." Then he asked, "Tell me what's got you so outraged?" ⁶He replied, "Where do I begin? My issues are legion!" ⁷He then begged Jesus to help him find a way to remain among his people even though they considered him unclean and crazy. ⁸It just so happened that a nearby herd of pigs got spooked by all the commotion and stampeded blindly off a cliff into the sea and drowned.

9 The herdsman ran into town to report the incident, and everyone ran out to see what was happening. ¹⁰When they arrived they couldn't believe their eyes. ¹¹There was the demonized man sitting with Jesus, dressed and in his right mind, having a friendly conversation. ¹²They were very superstitious and figured Jesus' kindness toward this outcast must have had something to do with what happened to the pigs, so they pleaded with him to leave the area. ¹³As Jesus got into the boat, the man asked if he could come with him, ¹⁴but Jesus responded, "You should go home to your friends and let them know that you are a child of God and deserve the same love and respect as anyone else." ¹⁵So he began telling everyone in the region about his encounter with Jesus, and they were all astounded.

Jesus Engages with a Girl and a Woman

16 Another time, when he was among a large crowd, he was approached by a respected religious leader named Jairus. ¹⁷He fell at Jesus' feet and began pleading with him, "Please, my little girl is dying. Won't you come and see if you can help her?" ¹⁸So Jesus went with him.

19 The eager crowd followed him and pressed in on him. ²⁰There happened to be a woman among them who was considered unclean because of her unusual menstrual cycles.

²¹She spent everything she had on doctors, but her condition only grew worse. ²²She had heard about Jesus' healing touch and snuck up behind him in the crowd just to feel his cloak. ²³"If I can just touch him, maybe some of his magic will rub off on me," she thought. ²⁴But Jesus noticed and turned around saying, "Who just touched me?" ²⁵But his followers responded, "Everyone is touching you. Look at the mob around us!" ²⁶But the woman, knowing she had done something considered inappropriate, especially in light of her condition, came forward and admitted what she had done. ²⁷But Jesus did not seem to mind. ²⁸He said, "You are one of God's precious daughters. There's nothing unclean about you. Understand this and you'll find peace and can feel good about yourself."

29 Before long, some others arrived from the leader's house saying, "It's too late. ³⁰Your daughter has died. Don't waste anymore of this man's time." ³¹But Jesus heard what they had to say and decided to continue anyway. ³²"Let's go see for ourselves," he told the man. ³³By the time they entered the house people had already begun the mourning process, weeping and wailing aloud. ³⁴But when Jesus examined the little girl he said, "What's all the commotion about, this child isn't dead, she's just sleeping." ³⁵They thought he was joking, but he had all of them leave the house. ³⁶Afterward he and the parents approached the little girl. ³⁷Jesus took her by the hand and tried arousing her, saying, "Talitha cum," meaning, "Little girl, little girl, wakeup." ³⁸Soon she began responding to his voice, stood, and had enough strength to begin walking around. ³⁹Her parents were overcome with joy. ⁴⁰Jesus asked them not to make a big deal about it and to give the child something good to eat.

Jesus' Female Followers

41 Jesus always had lots of female students, including many who had been demonized, like Mary, also called Magdalene. ⁴²Many prominent women also followed him, like Joanna, the wife of one of Herod's stewards, and Susanna, along with many others, who gave of their resources to help back his ministry. ⁴³Whenever the

legalists and literalists criticized him for this he simply responded, [44]"Truth be told, those you like to condemn, men and women desperate to make a living any way they can, understand much better than you what it means to live in God's community. [45]Those you consider the least are really the greatest."

Jesus Encourages a Woman to Stand

46 One Sabbath, when he was teaching some men in one of the synagogues, a woman had the audacity to intrude. [47]She'd been bent out of shape most of her life and was unable to stand up for herself. [48]When Jesus saw her courage he praised her, saying, "You are one liberated woman!" [49]This made her proud and she stood up straight for the first time in years, and began talking theology in this all male forum. [50]This did not please the leader of the synagogue, who became angry with Jesus for not chiding her. [51]"Why are you encouraging her to violate our laws, especially on the Sabbath of all days?" [52]Jesus responded, "How hypocritical! Don't you at least meet the needs of your animals on the Sabbath, your ox and donkey, making sure they have enough water? [53]Why shouldn't this lovely woman, this daughter of God who has been unjustly oppressed her entire life, not be free to express herself on such a holy day? In a Godly community there's no difference between men and women. They're all treated like angels." [54]Afterward, all who had opposed her participation felt ashamed, and everyone present welcomed her and thanked Jesus for setting them straight.

Visiting Two Sisters

55 Another time, as he and his students were passing through a certain village, a woman named Martha invited them to visit her home. [56]She had a sister named Mary who was fascinated with what Jesus had to say and sat at his feet listening the entire time. [57]Martha, who couldn't pay attention because she was so busy playing hostess, interrupted, [58]"Rabbi, don't you care that my sister has left me to do all this womanly work by myself? Command her to get up and help." [59]But Jesus responded, "Martha,

Martha, don't you see how your obsession with all these pointless tasks distracts you from what's really important? [60]Mary has every right to choose what's best for her! Who am I to try to take that away from her?"

Jesus Visits his Hometown

10 Once, while he was visiting his hometown, Jesus surprised many who had come to hear him speak in their synagogue. [2]They asked themselves, "Who does this guy think he is? What makes him think he's so smart and so important? [3]Isn't he that lowly artisan, the fatherless son of Mary, whose lowlife brothers and sisters live here among us?" [45]Jesus got the picture and responded, "It's hard to find respect among those who know you best, especially among your own neighbors, relatives, and immediate family." [46]He wasn't able to accomplish much during this visit because the folks there weren't very impressed by him.

Take Nothing and Go Only Where You're Welcome

[47] So he moved on to other towns where his teachings were better received. [48]He eventually even began sending his students out, telling them to make God's kingdom real by caring for the sick and diseased, and welcoming those who had been demonized and ostracized. [49]"Just as all you really need is provided freely, give freely and ask for nothing in return. [50]Don't take any money with you, or luggage, or extra clothes, or even shoes and a walking stick. [51]Go where you are welcome and bless those who welcome you into their homes. [52]If your blessing is not welcome, take it and move on. [53]Don't try to force your beliefs on those who disagree with you, just shake the dust from your feet and move on. [54]Truth be told, everyone has the right and responsibility to make their own choices."

Sharing Resources

[55] Because he and his followers were so popular and so busy all the time, Jesus used to say, [56]"You've got to find time to be alone in the wilderness now and again to rejuvenate yourselves." [57]Sometimes they were so busy

237

with the crowds that they didn't even have time to think about eating. [58]One time in particular, while he and his students were returning from a break in the countryside, they were met by a huge crowd that heard he was in the area. [59]He loved them very much and was eager to teach all of them. [60]But, as evening came, he realized the crowd had gone without eating anything for some time. [61]His students said, "Send them into the neighboring towns where they can buy something to eat." [61]But Jesus asked, "Why don't you give them something to eat?" [62]But they answered, "Are you kidding? How are we supposed to afford enough food for a crowd this size?" [63]Jesus responded, "Well go see exactly what we do have." [64]They returned with a few loaves and a few fish. [65]Jesus then asked the crowd to sit in groups on the grass. [66]He then gave thanks for the food and began sharing what little he and his students had with the enormous crowd. [67]Everyone was very touched by this selfless act of kindness and must have begun pitching in whatever they had too, [68]because somehow everyone had enough to eat, and at the end of the day there was more left over than they started with.

Uncleanness Comes from Within

11 Now the legalists and the literalists never cared much for Jesus and his students because they never washed their hands in the proper ritualistic way. [2](The legalists tried to convince all Jews that they should practice the same strict table rituals expected of the Temple Priests; [3]and they do not eat anything unless they wash it in just the right way, in addition to observing all the proper rituals for cleaning cups, and pots, and kettles.) [4]Sometimes they would ask him, "Why don't you or your students observe our traditions about eating? Why do you prefer to eat with unholy hands?" [5]Jesus would respond, "The prophet Isaiah guessed right about you hypocrites when he said,

[6]*'You honor me with*
your lips,
but your hearts
aren't in the right place;
[7]*Your worship is*
pointless if all you do is
focus on your own ridiculous
rules and teachings.'

238

⁸Why ignore God's command to love your neighbor in favor of human traditions?"

9 Sometimes he would say, "You reject this commandment in favor of your own rules. ¹⁰The Law of Moses says, 'Care for your elderly parents,' and 'whoever doesn't give them this respect will surely suffer themselves one day.' ¹¹But you spin things around to suggest that it's okay to ignore the needs of your senior citizens as long as you're making your offerings to God. ¹²This is just one example of how you manage to ignore God's commands in favor or your own traditions."

13 This is why he sometimes taught his followers, "Listen up! All of you need to understand that there is nothing external that can make God stop loving you! ¹⁴Sin is a state of mind that expresses itself in the way we treat others.

15 "If you don't understand this," he sometimes explained, "then what do you understand? ¹⁶Don't you see that food enters the stomach, not the heart, then passes out again? ¹⁷There's really nothing you can eat that makes you unworthy of God's love." ¹⁸Then he said, "The question is really what's coming out of you? ¹⁹For it is from within, from the human heart, that injustice comes: rape, theft, killing, sexual abuse, greed, hatred, deception, selfishness, jealousy, arrogance, and ignorance. ²⁰All these injustices come from within, and cause a person to do harm."

Giving Voice to a Quiet Man

21 Once, while in the region of the Decapolis, he encountered a man who seemed despondent and unable to communicate. ²²Jesus took him aside privately and put his fingers in his ears, and touched his tongue, then made a big sigh and said, "Ephphatha," meaning, "Open up." ²³And the man opened up to Jesus and began speaking out. ²⁴Jesus told the others not to make a big deal of it, but they couldn't help themselves. ²⁵They started telling everyone, "This guy is amazing. ²⁶He even gets those who have been silenced to start speaking again."

More than Enough for Everyone

12 Once when he was among a crowd of people that

hadn't eaten for days, Jesus said to his students, [2]"Such suffering makes me sick to my stomach. Isn't there anything we can do to help? [3]What good are my teachings if I have to send them away hungry? [4]Some of them are likely to die before they get very far." [5]His students replied, "What can we possibly do out here in the desert?" Jesus asked, "What do we have?" [6]After they had counted seven loaves, Jesus asked the people to sit down, gave thanks, then began dispersing what little resources he and his followers had of their own among the crowd. [7]Some in the crowd had a few small fish and began sharing those too. [8]Before it was over everyone had more than enough to eat with plenty of leftovers.

Give us a Miracle

9 The legalists were seldom impressed with all the good things Jesus did for people. [10]"A real man of God makes miracles," they said. This always made Jesus sad. [11]"Why do people demand miracles as proof of God's presence?" he asked, "I'm afraid they'll always be disappointed."

Beware the Spread of Legalism

12 Once he overheard his students complaining about not having any bread to eat. [13]Jesus said, "Beware the yeast of the legalists and the literalists." [14]They wondered what he meant. "Is it because we don't have bread?" [3]Jesus responded, "I'm not talking about bread. Don't you get it? Open your hearts! Open your eyes! Open your ears! [16]Don't you remember the way we managed to feed those hungry crowds and had plenty left over?"

Looking with Intention

17 Once, while in Bethsaida, Jesus encountered a man blind to others. [17]He took him by the hand and led him to a private place outside the village. [18]"What do you see?" he asked. [19]The man responded, "I can see people, but they look more like trees to me." [20]Then Jesus touched him compassionately, and the man took a deeper look and was able to see people clearly.

A Failed Healing

21 Another time, when he saw his students arguing with

some literalists in a large crowd, he approached to see what the commotion was about. ²²When the crowd saw him they were eager to hear what he had to say. ²³He asked, "What are you arguing about?" ²⁴A man from the crowd answered, "Rabbi, I brought you my son. He has been demonized because he is unable to speak; ²⁵and sometimes he falls to the ground, foams at the mouth, grinds his teeth, and his entire body becomes tense. I asked some of your students to heal him, but they can't seem to help." ²⁶It so happened that as soon as Jesus saw the boy he began convulsing and fell to the ground, foaming at the mouth, just as his father had described. ²⁷ "How long has he been like this?" Jesus asked. ²⁸He answered, "Since he was a small child. Sometimes he falls into the fire, or into the water. I'm afraid it's going to kill him someday. ²⁹If you can do anything at all, please have pity and help us." ³⁰Jesus said, "Isn't it up to you? Isn't your faith supposed to be enough? Isn't it just mind over matter?" ³¹The father of the boy cried, "My mind isn't strong enough. Please help me believe harder." ³²Suddenly the boy became completely rigid and looked like a corpse. ³³"He's dead," some of them said. ³⁴But Jesus took his hand and lifted him up until he was able to stand on his own again. ³⁵Later, when they were alone, his students asked him privately, "How come we couldn't heal him?" ³⁶He said to them, "Sometimes all we can do is pray."

A False Student

37 Once his student John said to him, "Rabbi, we witnessed a man falsely claiming to be one of your students giving those considered unclean a clean bill of health." ³⁸Jesus said, "Leave him alone. If he's claiming to do good things in my name, he won't speak ill of me. ³⁹Whoever isn't against us is for us."

Bless the Children

40 People liked bringing their children for him to bless; but his students discouraged them from doing so because he was always so busy. ⁴¹But Jesus rebuked them, "Let the little ones come to me, don't try to stop them, for God dwells most among the little children. ⁴²I'm telling you the

truth, if you can't enter God's community like a child, you can't enter it at all." ⁴³And he took them in his arms, hugged them, and blessed them. ⁴⁴Then he said, "If you make life difficult for one of these precious little ones, believe me, you'd be better off being thrown into the sea with a big rock tied around your neck!"

Give Everything Away

45 Once he was approached by an eager young man who asked, "Good Rabbi, what must I do to gain eternal life?" ⁴⁶Jesus answered him, "Why call me good? Isn't God the only good? You know God's law; don't kill, don't commit adultery, don't steal, don't lie, don't cheat, care for your elders." ⁴⁷The man responded, "Rabbi, I've kept all these laws since childhood, but am not fulfilled." ⁴⁸Jesus looked at him with love and said, "You lack only one thing; Go and sell everything you own and give the money to the poor, and your reward will be great. ⁴⁹Then come and be my student." ⁵⁰When he heard this he was shocked and went away very sad, for he was very wealthy.

51 Then Jesus said to his students, "How hard it is for those who have great wealth to dwell with others in a Godly way." ⁵²This confused some of them. ⁵³So Jesus explained, "Little ones, it's difficult enough to live in God's community because you must let go of so much. ⁵⁴For the wealthy especially, I suppose, it would be easier for a camel to squeeze through the eye of a needle."

Who is Greatest?

55 Once some of his students were arguing over who is the greatest in God's community. ⁵⁶Jesus told them, "In the dominator culture those who are the rulers are considered the greatest, even if they're cruel tyrants. ⁵⁶But it mustn't be this way among you; whoever wants to be the greatest among you must become your servant, ⁵⁷and whoever wishes to be first among you must be a slave to everyone. ⁵⁸To be human is to be humble and giving."

Jesus Washes his Students' Feet

59 Jesus loved his students and often treated them like they were his masters. ⁶⁰On

occasion he would wrap a towel around himself, pour water into a basin, and begin washing their feet. [61]Sometimes they would protest, "Rabbi, you are our superior, and you're going to wash our feet?" [62]But Jesus responded, "Unless you let me wash your feet, you'll never understand what I'm all about."

Love One Another

63 Sometimes he told them, "God is glorified when human beings are at their best. [64]And human beings are at their best whenever they obey the most important commandment, 'Love one another.' [65]Just as I have loved you, you must also love one another. [66]This is the only way anyone will know that you are truly my student, if you love one another."

The Stoning of a Man

67 Jesus often said, "Judge not, unless you want to be judged." [68]Once, after he and his students had entered Jerusalem for the Passover festival, they encountered an angry mob about to stone a man they had already nearly beaten to death. [69]Nearby was the corpse of another man who they had thrown from the temple. [70]"What have they done?" Jesus asked. [71]Someone answered, "We found them defiling the Temple; laying with one another in the same way a man lays with a woman." [72]When some literalists recognized who it was, they said to Jesus, "The Law says both of them should be put to death. What do you say holy man?" [73]Jesus looked at the frightened man, then at the dead man, then said to the crowd, [74]"Let the one among you who is perfect when it comes to strictly keeping all our laws cast the first stone." [75]The crowd stood silent for a few moments, then slowly dispersed.

76 Finding himself left alone with the frightened humiliated fellow, Jesus said, "It's okay now. [77]Those who would condemn you are gone, and I'm certainly nobody to judge you. [78]Leave here and be careful, for there are many who do not understand that God's love is universal."

Love as Predicate

13 This didn't make the literalists very happy. [2]They came to him and demanded that he account for himself.

³"Have you no regard at all for our laws?" they asked. ⁴But Jesus answered, "Love precedes all laws. ⁵Haven't you read the commandment, 'Hear, O Israel, the Lord our God, the Lord is one; ⁶you shall love the Lord your God with all your heart, and with all your soul, and with all your mind, and with all your strength,' ⁷and, 'You shall love your neighbor as yourself.' ⁸There are no other commandments greater than these." ⁹One of them was so moved that even he had to admit, "You may be right Rabbi. ¹⁰It is written as you said, 'God is one, there are no others,' ¹¹and 'to love God with all your heart, mind, and strength,' ¹²and 'to love your neighbor,'—this is worth a whole lot more than all our rituals." ¹³Jesus was pleased with his response, and said, "You have what it takes to make God's community right here right now." ¹⁴The literalists didn't bother him much after that.

Jesus Denounces Religiosity

15 He later told his students, "Watch out for literalists, who like to walk around in religious garb, and enjoy the recognition they get from others, ¹⁶and use their positions to get the best seats at public events and enjoy banquets in their honor! ¹⁷Yet they use their positions of religious honor to help exploit the poor. ¹⁸It's a hell of a thing!"

A Poor Woman Gives Everything

19 While at the Temple he sat down opposite the treasury and watched as everyone gave offerings. ²⁰The richest among them put in large amounts. ²¹But a poor widow showed up and contributed two small copper coins, worth about a penny. ²²Jesus said to his students, "This poor woman has given away everything she has, and it's cost her more than anyone else. ²³The wealthy can afford to give plenty, and still have plenty left over, but she gave everything she had, and now has nothing left to live on." ²⁴Jesus wept.

A Ruckus in the Temple

25 It was shortly afterward that Jesus entered the Temple and began driving out those who were using it as a marketplace—selling and buying merchandise. ²⁶He went so far as to turn over the chairs

and tables belonging to some of the merchants, and obstructed people from carrying merchandize through the Temple. [27]He shouted out, "God's house should be a house of prayer for all people; but you have turned it into a hideout for greedy crooks!" [28]When the legalists and literalists heard about the ruckus, they sent the authorities looking for him. [29]Jesus and his students had to flee the city.

A Question about Taxes

30 When the authorities began investigating what had happened, they learned of Jesus' subversive teachings about the Roman economy. [31]Some of the legalists and literalists had asked him, "Rabbi, we understand you to be a fair minded person who shows preference to no one, [32]and teaches the ways of God without partiality, unafraid to speak your mind. [33]So tell us, do you think it is right that Jews should pay tribute to the emperor? [34]Jesus knew what they were getting at so he responded, "I'm the wrong guy to ask. I have no money to give to anyone." [35]So they gave him a coin, but Jesus asked,

"Whose face and name is on this coin?" [36]They answered, "The emperor's, of course." [37]Then Jesus said, "Then it must belong to the emperor. You should give it to him, and give to God what belongs to God." [38]His quick thinking amazed just about everyone!

The Authorities Intend to Capture and Kill Jesus

14 The authorities were now on high alert, and were determined to capture Jesus before he could create any more problems, [2]especially by disrupting the commerce of those expecting to make big profits during the annual Passover festival. [3]But the authorities knew they would have to be covert so as not to start a riot among the masses.

Jesus has Passover with his Students

4 Jesus had been laying low with his students, but on the first day of the festival they asked him, "Where should we go to prepare our Passover meal?" [5]Jesus instructed them, "Return to the city and find someone who will welcome us. Say, 'Our Rabbi needs a room to have Passover with his

students." [6]They did as he said, found a place, and prepared the Passover meal. [7]Jesus waited until it was dark to join them. [8]Once there, they all enjoyed a simple meal of bread and wine together, but nobody suspected it would be their last supper together. [9]That was the same night he told them, "I'm with you whenever you practice my teachings among yourselves."

The Arrest of Jesus

10 Later that night Jesus and some of his student went to a quiet place called Gethsemane to pray. [11]He was worried about the authorities and warned his students to remain alert while he prayed. [12]When he was alone, he said, "Daddy, my Father, please keep me safe. I'm a little scared, but I'm going to continue standing against oppression no matter what." [13]When he returned, he found his students sleeping, for they did not realize the magnitude of the situation and the danger they were in. [14]Jesus woke them, but not before it was too late.

15 Suddenly they found themselves surrounded by men with swords and clubs sent by the authorities. [16]It turns out that one of Jesus' own students, a fellow named Judas who favored the militants, had devised a plan to point out Jesus with a secret sign. [17]He approached Jesus and said, "Rabbi!" then he kissed him. [18]Some of the men then seized hold of Jesus to arrest him. But one of his students grabbed a sword and took a swipe at them. [19]But Jesus said, "There's no need for any of this! I'm not a bandit. You don't need weapons; put away your swords. [20]Violence begets violence. Those who live by the sword die by the sword." [21]Having so easily captured Jesus, the one they came after, they were not interested in pursuing his students when they fled.

22 One of them in particular was wearing nothing but a linen cloth. [23]When they grabbed hold of him, it slipped off and he ran away naked.

Jesus before the Tribunal

24 After he had been delivered before the authorities he was asked to account for his reckless behavior at the Temple. [25]Some stood up and gave false testimony saying, "We heard him plotting to destroy the Temple." [26]But

Jesus remained silent and would not respond to their unfounded accusations. [27]"We've heard enough," they said, "He should be put to death as a terrorist!"

Jesus is Crucified

28 After beating him severely, he was handed over to the Romans who were quick to have him crucified along with numerous other Jews on Golgotha, the "hill of death." [29]After he was crucified, his executioners cast lots among themselves for his clothes. [30]As he hung there, many passed by and insulted him mercilessly, saying, "Who do you think you are, terrorist!"

The Death and Burial of Jesus

31 A few hours later Jesus cried out in agony and died. [32]A few of his female students were able to safely observe what had happened to him from a distance. [33]Although it was unusual, they gained permission with the help of a prominent man, to remove Jesus' body and give him a proper burial by wrapping him in linen and laying him to rest in a tomb hewn of rock.

The Missing Body

15 When the Sabbath was over, the women who had cared for his body went to the tomb to anoint him with spices. [2]It was just after sunrise when they arrived. [3]They had been discussing among themselves, "Who will we find to roll the heavy stone away from the entrance for us?" [4]But when they looked up they saw that the stone had already been rolled back. [5]They looked in and saw that the tomb was empty and wondered what it could possibly mean.

EPILOGUE

Would the Real Jesus Please Rise?

"Everyone then who hears these words of mine and acts on them will be like a wise man who built his house on rock."

I have a friend, an artist, who many years ago painted a portrait of Jesus, which is, simultaneously, his own self-portrait. For some, this artistic interpretation might seem arrogant at best, and blasphemous at its worst. But I personally find it to be no different than how any of us treat Jesus. He always ends up looking and sounding like us. Hollywood, for instance, has a notorious history of casting blue-eyed, blond-headed actors like Max von Sydow, Jeffrey Hunter, and Ted Neeley in the role of Jesus. This might be expected, given what little information we have about Jesus' life and teachings is unreliable at best. Even theologians, like artists and actors, end up portraying him in their own images. As Albert Schweitzer once noted, "There is no historical task which reveals [one's] true self as the writing of a Life of Jesus."[1]

I have found this to be so in my own study of various theologians, including some of those mentioned in this book. John Dominic Crossan, for example, who was raised in poverty at a time of fearful revolution in Ireland, portrays Jesus as a nonviolent revolutionary raised in poverty. Professor Hyam Maccoby, a contemporary Jewish scholar portrays him as an ancient Jewish scholar. Walter Wink, a Peace Fellow at the U.S. Institute of Peace, writes of a peaceful Jesus who came to help us break our spiral of violence. In the end, I have proven no different in my own treatment of Jesus. I could say all the things I've claimed about Jesus in these pages about myself. I am a man who is political. I'm a situation ethicist in support of reproductive freedom, and against the death penalty. I also oppose war and support nonviolence. I value civil disobedience as a tool of social

---

[1] Herzog, William R., *Jesus, Justice and the Reign of God*, ibid., p. 5f.

transformation, and I find modern Capitalism to be extremely unjust. I'm an environmentalist and a vegetarian, a feminist and a gay rights activist, support universal healthcare, and even worked many years of my life as a TV reporter. The resemblance between Jesus and me is remarkable!

But the Jesus I've portrayed herein represents only my ideal self, not someone I'm always able to imitate. Surely this is what Schweitzer was getting at by suggesting our images of Jesus end up reflecting our "true self." Carl Jung said, "In the final analysis, we count for something only because of the essential we embody, and if we do not embody that, life is wasted,"[2] implying that it's possible we don't always embody our essence, express our truth, or put our faith into action. Each of us has a true Self, the person we are at the core of our being who thrives on authentic expression, and a false self, or ego, who learns to think, feel, desire, and do what is expected. Jung called this pseudo-self the *persona*, referring to the masks worn by ancient Greek actors. "In order to move into the world," he said, "we have need of a certain attitude or persona, the mask we turn toward the world."[3] There's nothing wrong or misleading about this. Each of us must learn to compromise with others in order to get along. In developmental psychology this is considered midlevel morality, the *conventional* level. Children achieve it when they learn to share, take turns, and play by the rules. Adults functioning at this level are typically law abiding and affirm traditional mores and conventional wisdom. This is normal and necessary, to a degree. The problem arises only when we mistake our true Self for the shells we wear. As Jung put it, "In doing all their small tasks, most people believe that they are their masks, and thus they become neurotic."[4] The only way around this is to remain conscious that we are only playing a role, that there is more to us than meets the eye, that the ego does not represent the whole Self, and that the expectations of others do

---

[2] Jung, C.G., *Memories, Dreams, Reflections*, ed. Aniela Jaffé, trans. Richard and Clara Winston, Vintage Books, New York, NY, 1989, p. 325.

[3] Jung, C.G., *Dream Analysis*, Bollingen Series XCIX, Princeton University Press, Princeton, NJ, 1984, p. 51.

[4] Ibid., p. 74.

not reflect our innermost calling. "If I should believe I was exactly what I am doing, it would be a terrible mistake, I would not fit that fellow." Jung said, "As soon as I say that I am only playing a role for the time being to please you, I am all right."[5]

Perhaps it is necessary then, that Jesus, like all great souls, Buddha, Mohammed, Krishna, functions as a mirror upon which to project our highest aspirations, reflecting back all the goodness, courage, compassion, and truth that is inside each of us. We can't always live up to these ideals because we get lost along the way, forgetting the divine life-sustaining presence coursing through our veins, the *pneuma* (Divine breath) that animates us (*anima*/soul) with each inhalation. "We are not human beings having a spiritual experience," Teilhard de Chardin once said, "We are spiritual beings having a human experience." Yet we come into this world forgetting our divine truth, essence, and origin. There's an old Jewish legend, for instance, that suggests the *philtrum*, that indention between our nose and upper lip, is placed there just before we're born by an angel who presses his finger over our mouths and whispers, "shush," reminding us not to tell the secret of our true identity. The Huichol Indians of northern Mexico have a similar myth suggesting we are all gods before we are born, but once we pass through a tunnel of light into this world (the birth canal) we forget who we are and where we're from. This idea that there's more to us than our individual self (*jivatman* in Hinduism), that there's also a larger Self (*Atman*), is the concept behind *reincarnation* in eastern philosophy. Even Christianity, here in the west, tells us we must be born again, that another Self must emerge. This Self, this truth, sometimes dormant, but always present in the heart of each of us, longs for an empty mirror upon which to see itself. And it is this eternal longing for our own authentic lives that moves us toward the likes of Jesus, to see, in him, our own divine face peering out from behind our masks.

There is a beautiful story in the Gospels in which Jesus is accused of blasphemy for telling a paralytic man that his sins have been forgiven. "Which is easier, to say to the paralytic, 'Your sins are forgiven,'" he responds, "Or to say, 'Stand up and take

---

[5] Ibid.

your mat and walk.'"[6] To prove that human beings have the power to forgive sins, this self affirmed "Son of Man," turns to the paralytic and says, "stand up, take up your mat and go to your home."[7] Our weaknesses often paralyze us in life, so much so that we sometimes cannot bring ourselves to genuine self-reflection, to face our failure, to take an honest look at ourselves in the mirror. So, the true Self inside us, like the man in this story, becomes paralyzed and ineffectual in the world. Jesus understood forgiveness is necessary to cure such paralysis, that we must learn to look beyond our failures, our wounds, our weaknesses, to find the strength and the courage to "Stand up, pick up our mats, and walk." Each of us has the power to stand up and be the true person we are meant to be, to take up the beds we have made for ourselves to lie in, and to become truly present in this world. But first we must let go of the false self that keeps us crippled and immobile by remembering we are so much more than our failures and weaknesses.

Unfortunately, finding such strength is difficult in a culture that counts on everyone towing the line, adhering to norms, respecting conventions, and meeting expectations. Speaking our truth, claiming the power to grow beyond our failures, and suggesting the Divine looks just like us, is considered blasphemy by those who would discourage us from removing the masks they have had a part in shaping. They have substituted the malleable image of historic Jesus with the unyielding Christ of faith. And because this Christ is so high above us, so out of reach and out of touch, there is nothing we can ever do to be like him, especially during our lives here on Earth. We will always remain paralyzed failures compared to this uplifted Christ, incapable, and, ultimately, unexpected to make any real attempt to manifest God's kingdom among us.

Recently, after I'd participated in an environmental action that got a small amount of media attention, I received an angry phone call from a Christian who said, "I wish you would put the same effort and the same energy to leading unborn people to Jesus Christ our Lord and Savior. It's going to effect them for eternity,

---

[6] Mark 2:9.
[7] Mark 2:11.

and what your doing is not going to effect eternity at all." You'll notice this man's faith, without apology on his part, is no earthly good whatsoever! His only concern is for people who aren't born, and for those who are dead. Nothing between birth and death counts for him. This is what results from worshipping Christ, rather than following Jesus. As a man, Jesus' teachings emphasize life in this world, not the unborn and the dead. "Let the dead bury the dead," he said. Yet this angry caller left me a message shaming me for trying to make this world a better place.

So, it is also without apology that I admit my Jesus looks a lot like me, just, as I suspect, your Jesus looks a lot like you. This is so because, on the one hand, the historical Jesus is lost to us forever, buried beneath 2000 years of forgotten time, bias, and unreliable reports. We simply cannot know who Jesus, the man, was. But, on the other hand, we can recognize his soul, for he didn't teach us anything that doesn't resonate as true within our own hearts. As Thomas Jefferson put it, "The doctrines which flowed from the lips of Jesus himself are within the comprehension of a child." This is especially true for children because they are less corrupted by the social conventions and expectations of others than are adults, and closer still to the "heart of flesh" God puts in each of us to remind us how we ought to treat each other. **"I will put my Spirit in you and move you to follow my decrees and be careful to keep my laws."**[8] As we have seen, Jesus' teachings are based on the Golden Rule, the pleasure principle, that the abundance we want for ourselves we must seek also for others—food, clothing, shelter, health, security, meaning, compassion, forgiveness, acceptance, joy, life, love! This simple truth dwells naturally inside each of us and ought to be the basis of all our actions. Yet, almost inexplicably, we have circumvented this deepest and most basic awareness with the meaningless jargon of Christianity, with jots and tittles that don't amount to anything!

It is my hope that *A Gospel for Liberals* might challenge us to set aside such arrogant commentary and seek, instead, to create the kind of abundant life Jesus taught is possible. Though reports about him are sketchy and unreliable at best, we can turn to

---

[8] Ezekiel 37:27.

the natural world, to the Living Word, that inspired him to help guide our way, and to our own natural inclinations toward justice and compassion to guide our relations with others. It is no longer enough to claim the name of Jesus and act like brutes. It is no longer possible to claim the moral high ground, yet support inequality, discrimination, poverty, violence, destruction, and death. Jesus has been wrested from the hands of Christ at long last! If you have been a Christian who long ago learned to stop your own beating heart in the name of hypocrisy and hate, "Your sins are forgiven." If, like me, you once abandoned your right to reflect on Jesus in order to free yourself from so much Christian baggage, I say, "Stand, pick up your mat, and walk."

APPENDIX

Scriptures Cited by Chapter

CHAPTER I
Jesus Was a Man

Mark 1:10-11
And just as he was coming up out of the water, he saw the heavens torn apart and the Spirit descending like a dove on him. And a voice came from heaven, "You are my Son, the Beloved; with you I am well pleased."

Matthew 1:1
An account of the genealogy of Jesus the Messiah, the son of David, the son of Abraham.

Luke 1:30-33
Do not be afraid Mary for you have found favor with God. And now you will conceive in your womb and bear a son, and you will name him Jesus. He will be great, and will be called the Son of the Most High, and the Lord God will give him the throne of his ancestor David.

John 1:1-2, 14
In the beginning was the Word, and the Word was with God, and the Word was God. He was in the beginning with God... And the Word became flesh and dwelt among us..."

Philippians 2:8-9
...and he became obedient to the point of death—even death on a cross. Therefore God also highly exalted him and gave him the name that is above every name.

Mark 16:1
When the Sabbath was over, Mary Magdalene, Mary the mother of James, and Salome brought spices, so that they might go and anoint him.

Mark 16:8
So they went out and fled from the tombs, for terror and amazement had seized them; and they said nothing to anyone, for they were afraid."

Matthew 28:20
And remember, I am with you always, to the end of the age.

Luke 24:51
While he was blessing them, he withdrew from them and was carried up to heaven.

Deuteronomy 5:9
I the Lord your God am a jealous God, punishing children for the iniquity of parents, to the third and fourth generation of those who reject me.

Ezekiel 37:12
I will open your graves, and cause you to come up.

Matthew 8:26
Why are you afraid, you of little faith?

Matthew 8:27
What sort of man is this, that even the winds and seas obey him?

Matthew 16:23
Get behind me, Satan!

Matthew 17:20
He said to them, "Because of your little faith. For truly I tell you, if you have the faith the size of a mustard seed, you will say to this mountain, 'Move from here to there,' and it will move; and nothing will be impossible for you."

I Corinthians 2:2
I decided to know nothing among you except Christ and him crucified.

Acts 9:26
...they were all afraid of him,

I Corinthians 10:23
Everything is permissible.

Acts 10:45
The circumcised believers who had come with Peter were astonished that the gift of the Holy Spirit had been poured out even on the Gentiles.

Galatians 2:11
When Peter came to Antioch, I opposed him to his face, because he was in the wrong.

Romans 3:28
We maintain that a man is justified by faith apart from observing the law.

James 2:24
A person is justified by what he does and not by faith alone.

CHAPTER II
Jesus Was Political

Genesis 3:17
Cursed is the ground because of you; in toil you shall eat of it all the days of your life.

Deuteronomy 23:3
"No bastard shall enter the assembly of YHVH, even to the tenth generation.

Exodus 20:2-3
I am the Lord your God, who brought you out of the land of

**Egypt, out of the house of slavery. Have no other gods before
me.**

Matthew 20:1-16
For the kingdom of heaven is like a landowner who went out
early in the morning to hire laborers for his vineyard. Now
when he had agreed with the laborers for a denarius a day, he
sent them into his vineyard. And he went out about the third
hour and saw others standing idle in the marketplace, and said
to them, "You also go into the vineyard, and whatever is right
I will give you." And they went. Again he went out about the
sixth and the ninth hour, and did likewise. And about the
eleventh hour he went out and found others standing idle, and
said to them, "Why have you been standing here idle all day?"
They said to him, "Because no one hired us." He said to them,
"You also go into the vineyard and whatever is right you will
receive." So when evening had come, the owner of the
vineyard said to his steward, "Call the laborers and give them
their wages, beginning with the last to the first." And when
those came who were hired about the eleventh hour, they each
received a denarius. But when the first came, they supposed
that they would receive more; and they likewise received each
a denarius. And when they had received it, they murmured
against the landowner, saying, "These last men have worked
only one hour, and you made them equal to us who have borne
the burden and the heat of the day." But he answered one of
them, "Friend, I am doing you no wrong. Did you not agree
with me for a denarius? Take what is yours and go your way.
I wish to give to this last man the same as to you. It is not
lawful for me to do what I wish with my own things? Or is
your eye evil because I am good?" So the last will be first, and
the first will be last. For many are called, but few are chosen.

Exodus 20:17
**You shall not covet your neighbor's house; you shall not covet
your neighbor's wife or his male servant or his female servant
or his ox or his donkey or anything that belongs to your
neighbor.**

Isaiah 3:14-15
"It is you who have devoured the vineyard; the plunder of the poor is in your houses. What do you mean by crushing my people and grinding the face of the poor?" Declares the Lord God of hosts.

Micah 2:2
They covet fields, and seize them; houses, and take them away, they oppress householder and house, people and their inheritance.

Micah 3:2-3
Hear now you *heads* of Jacob and *rulers* of the house of Israel, is it not for you to know justice? You who hate the good and love the evil, who tear the skin off my people, and the flesh off their bones; who eat the flesh of my people, flay their skin off them, break their bones in pieces, and chop them up like meat in a kettle, like flesh in a caldron.

Amos 5:12
I know how many are your transgressions, and how great are your sins—you who afflict the righteous, who take a bribe, and push aside the needy at the gate.

Matthew 21:33-39
There once was a landowner who planted a vineyard, put a fence around it, dug a wine press, and built a watchtower. Then he leased it to tenants and went to another country. When the harvest time had come, he sent his slaves to the tenants to collect his produce. But the tenants seized his slaves and beat one, killed another, and stoned another. Again he sent other slaves, more than the first; and they treated them in the same way. Finally he sent his son to them, saying, "They will respect my son." But when the tenants saw the son, they said to themselves, "This is the heir; come, let us kill him and get his inheritance." So they seized him, threw him out of the vineyard, and killed him.

CHAPTER III
Jesus Was a Situation Ethicist

Luke 6:9
Is it lawful to do good or harm on the Sabbath, to save life or to destroy it?

Luke 15:4
Which of you, having a hundred sheep and losing one of them, does not leave the ninety-nine in the wilderness and go after the one that is lost until he finds it?

Matthew 22:39
Love your neighbor as yourself.

Matthew 22:37-40
'You shall love the Lord your God with all your heart, and with all your soul, and with all your mind.' This is the greatest and first commandment. And the second is like it: 'You shall love your neighbor as yourself.' On these two commandments hang all the law and the prophets.

Mark 2:27
The Sabbath was made for humankind, and not humankind for the Sabbath.

Matthew 5:17
Do not think that I have come to abolish the law or the prophets. I have come not to abolish but to fulfill.

Mark 2:28
So the Son of Man is lord even of the Sabbath.

I Corinthians 10:23-24
"All things are lawful," but not all things are beneficial. "All things are lawful," but not all things build up. Do not seek your own advantage, but that of the other.

Amos 5:23-24

Take away from me the noise of your songs; I will not listen to the melody of your harps. But let justice roll down like waters, and righteousness like an ever-flowing stream.

Micah 6:6-7
With what shall I come before the Lord, and bow myself before God on high? Shall I come before him with burnt offerings, with calves a year old? ...with thousands of rams... thousands of rivers of oil? Shall I give my firstborn for my transgression, the fruit of my body for the sin of my soul?

Micah 6:8
He has told you, O mortal, what is good; and what does the Lord require of you but to do justice, and to love kindness, and to walk humbly with your God?

Mark 7:6-7
Isaiah prophesied rightly about you hypocrites, as it is written, "This people honors me with their lips, but their hearts are far from me; in vain they worship me, teaching human precepts as doctrines."

Ezekiel 11:19-20
I will give them one heart and put a new spirit within them; I will remove the heart of stone from their flesh and give them a heart of flesh, so that they may follow my statutes and keep my ordinances and obey them. Then they shall be my people, and I will be their God.

Ezekiel 36:26
A new heart I will give you, and a new spirit I will put within you; and I will remove from your body the heart of stone and give you a heart of flesh. I will put my spirit within you, and make you follow my statutes and be careful to observe my ordinances.

Matthew 5:20

For I tell you, unless your righteousness exceeds that of the scribes and Pharisees, you will never enter the kingdom of heaven.

Matthew 5:46
For if you love those who love you, what reward do you have?

Wisdom of Solomon 7:25-26
Therefore nothing defiled gains entrance into her. For she is the reflection of the working of God, and an image of his goodness.

Luke 6:31
Do unto others as you would have them do unto you.

Psalms 37:31
The law of their God is in their hearts.

CHAPTER IV
Jesus Was Pro-Choice

Matthew 7:2-3
Do not judge, so that you may not be judged... Why do you see the speck in your neighbor's eye, but do not notice the log in your own eye?

Mark 2:27
The Sabbath was made for people, not people for the Sabbath.

John 10:10
I came that they may have life, and have it abundantly.

Matthew 16:25
Whoever wants to save his life will lose it, but whoever loses his life for me will find it.

John 15:13
There is no greater love than to lay down your life for your friends.

Matthew 26:39
My Father, if it is possible, let this cup pass before me.

I Corinthians 13:11
When I was a child, I talked like a child, I thought like a child, I reasoned like a child. When I became a man, I put childish ways behind me.

CHAPTER V
Jesus Was Pro-Life

Galatians 2:15
We know that a person is not justified by the works of the law but through faith in Jesus Christ.

James 2:26
Faith without works is dead.

John 3:16
Whosoever *believeth* **in him shall not perish but have everlasting life.**

Matthew 5:38-45
You have heard that it was said, 'an eye for an eye and a tooth for a tooth,' But I say to you, do not resist an evildoer. But if anyone strikes you on the right cheek, turn the other also: and if anyone wants to sue you and take your coat, give your cloak as well; and if anyone forces you to go one mile, go also the second mile. Give to everyone who begs from you, and do not refuse anyone who wants to borrow from you. You have heard it said, 'You shall love your neighbor and hate your enemy.' But I say to you, Love your enemies and pray for those who persecute you, so that you may be children of your Father in heaven; for he makes his sun to rise on the evil and on the good, and sends rain on the righteous and on the unrighteous.

Matthew 6:14
For if you forgive others their trespasses, your heavenly Father will also forgive you.

Matthew 18:21
"Lord, if another member of the church sins against me, how often should I forgive? As many as seven times?" Jesus said to him, "Not seven times, but, I tell you, seventy-seven times."

John 8:7
Let those who have not erred, cast the first stone.

CHAPTER VI
Jesus Was a Draft Dodger

Matthew 5:39
But if anyone strikes you on the right cheek, turn the other also.

Matthew 5:44
Love your enemies and pray for those who persecute you.

Matthew 25:52
Put away your sword back into its place. For all who take the sword will perish by the sword.

Mark 3:5
He looked around at them with anger.

Matthew 10:34
I have not come to bring peace but a sword.

Matthew 10:36
...and one's foes will be members of one's own household.

Matthew 7:13
For the gate is narrow and the road is hard that leads to life, and there are few who find it.

CHAPTER VII
Jesus Was Civilly Disobedient

Matthew 22:21
Render unto Caesar what is Caesar's.

Romans 13:1
Let every person be subject to the governing authorities; for there is no authority except from God, and those authorities that exist have been instituted by God.

I Timothy 2:1-2
I urge that supplications, prayers, intercessions, and thanksgivings be made for everyone, for kings and all who are in high positions, so that we may lead a quiet and peaceable life in all godliness and dignity.

Mark 2:27
The Sabbath was made for humankind, not humankind for the Sabbath.

Mark 3:4
"Is it lawful to do good or to do harm on the Sabbath," **he responded,** "to save a life or to kill?"

Matthew 12:13
Stretch out your hand.

Matthew 5:17
Do not think that I have come to abolish the law or the prophets; I have come not to abolish but to fulfill.

Matthew 5:21-22
You have heard that it was said to those of ancient times, "You shall not murder"; and "whoever murders shall be liable to judgment." But I say to you that if you are angry with a brother or sister, you will be liable to judgment; and if you insult a brother or sister, you will be liable to the council; and if you say, "You fool," you will be liable to the hell of fire.

I John 4:16
God is love.

Mark 3:5
He was grieved at their hardness of heart.

Exodus 9:35
The heart of the Pharaoh was hardened, and he would not let the Israelites go.

Ezekiel 36:26
I will remove from you your heart of stone and give you a heart of flesh.

Matthew 7:12
In everything do to others as you would have them do to you; for this is the law and the prophets.

CHAPTER VIII
Jesus Was a Member of the Liberal Media

Mark 1:15
Now after John was arrested, Jesus came to Galilee, proclaiming the good news of God, and saying "The time has come, the kingdom of God is at hand."

Matthew 10:7
As you go, proclaim the good news, "The kingdom of heaven has come near."

Matthew 13:34
Jesus told the crowd all these things in parables; without a parable he told them nothing.

Matthew 9:32-33
A demoniac was brought to him. And, when the demon had been cast out, the one who had been mute spoke.

Luke 8:27-31
For a long time he had worn no clothes, and he did not live in a house but in the tombs. When he saw Jesus, he fell down before him and shouted at the top of his voice, "What have you to do with me, Jesus, Son of the Most High God? I beg you, do not torment me"—for Jesus had commanded the unclean spirit to come out of the man. (For many times it had seized him; he was kept under guard and bound with chains and shackles, but he would break the bonds and be driven by the demon into the wilds.) Jesus then asked him, "What is your name?" He said, "Legion"; for many demons had entered him. They begged him not to order them to go back into the abyss.

Matthew 9:24
It is only by Beelzebub, the prince of demons, that this fellow drives out demons.

Mark 8:24-25
"Can you see anything?" And the man looked up and said, "I can see people, but they look like trees walking." Then Jesus laid his hands on his eyes again; and he looked intently and his sight was restored, and he saw everything clearly.

Mark 7:32-35
They brought to him one who was deaf and spoke with difficulty, and they implored him to lay his hand on him. Jesus took him aside from the crowd, by himself, and put his fingers into his ears, and after spitting, he touched his tongue with the saliva; and looking up to heaven with a deep sigh, he said to him, "Ephphatha!" that is, "Be opened!" And his ears were opened, and the impediment of his tongue was removed, and he began speaking plainly.

Mark 7:37
He makes even the deaf to hear and the mute to speak.

CHAPTER IX
Jesus Was a Universal Healthcare Provider

Matthew 15:30
Great crowds came to him, bringing with them the lame, the maimed, the blind, the mute and many others. They put them at this feet and he cured them.

Mark 1:35
In the morning, while it was still very dark, he got up and went out to a deserted place, and there he prayed.

Mark 1:37-38
When they found him, they said, "Everyone is searching for you." He answered, "Let us go on to the neighboring towns, so that I may proclaim the message there also; for that is what I came out to do."

Matthew 10:8
Cure the sick.

Matthew 7:20
You will know them by their fruits.

Matthew 10:35-36
For I have come to set a man against his father, and a daughter against her mother, and a daughter-in-law against her mother-in-law; and one's foes will be members of one's own household.

Mark 1:32-33
That evening, at sundown, they brought to him all who were sick or possessed with demons. And the whole city was gathered around the door.

Matthew 25:43-45
"I... was sick and in prison and you did not visit me..." **"Lord, when was it that we saw you... sick or in prison and did not take care of you?" Then he answered them,** "Truly I tell you, just as you did not do it to one of the least of these, you did not do it to me."

Mark 1:23
Just then there was in the synagogue a man with an unclean spirit.

Mark 9:25
When Jesus saw that a crowd came running together, he rebuked the unclean spirit, saying to it, "You spirit that keeps this boy from speaking and hearing, I command you, come out of him and never enter him again."

Leviticus 13:46
He shall remain unclean as long as he has the disease; he is unclean. He shall live alone; his dwelling shall be outside the camp.

Matthew 8:1-3
When Jesus had come down from the mountain, great crowds followed him; and there was a leper who came to him and knelt before him, saying, "Lord, if you choose, you can make me clean. He stretched out his hand and *touched* him, saying, "I do choose. Be made clean."

Job 27:5-6
Far be if from me to say that you are right; until I die I will not put away my integrity from me. I hold fast my righteousness, and will not let it go; my heart does not reproach me for any of my days.

Leviticus 15:19
When a woman has a discharge of blood that is her regular discharge from her body, she shall be in impurity for seven days, and whoever touches her shall be unclean until the evening.

Matthew 9:22
Take heart daughter, your faith has made you well.

Mark 5:39
The child is not dead but sleeping.

Mark 9:18
Whenever it seizes him, it dashes him down; and he foams and grinds his teeth and becomes rigid.

Mark 9:27
But Jesus took him by the hand and lifted him up, and he was able to stand.

Mark 2:9
Your sins are forgiven.

Luke 13:13
When he laid his hands upon her, immediately she stood up straight and began praising God.

Luke 14:4
So Jesus took him, healed him, and sent him on his way.

CHAPTER X
Jesus Was a Communist

Luke 24:51-52
While he was blessing them, he withdrew from them and was carried up into heaven. And they worshipped him...

Colossians 1:18
He is the head of the body, the church.

Matthew 28:20
And remember, I am with you always, to the end of the age.

Matthew 18:20
Where two or more are gathered in my name, I am there among you.

Luke 17:21
For in fact, the kingdom of God is among you.

Matthew 8:20
Foxes have holes, and birds of the air have nests; but the Son of Man has nowhere to lay his head.

Mark 10:22-22
"You lack one thing: go, sell what you own, and give the money to the poor, and you will have treasure in heaven; then come, follow me." When he heard this, he was shocked and went away grieving, for he had many possessions.

Matthew 3:13-15
Then Jesus came from Galilee to John at the Jordon, to be baptized by him. John would have prevented him, saying, "I need to be baptized by you, and do you come to me?" But Jesus answered him, "Let it be so for now; for it is proper for us in this way to fulfill all righteousness." Then he consented.

Mark 1:7-8
[John] proclaimed, "The one who is more powerful than I is coming after me; I am not worthy to stoop down and untie the thong on his sandals. I have baptized you with water but he will baptize you with the Holy Spirit."

Luke 3:16
John answered all of them saying, "I baptize you with water; but one who is more powerful than I is coming; I am not worthy to untie the thong of his sandals. He will baptize you with the Holy Spirit and fire."

John 1:26-27
John answered them, "I baptize with water. Among you stands one whom you do not know, the one who is coming after me; I am not worthy to untie the thong of his sandal."

Matthew 10:9-10
Take no gold, or silver, or copper in your belts, no bag for your journey, or two tunics, or sandals, or a staff.

Luke 9:3
He said to them, 'Take nothing for your journey; no staff, nor bag, nor bread, nor money—not even an extra tunic.'"

Mark 6:8-9
He ordered them to take nothing for their journey *except a staff*; no bread, no bag, no money in their belts; but to *wear sandals* and not to put on two tunics.

Mark 10:21
Jesus looking upon him loved him.

Mark 14:51-52
A certain young man was following him, wearing nothing but a linen cloth. They caught hold of him, but he left the linen cloth and ran off naked.

Luke 12:15
A man's life consists not in having more possessions than he needs.

Matthew 6:19
Do not store up for yourselves treasures on Earth.

James 1:9-11
The rich will disappear like a flower in the field. For the sun rises with its scorching heat and withers the field; its flower falls, and its beauty perishes. It is the same way with the rich; in the midst of a busy life, they will wither away.

Acts 2:44-45
All who believed were together and had all things in common; they would sell their possessions and goods and distribute the proceeds to all as any had need.

Galatians 3:28
There is no longer Jew or Greek, no longer slave or free, no longer male of female, for all of you are one in Christ Jesus.

John 10:10
I came that they may have life, and have it abundantly.

Matthew 6:25-34
Therefore I tell you, do not worry about you life, what you will eat or what you will drink, or about your body, what you will wear. Is not life worth more than food, and the body more than clothing? Look at the birds of the air; they neither sow nor reap nor gather into barns, and yet your heavenly Father feeds them. Are you not of more value than they? And can any of you by worrying add a single hour to your span of life? And why do you worry about clothing? Consider the lilies of the field, how they grow; they neither toil nor spin, yet, I tell you, even Solomon in all his glory was not clothed like one of these. But if God so clothes the grass of the field, which is alive today and tomorrow is thrown into the oven, will he not much more clothe you—you of little faith? Therefore, do not worry, saying "What will we eat?" or "What will we drink?" or "What will we wear?" For it is the Gentiles who strive for all these things; and indeed your heavenly Father knows that you need all these things. But strive first for the kingdom of God and his righteousness, and all these things will be given to you as well. So do not worry about tomorrow, for tomorrow will bring worries of its own. Today's trouble is enough for today.

Mark 8:2
I have compassion for the crowd... because they have nothing to eat.

Matthew 10:8
You received without payment; give without payment.

Mark 10:23
How hard it will be for those who are rich to enter the kingdom of God.

Mark 10:25
It's easier for a camel to go through the eye of a needle than for someone who is rich to enter the kingdom of God.

Mark 6:24
You cannot serve God and wealth.

Matthew 22:20
Whose head is this, and whose title?

Luke 10:7
The laborer deserves to be paid.

Mark 8:8
They ate and they were filled; and they took up the broken pieces left over, seven baskets full.

I Timothy 6:10
Money is the root of all evil.

Matthew 6:24
No one can serve two masters; for a slave will either hate the one and love the other, or be devoted to the one and despise the other.

Luke 16:26
Between you and us a great chasm has been fixed, so that those who might want to pass from here to you cannot do so, and no one can cross from there to us.

Mark 6:19-21
Do not store up for yourselves treasures on earth, where moth and rust consume and where thieves break in and steal; but store up for yourselves treasures in heaven, where neither moth nor rust consumes and where thieves do not break in and steal. For where your treasure is, there your heart will be also.

CHAPTER XI
Jesus Was an Environmentalist

Proverbs 8:1

Does not wisdom call, and does not understanding raise her voice?

Proverbs 8:22-31

> **The Lord created me at the beginning of his work,**
> **the first of his acts of long ago.**
> **Ages ago I was set up, at the first,**
> **before the beginning of the earth...**
> **When he established the heavens, I was there,**
> **when he drew a circle on the face of the deep,**
> **when he made firm the skies above,**
> **when he established the fountains of the deep,**
> **when he assigned to the sea its limit,**
> **so that the waters might not transgress his command,**
> **when he marked out the foundations of the earth,**
> **then I was beside him like a master worker;**
> **and I was daily his delight,**
> **rejoicing before him always,**
> **rejoicing in his inhabited world**
> **and delighting in the human race.**

Exodus 33:19-23

Moses said, "Show me your glory, I pray." And he said, "I will make all my goodness pass before you, and will proclaim before you the name, 'The Lord:' and I will be gracious, and will show mercy on whom I will show mercy. But," he said, "you cannot see my face; for no one shall see me and live." And the Lord continued, "See, there is a place by me where you shall stand on the rock; and while my glory passes by I will put you in a cleft of the rock, and I will cover you with my hand until I have passed by; then I will take away my hand, and you shall see my back; but my face shall not be seen."

Psalms 104:24-30

> **O Lord, how manifold are your**
> **Works!**
> **In wisdom you have made**
> **them all;**

the earth is full of your
creatures,
Yonder is the sea, great and wide,
creeping things innumerable
are there,
living things both small and
great.
Where ships sail,
and whales play.

These all look to you
To give them their food in due
Season;
when you give to them, they
gather it up;
when you open your hand, they
are filled with good things.
When you hide your face, they
are dismayed;
when you take away their
breath, they die
and return to their dust.
When you send forth your
Spirit, they are created;
And you renew the face of the
ground.

Matthew 6:34
Do not worry about tomorrow, for tomorrow will worry about
itself.

Matthew 5:3-10
Blessed are the poor in spirit, for theirs is the kingdom of
heaven.
Blessed are those who mourn, for they will be comforted.
Blessed are the meek, for they will inherit the earth.
Blessed are those who hunger and thirst for righteousness, for
they will be filled.
Blessed are the merciful, for they will be shown mercy.

Blessed are the pure in heart, for they will see God.
Blessed are the peacemakers, for they will be called sons of
God.
Blessed are those who are persecuted because of righteousness,
for theirs is the kingdom of heaven.

Matthew 5:45
For [God] makes the sun rise on the evil and on the good, and
sends rain on the righteous and on the unrighteous.

John 3:3
You must be born again.

Amos 5:22-24
**Take away from me the noise of your songs; I will not listen to
the melody of your harps. But let justice roll down like waters,
and let righteousness like an ever-flowing stream.**

Matthew 6:26
Look at the birds of the air.

Matthew 6:28
Consider the lilies of the field.

Matthew 8:20
Foxes have holes, and birds of the air have nests; but the Son
of Man has nowhere to lay his head.

Matthew 7:16-17
You will know them by their fruits. Are grapes gathered from
thorns, or figs from thistles? In the same way, every good tree
bears good fruit, but every bad tree bears bad fruit.

Matthew 13:45-46
The kingdom of heaven is like a merchant looking for fine
pearls. When he found one of great value, he went away and
sold everything he had and bought it.

Genesis 1:31
God saw everything that had been made, and indeed, it was very good.

CHAPTER XII
Jesus Was a Person for the Ethical Treatment of Animals

John 2:15
Making a whip of cords, he drove all of them out of the temple, both the sheep and the cattle.

Proverbs 12:10
The righteous know the needs of their animals, but the mercy of the wicked is cruel.

Luke 15:4
Which one of you, having a hundred sheep and losing one of them, does not leave the ninety-nine in the wilderness and go after the one that is lost until you find it?

Matthew 5:48
Be perfect, therefore, even as your heavenly Father is perfect.

Matthew 7:7-8
Ask and it will be given to you; seek and you will find; knock and the door will be opened to you. For everyone who asks receives; one who seeks finds; and to one who knocks, the door will be opened.

Matthew 15:11
It is not what goes into the mouth that defiles a person, but it is what comes out of the mouth that defiles.

Matthew 26:26-28
While they were eating, Jesus took a loaf of bread, and after blessing it he broke it, gave it to his disciples and said, "Take, eat; this is my body." Then he took a cup, and after giving thanks gave it to them, saying, "Drink from it, all of you, for this is my blood..."

Mark 8:2
I have compassion for the crowd... because they have nothing
to eat.

Matthew 6:11
Give us this day our daily bread.

Matthew 19:14
Let the little children come to me, and do not stop them.

Matthew 18:6
If any of you put a stumbling block before one of these little
ones who believe in me, it would be better for you if a great
millstone were fastened around your neck and you were
drowned in the depth of the sea.

Matthew 18:7
Occasions for stumbling blocks are bound to come, but woe to
the one by whom the stumbling block comes!

Matthew 5:7
Blessed are the merciful, for they will receive mercy.

Luke 17:21
The kingdom of God is among you.

CHAPTER XIII
Jesus Was a Feminist

Genesis 3:16
**I will greatly multiply your pain in childbirth, in pain you will
bring forth children. Yet your desire will be for your husband
and he will rule over you.**

Ephesians 5:22-23
**Wives should be subject to their husbands as to the Lord, since
as Christ is head of the Church and saves the whole body, so is**

a husband the head of his wife; and as the Church is subject to Christ, so should wives be to their husbands, in everything.

Galatians 3:28
There is neither Jew nor Greek, slave nor free, male nor female, for you are all one in Christ Jesus.

Luke 8:1-3
The twelve were with him, as well as some women who had been cured of evil spirits and infirmities: Mary, called Magdalene, from whom seven demons had gone out, and Joanna, the wife of Herod's steward Chuza, and Susanna, and many others, who provided for them out of their resources.

Matthew 21:31
I tell you the truth, the tax collectors and the prostitutes are entering the kingdom of God ahead of you.

Luke 9:48
Whoever is least among you all is the greatest.

Matthew 1:16
Joseph, the husband of Mary, of whom was born Jesus, who is called Christ.

Matthew 5:28
Anyone who looks at a woman lustfully has already committed adultery in his heart.

Matthew 5:32
I tell you that anyone who divorces his wife, except for marital unfaithfulness, causes her to become an adulteress.

Matthew 9:22
Take heart daughter, your faith has healed you.

Genesis 24:14
Let the girl to whom I shall say, "Please offer your jar that I may drink," and who shall say, "Drink, and I will water your

camels"—let her be the one whom you have appointed for your servant Isaac.

Genesis 24:28
She ran and told her mother's household about these things.

Genesis 29:10-12
Now when Jacob saw Rachel... Jacob went up and rolled the stone from the well's mouth, and watered the flock... Then Jacob kissed Rachel, and wept aloud... and she ran and told her father.

Luke 7:39
If this man were a prophet, he would have known who and what kind of woman this is who is touching him—that she is a sinner.

Luke 10:40
"Lord, do you not care that my sister has left me to do all the work by myself? Tell her then to help me." "Martha, Martha, you are worried and distracted by many things; there is need of only one thing. Mary has chosen the better part, which will not be taken away from her."

Luke 13:10-13
Now he was teaching in one of the synagogues on the Sabbath. And just then there appeared a woman who had been crippled by a spirit for eighteen years. She was bent over and unable to stand up straight. When Jesus saw her, he called her over and said, "Woman, you are set free from your ailment." When he laid his hands on her, immediately she stood up straight and began praising God.

Luke 13:16
And ought not this woman, a daughter of Abraham whom Satan bound for eighteen long years, be set free from this bondage on the Sabbath day?

John 1:1-3

In the beginning was the Word, and the Word was with God, and the Word was God. He was in the beginning with God. All things came into being through him, and without him not one thing came into being.

Proverbs 8:22-23
The Lord created me at the beginning of his work, the first of his acts of long ago. Ages ago I was set up, at the first, before the beginning of the earth

Matthew 22:30
For in the resurrection they will neither marry nor be given in marriage, but are like the angels.

Matthew 12:49-50
Here are my mother and my brothers. For whoever does the will of my Father in heaven is my brother and sister and mother.

Matthew 13:33
The kingdom of heaven is like yeast that a woman took and mixed into a large amount of flour until it worked all through the dough.

CHAPTER XIV
Jesus Was a Gay Rights Advocate

Romans 3:23
All have sinned and fall short of the glory of God.

Matthew 22:37-40
"You shall love the Lord your God with all your heart, and with all your soul, and with all your mind." This is the greatest and first commandment. And a second is like it: "You shall love your neighbor as yourself." On these two commandments hang all the law and the prophets.

Luke 15:20

But while he was still far off, his father saw him and was filled with compassion; he ran and put his arms around him and kissed him.

Mark 3:32-35
"Who are my mother and my brothers?" **And looking at those who sat around him, he said,** "Here are my mother and my brothers! Whoever does the will of God is my brother and sister and mother."

Matthew 23:9
Call no one your father on earth, for you have one Father—the one in heaven.

Genesis 19:24
The Lord rained on Sodom and Gomorrah sulfur and fire from the Lord of heaven.

Exodus 23:9
You shall not oppress a stranger. You know the heart of a stranger, for you were strangers in the land of Egypt.

Mathew 25:43
I was a stranger and you welcomed me.

Ezekiel 22:7
The stranger has been oppressed in your midst.

Ezekiel 16:49
Now this is the sin of your sister Sodom, she and her daughters were arrogant, overfed and unconcerned; they did not help the poor and needy.

Leviticus 18:22
Do not lie with a man as one lies with a woman; that is detestable.

Leviticus 20:13

If a man lies with a man as one lies with a woman, both of them have done what is detestable. They must be put to death; their blood will be on their own heads.

Deuteronomy 23: 17-18
There shall be no whore of the daughters of Israel, nor a sodomite of the sons of Israel. Thou shall not bring the hire of a whore, or the price of a dog, into the house of the Lord thy God for any vow: for even both these are abominations unto the Lord thy God.

Exodus 20:2-3
I am the Lord your God, who brought you out of the land of Egypt, out of the house of slavery. You shall have no gods before me.

Romans 1:26-27
For this reason God gave them up to degrading passions. Their women exchanged natural intercourse for unnatural, and in the same way also the men, giving up natural intercourse with women, were consumed with passion for one another.

Romans 7:7
If it had not been for the law, I would not have known sin.

Romans 2:1
Therefore you have no excuse, whoever you are, when you judge others; for in passing judgment on another you condemn yourself.

Romans 8:1
There is therefore now no condemnation for those who are in Christ Jesus.

I Corinthians 6:9
Know ye not that the unrighteous shall not inherit the kingdom of God? Be not deceived: neither fornicators, nor idolaters, nor adulterers, nor effeminate, nor abusers of

themselves with mankind, nor thieves, nor covetous, nor drunkards, nor revilers, nor extortioners, shall inherit the kingdom of God.

Romans 14:10
Why do you pass judgment on your brother or sister?

John 15:12
Love one another, even as I have loved you.

EPILOGUE
Would the Real Jesus Please Rise?

Mark 2:9-11
"Which is easier, to say to the paralytic, 'Your sins are forgiven,' or to say, 'Stand up and take your mat and walk?' But so you know that the Son of Man has authority on earth to forgive sins"—**he said to the paralytic**—"I say stand up, take up your mat and go to your home."

Matthew 8:22
Follow me and let the dead bury the dead.

Ezekiel 37:27
I will put my Spirit in you and move you to follow my decrees and be careful to keep my laws.

WORKS CITED

Alter, Robert, *The Art of Biblical Narrative*, Basic Books, Perseus Books Group, U.S., 1981

Armstrong, Karen, *The Great Transformation*, Alfred A. Knopf, New York, NY, 2006

Armstrong, Karen, *Visions of God*, Bantam Books, New York, NY, 1994

Ayers, "Will We Still Eat Meat?" *Time* Magazine, 1999

Audubon, December 1999

Beard, Ruth M., *An Outline of Piaget's Developmental Psychology*, A Mentor Book, Basic Books, Inc., New York, NY, 1972

Berry, Thomas, & Swimme, Brian, *The Universe Story*, Harper Collins, New York, NY, 1992

Bly, Robert, trans. & ed., *Selected Poems of Rainer Maria Rilke*, HarperCollins Publishers, New York, NY, 1981

Brenan, Gerald, *St. John of the Cross: His Life and Poetry*, Cambridge University Press, London, 1973

Brodie, Fawn M, *Thomas Jefferson, an Intimate History*, Norton and Co., Inc., New York, NY 1974

Buber, Martin, *I and Thou*, Charles Scribner & Sons, New York, NY, 1970

Cahill, Thomas, *How the Irish Save Civilization*, Random House, Inc., New York, NY, 1995

Ceresko, Anthony, *Introduction to the Old Testament*, Orbis Books, Maryknoll, NY, 1992

Chadwick, Owen, *A History of Christianity*, St. Martin's Press, New York, NY, 1995

Chidester, David, *Christianity: A Global History*, HaperCollins Publishers, New York, NY, 2000

Crossan, John Dominic & Reed, Jonathan L., *Excavating Jesus*, Harper Collins, New York, NY, 2001

Crossan, John Dominic, *Jesus: A Revolutionary Biography*, HarperCollins Publishers, New York, NY, 1995

Crossan, John Dominic, *The Birth of Christianity*, HarperCollins, New York, NY, 1998

Cullen, Francis T., & Unnever, James D., "Christian Fundamentalism and Support for Capital Punishment," *Journal of Research in Crime Delinquency*, 2006

de Nicolas, Antonio T., *St. John of the Cross: Alchemist of the Soul*, Paragon House, New York, NY, 1989

Durning, Alan, and Brough, Holly, "Taking Stock: Animal Farming and the Environment," *Worldwatch* Paper 103, July 1991

Eisler, Riane, *The Chalice and the Blade*, HarperCollins, New York, NY, 1987, 1995

Eisler, Riane, *The Power of Partnership*, New World Library, Novato, CA, 2002

Fehribach, Adeline, *The Women in the Life of the Bridegroom*, The Liturgical Press, Collegeville, Minnesota, 1998

Ferm, Vergilius, ed., *Classics of Protestantism*, Philosophical Library, New York, NY, 1959

Fletcher, Joseph, *Situation Ethics*, The Westminster Press, Philadelphia, PA, 1966

Fletcher & Montgomery, *Situation Ethics*, Bethany House Publishers, Minneapolis, MN, 1972

Fox, Matthew, *A New Reformation*, Wisdom University Press, Oakland, CA, 2005

Fox, Matthew, *Creation Spirituality*, Harper San Francisco, Harper Collins Publishers, New York, NY, 1991

Fox, Matthew, ed., *Hildegard of Bingen's Book of Divine Works*, Bear & Company, Santa Fe, NM, 1987

Fox, Matthew, *One River, Many Wells*, Jeremy P. Tarcher/Putnam, New York, NY, 2000

Fox, Matthew, *Original Blessing*, Tarcher/Putnam, New York, NY, 1983, 2000

Fox, Matthew, *Wrestling with the Prophets*, Jeremy P. Tarcher/Putnam, New York, NY, 1995

Freedman, Russell, *Indian Chiefs*, Scholastic Inc., New York, NY, 1987

Fromm Erich, *Escape from Freedom*, Avon Books, New York, NY, 1941, 1966

Fromm, Erich, *The Art of Loving*, Bantam Books, Harper & Row, New York, NY, 1956, 1972

Fromm, Erich, *The Dogma of Christ*, A Fawcett Premier Book, Holt, Rinehart and Winston, Inc., 1955, 1963, Printed in U.S., July 1973

Fromm Erich, *The Heart of Man*, Harper Colophon Edition, Harper & Row, New York, NY, 1980, copyright, 1964

Fukuoka, Masanobu, *The Natural Way of Farming*, Japan Publications, Inc., 1985

Funk, Robert W. & The Jesus Seminar, *The Acts of Jesus: The Search for the Authentic Deeds of Jesus*, HarperCollins, New York, NY, 1998

Gandhi, *All Men are Brothers*, Kripalani, Krishna, ed., Continuum Press, New York, NY, 1982

Grudem, Wayne, *Bible Doctrine*, Zondervan, Grand Rapids, MI, 1999

Hanh, Thich Nhat, *Anger*, Riverhead Books, New York, NY, 2001

Hanh, Thich Nhat, *Living Buddha, Living Christ*, Riverhead Books, Berkley Publishing Group, New York, NY, 1995

Harcourt, Bernard E., "The Mentally Ill, Behind Bars," *New York Times*, January 15, 2007

Harden, Blaine, "The Greening of Evangelicals: Christian Right Turns, Sometimes Warily, to Environmentalism" *Washington Post*, Sunday, February 6, 2005, Page A01

Harvey, Andrew, *Son of Man*, Jeremy P. Tarcher/Putnam, New York, NY, 1998

Herzog II, William R., *Jesus, Justice and the Reign of God*, Westminster Knox Press, Louisville, KY, 2000

Herzog II, William R., *Parables as Subversive Speech: Jesus as Pedagogue of the Oppressed*, Westminster/John Knox Press, Louisville, KY, 1994

Hill, Paul, *Defending the Defenseless*, August 2003, from a revised paper in an anthology in The Current Controversy Series: *The Abortion Controversy*, Greenhaven Press, 2001, found at www.armyofgod.com/PHill_ShortShot.html, December 1, 2006

Hitler, Adolph, *Mein Kampf*, Ralph Mannheim, ed., Mariner Books, New York, NY, 1999

Howe, Charles A., *For Faith and Freedom*, Skinner House Books, Boston, MA, 1997

Johnston, William, ed., *The Cloud of Unknowing & Book of Privy Counseling*, Doubleday, Random House, Inc., New York, NY, 1973, 1996

Jordan, Clarence, *The Cotton Patch Version of Luke and Acts*, A Koinonia Publication, Association Press, New York, NY, 1969, 1970

Jung, C.G., *Dream Analysis*, Bollingen Series XCIX, Princeton University Press, Princeton, NJ, 1984

Jung, C.G., *Memories, Dreams, Reflections*, ed. Aniela Jaffé, trans. Richard and Clara Winston, Vintage Books, New York, NY, 1989

Kennedy, Jr., Robert F. *Crimes Against Nature*, Harper Perennial, New York, NY, 2004, 2005

Kent, Charles Foster, *The Social Teachings of the Prophets and Jesus*, Charles Scribner & Sons, New York, NY, 1917

King, Martin Luther, *A Testament of Hope*, Washington, James, ed., HarperCollins, New York, NY, 1986, 1981

Koch, G. Adolph, *Religion in the American Enlightenment*, Thomas Crowell Co., New York, NY, 1968

Korten, David C., *When Corporations Rule the World*, Kumarian Press, Inc., Berrett-Koehler Publishers, New York, NY, 1995

Lang, John, "Environmentalists Rap Factory Farms for Manure Productions," Scripps Howard News Service, June 9, 1998

Lakoff, George, *Don't Think of an Elephant*, Chelsea Green Publishing, White River Junction, VT, 2004

Lakoff, George, *Moral Politics*, 2nd ed., The University of Chicago Press, Chicago, IL, 1996, 2002

Lenski, Gerhard E., *Power and Privilege: A Theory of Social Stratification*, McGraw-Hill, New York, NY, 1966

Maccoby, Hyam, *The Mythmaker: Paul and the Invention of Christianity*, HarperCollins, 1986, Barnes & Noble, Inc., New York, NY, 1998

Matt, Daniel C., *The Essential Kabbalah*, Quality Paper Back Book Club, New York, NY, 1995

McKibben, Bill, *Deep Economy*, Times Books, Henry Holt and Company, New York, NY, 2007

Mitchell, Stephen, *The Gospel According to Jesus*, HarperCollins, New York, NY, 1991

Moore, Thomas, *The Soul of Sex*, HarperCollins Publishers, New York, NY, 1998

Moore, Virginia, *The Madisons*, McGrall-Hill Co., New York, NY, 1979

Olson, Sarah, "Why Iraq Veterans Can't Stay Silent," *Yes!* Magazine, Summer, 2007

Ortiz, Brandon, *Lexington Herald-Leader*, July, 2006

Paine, Thomas, *The Age of Reason*, Pormetheus Books, Buffalo, NY, 1984

Peabody, James, ed., *A Biography of His Own*

Plato, *The Five Great Dialogues*, Walter J. Black – Roslyn, New York, NY, 1942

Residential Finance Survey: 2001, U.S. Department of Housing and Urban Development and U.S. Census Bureau

Robbins, John, *The Food Revolution*, Conari Press, Boston, MA, 2001

Romero, Oscar, *The Violence of Love*, Orbis Books, Maryknoll, NY, 1987, 2007

Ryan, John, and Durning, Alan, *Stuff: The Secret Lives of Everyday Things*, Seattle, Northwest Environment Watch, 1997

Schulbach, Herb, et al., in *Soil and Water* 38, Fall, 1978

Schut, Michael, ed., *Simpler Living, Compassionate Life*, Living the Good News, The Morehouse Group, Denver, CO, 1999, 2001

Shiva, Vandana, *Water Wars*, Pluto Press, London, 2002

Stumpf, Samuel E., *Philosophy, History and Problems*, 3rd ed., McGraw-Hill Book Company, New York, NY 1971, 1983

Suzuki, David, *The Sacred Balance: Rediscovering Our Place in Nature*, Vancouver, BC, Greystone Books, 1997

Tillich, Paul, *Systematic Theology*, Vol. I, 1951, p. 152

Treaty of Tripoli (Treaty of Peace & Friendship), 1796, Article XI

Twain, Mark, *The Adventures of Huckleberry Finn*, Bantam Books, New York, NY, 1884, 1986

Ueshiba, Morihei, *The Art of Peace*, Stevens, John, trans., Shambhala, Boston, MA, 1992

Vermes, Geza, *The Changing Faces of Jesus*, Penguin Compass, New York, NY, 2000

Wink, Walter, *The Powers that Be*, A Galilee Book published by Doubleday, New York, NY, 1998

Wolff, Edward, N., *The American Prospect*, vol. 6, Issue 22, June 23, 1995

www.creationcare.org

www.juntosociety.com/guest/falwell/jf_tyoa010303.html, November 29, 2006

www.mayoclinic.com/health/childhood-obesity/DS00698, 2007

www.pbs.org/wgbh/pages/frontline/shows/religion/portrait/religions.html

www.worldnetdaily.com/news/article.asp?ARTICLE_ID=36859, *God is Pro-War*, posted January 31, 2004

Zicree, Mark Scott, *The Twilight Zone Companion*, 2nd ed., Silman-James Press, Los Angeles, CA, 1982, 1989

INDEX

Made in the USA
Lexington, KY
07 March 2010